I Always Wanted to Fly

To Bob Brewer, a
fellow Raven — we
shared the, same
hostile skies,
Best,

[signature], USAF (Ret)
9/2003

I Always

Wanted to Fly

America's Cold War Airmen

Colonel Wolfgang W. E. Samuel

With a foreword by Ken Hechler

University Press of Mississippi
Jackson

www.upress.state.ms.us

Painting on pages ii and iii by George Back. A 1965 MiG-17 attack on an RB-47H
reconnaissance aircraft off the east coast of North Korea.

09   08   07   06   05   04   03   02   01   4   3   2   1
∞
Library of Congress Cataloging-in-Publication Data

Samuel, Wolfgang W. E.
I always wanted to fly : America's Cold War airmen / Wolfgang W. E. Samuel.
p.   cm.
ISBN 1-57806-399-X (cloth : alk. paper)
1. Air pilots, Military—United States—Biography.   2. Cold War.   3. United States Air
Force—Officers—Biography.   I. Title.

UG626.S26   2001
358.4′0092—dc21
[B]
2001026039

British Library Cataloging-in-Publication Data available

To the flyers who gave their lives during the Cold War from 1945 to 1991 in the service of their country.

In memory of the friends I served with who did not return from their last flights.

Contents

Contents

Contents

Part 4: Vietnam, 1965   257

14. Hambone 02   267
Colonel Ralph L. Kuster Jr.

15. Lincoln Flight   300
Colonel Kevin A. "Mike" Gilroy

16. Yellowbird   323
Major Fred E. "Ed" Rider

Foreword

I Always Wanted to Fly is a comprehensive collection of first-person narratives depicting the heroism of young men who grew up with a compelling desire to fly airplanes as well as of the changing nature of the U.S. Air Force during the Cold War. The author is a veteran of many reconnaissance missions against the Soviet Union and of air combat in the Vietnam War. I found this book to be a series of gripping stories, told in such remarkable detail that I felt I was alongside the pilots and crew members, living with them through every thrilling moment in the sky.

On March 7, 1945, I served as combat historian with III Corps, part of General Omar N. Bradley's 12th Army Group, as it advanced toward the Rhine River near the little town of Remagen, just a few miles south of Bonn. That afternoon I learned that the Remagen Bridge had been captured by U.S. forces before the Germans had a chance to blow it up. Second Lieutenant Karl H. Timmermann, the commander of A Company, 27th Armored Infantry Battalion, 9th Armored Division, had led his men in a death-defying charge across the bridge and gained a foothold on the east bank of the Rhine River, securing the bridge in the process. For his leadership and extraordinary heroism, Lieutenant Timmermann was subsequently awarded the Distinguished Service

Cross. When I found the lieutenant, he was calmly shaving in the shell of a bombed-out house. His reaction to my probing historian's questions? He wondered what all the excitement was about.

While reading *I Always Wanted to Fly,* I encountered Lieutenant Timmermann's selfless courage and uncommon ability in the individual flyers who tell their stories. These are the men who flew the Berlin Airlift, who stopped the North Korean People's Army in Korea, who probed the Soviet Union in secret reconnaissance flights, and who fought an air war over North Vietnam under incredibly confining restrictions. These flyers never hesitated to act when their country asked them to protect its vital interests. If I were to question them about their contributions, I am certain they too would ask me what all the excitement was about.

The reader will find that it is all about nerves-of-steel flyers like Sam Myers, who stole a city from the grasp of the Russians by carrying life-giving coal and food around the clock into a freezing and hungry Berlin. And it is all about Barney Dobbs, a veteran of the forgotten war in Korea, who spent nineteen months in a Chinese prisoner-of-war camp after his B-26 was shot down on a night-interdiction mission.

Author Samuel takes you to Thule, Greenland, a strategic reconnaissance base during the Cold War, to let you experience at that remote and unforgiving air base the bone-chilling forty degree below zero temperatures, the ice-fog obscured visibility, and the raging winds that meant near instant death to any air crew caught unprepared. As a historian, I find it remarkable that although there were many losses of aircraft—both U.S. Air Force and U.S. Navy—while flying the periphery of the Soviet Union and during shallow penetrations of their territory, in the many major overflights by both American and British military aircraft, not one aircraft was lost. The author not only presents the extent of our significant losses over the years in the secret war of reconnaissance but also lets the reader experience the near shootdown of a lone RB-47H reconnaissance aircraft by North Korean MiGs.

I found Ralph Kuster's narrative particularly riveting as I remember quite well the anguish of the Vietnam War, having served as a member of the U.S. Congress during that period. Kuster flew an F-105 Thunderchief over North Vietnam, experiencing the helplessness and loneliness that engulfs a pilot when his aircraft is hit and he is forced to eject over enemy territory. The story of his rescue is a graphic account of courage and determination, underlining the importance and value of training in meeting emergencies.

Author Samuel gives his readers a framing section for the Vietnam period, as he does for all of the other segments of the Cold War he presents—the Berlin Airlift, Korea, and strategic reconnaissance—providing enough historical detail to illuminate the issues of the time and providing critical context for the airmen's stories that follow. He also depicts for us a changing air force, moving from slow, propeller-driven aircraft to jets, from youthful volunteers and citizen soldiers (Stephen Ambrose's characterization) to the largely professional, college-educated air force of the Vietnam era. The well-integrated coverage of the major conflicts of the Cold War period is presented logically and in a neutral style. Samuel acknowledges that there were varying opinions and divisions about the conduct of the Vietnam air war but remains personally neutral on the subject.

Most importantly for me, though, throughout my reading of *I Always Wanted to Fly,* I felt that I was listening to the conversations and vivid memories of real individuals, of human beings exposed to the immense stresses of armed conflict. I frequently felt I was sitting right in the cockpit with these remarkable flyers, and I understood clearly that they really had "always wanted to fly." Samuel has produced a well-integrated package of excitement and courage and aviation history.

Ken Hechler
Author of *The Bridge at Remagen*

Preface and Acknowledgments

I became aware of my first airplane on a sunny spring morning in 1940. I was five years old, a German child playing in my sandbox. The quiet of my world was suddenly shattered by a strange-looking machine flying noisily toward me. It had three engines and was flying very low and coming directly at me. I watched not in fear but in fascination. The airplane thundered by, no more than a hundred meters above me, disappearing beyond the Bober River. I imagined I saw the pilot looking down at me. That evening when my father, Willi, came home from work at the Sagan *Flugplatz* and took off his Luftwaffe tunic, I excitedly told him about what I had seen. "I know what I want to be when I grow up, Papa," I said. He laughed at my enthusiasm and replied, "You want to be a pilot, *Ja?*" "*Ja*, Papa, I want to fly airplanes when I grow up." And nothing ever changed that wish.

That airplane was a Junkers-52 trimotor transport. As the years passed my dream became more specific—first I wanted to be a Stuka pilot after seeing a war movie, and then I wanted to be a jet pilot after observing an Me-262 jet fighter passing overhead. Huge formations of B-17 bombers left me wondering as I watched them attack a nearby town. I tried to imagine what it was like to fly such a large airplane and what those men from America who were flying them were like. In 1945 my family fled from the advancing Red Army. We eventually ended up near the small town of Fassberg, south of Hamburg. Hundreds of abandoned airplanes stood at Fassberg, a former Luftwaffe base. On my way to school I often stopped at my favorite Junkers-88 bomber, climbed into the pilot's seat, and played at flying. In 1948, when the Soviets blockaded Berlin, a new airplane arrived—an American four-engine transport, the C-54 Skymaster. For more than a year I watched the American planes carrying coal to Berlin. Day after day they passed over the rotting former German army barracks I called home. For me, the men who flew those airplanes did not just fly coal to Berlin but represented all my hope for a better future. I admired the American flyers, and I wanted to be just like them.

In 1955, only four years after immigrating to the United States, I found myself as an American airman at RAF Sculthorpe in England, an air base from which RB-45 four-engine jets, manned by American and British airmen, flew night reconnaissance over the Soviet Union. In July 1960 I was commissioned a second lieutenant in the U.S. Air Force and soon left for flight training at bases in Texas and Mississippi. I ended up in a reconnaissance wing at Forbes Air Force Base near Topeka, Kansas, just in time for the Cuban Missile Crisis. There I flew with men who had flown the B-17 bombers I watched as a child. And I met some of the men who in 1948 saved the city of Berlin with their unarmed C-54 transports.

As I got to know those and other flyers, I learned that many of them once had childhood dreams just like mine. They were inspired by passing barnstormers, by World War I fighter legends about whom they read, by the legendary Charles Lindbergh, and some, just like me, by airplanes flying overhead. With the advent of World War II, many of these dreamers found themselves in cockpits soon after high school. They could not believe their good luck. Of those who survived World War II, some chose to continue to fly. In 1998 I met one of these men, a former 8th Air Force B-17 pilot who later flew in the Berlin Airlift, flew combat in Korea, and continued flying into the early days of the Vietnam War. I found his story so inspiring that I decided to write this book. Over a two-year period, I interviewed many men who went to war as teenagers against Nazi Germany and then stayed around to fly for their country. I heard a common refrain: "I always wanted to fly," they said again and again, "I always wanted to fly."

I believe these men are a unique generation. Inspired to fly as children by the mystique and aura of adventure surrounding the airplane, they followed their dreams with tenacity and dedication for much of their adult lives. I did not meet one who said he wished he had done something else. Their only regret was that their flying careers ended all too soon: they loved military flying and all the dangers they survived. In our talks, if I referred to them as anything other than "average" men, they raised their eyebrows. Maybe in their own minds they were average, but I know they did extraordinary things when called upon to do so. They certainly inspired those of us who followed.

The first overt Cold War confrontation between the United States and the Soviet Union, the Berlin blockade, was not the beginning of the Cold War but rather was the first manifestation of long-standing conflict between East and West. The Cold War likely began as early as April 1945, before World War II in Europe had ended, when Marshal Konstantin K. Rokossovski's second Belorussian front swept across the north German plain and made a grab for Denmark. American and British Intelligence intercepted Russian communications revealing their intentions, and troops of General Matthew B. Ridgway's XVIII Corps cut the Russians off. On May 2, 1945, on the shore of the Baltic Sea east of Wismar, Ridgway's troops made contact with the Russians. Ridgway and one of his division commanders, General James M. Gavin, met their first Russian general on May 3. The Russian seemed displeased. The furtive attempt to grab Denmark had failed. As World War II in Europe came to an end on May 7, 1945, a new conflict between former allies had begun. It would be called the Cold War. The Berlin Airlift, Korea, and Vietnam were some of the most salient hot spots of this protracted conflict. The fall of the Berlin Wall in 1989 signaled its end. Only two years later the USSR ceased to exist when the communist giant fell as a result of economic exhaustion and intellectual sterility. The contribution of America's flyers to the downfall of the Soviet Union was pivotal. The boys who always wanted to fly got all the flying they ever imagined they would—and more. Many of them were there not only for World War II but also for the Berlin crisis of 1948, for the war in Korea in 1950, for the Cuban Missile Crisis in October 1962. A few of the old warriors were even still around in the early days of the Vietnam War, but by then, a younger generation of flyers had largely taken over to fly America's warplanes.

Although the Cuban Missile Crisis was an encounter between the two nuclear superpowers with the potential for a world-embracing nuclear holocaust, the conflict resulted in a mutually agreed-upon standoff. No direct combat or engagement between American and Soviet forces took place. I therefore did not include that episode in this book, recognizing that the Cuban Missile Crisis was a Cold War watershed. Although the confrontation was exceedingly brief and no shots were fired in anger by either side, there were losses. Cuban SA-2 missile batteries shot down a U-2 photo-reconnaissance plane from the 4080th Strategic Reconnaissance Wing, and two RB-47H electronic-reconnaissance aircraft from the 55th Strategic Reconnaissance Wing crashed while attempting to perform reconnaissance missions. The flyers of the three aircraft died. They, like so many others who perished in various large and small Cold War encounters, are part of the price we paid to preserve our way of life.

Included with each major section of the book—the Berlin Airlift, Korea, strategic reconnaissance, and Vietnam—is a brief summary of how the conflicts came about to assist the reader contextually and to provide compelling historical background. For each flyer I show the highest rank held at the time of retirement or discharge from the U.S. Air Force as well as combat decorations earned. The highest recognition, the Medal of Honor, is most often given posthumously. The Medal of Honor is followed in order by the Air Force Cross, the Silver Star, the Distinguished Flying Cross, and the Air Medal, all awarded in recognition of risks taken while flying. The Bronze Star may be awarded for nonflying activities in direct support of combat operations. And the

Purple Heart is earned for wounds sustained in wartime combat. If I collected the medals of all the men I wrote about, I would hold in my hands every one of these decorations, in many instances awarded more than once. Behind these small pieces of metal dangling from colorful ribbons lie the stories of the boys who always wanted to fly.

I thank all of the men who so openly and generously shared with me events in their lives. At times, our conversations forced them to reach deep into recesses of the past. It was not easy for some to talk to me, but they did, as one flyer to another. They freely shared documentation and personal photographs and allowed me unencumbered access to the precious records of their ever more distant pasts. I offer special recognition to Colonel David M. Taylor, whose experiences as a B-17 pilot over Europe originally inspired me to write this book, and to Colonel Howard S. "Sam" Myers Jr., who so generously supported me with background material, gave freely of his time and knowledge of reconnaissance operations, and provided support to me in many other areas. Without Sam's generous help, locating the men who fought the Cold War from the sky would have been immensely more difficult. My thanks also go to Dr. Ken Hechler, a soldier, statesman, author, and longtime public servant in both the U.S. Congress and the state of West Virginia, for writing the foreword to *I Always Wanted to Fly*. I thank my wife, Joan Powers, for her dispassionate and critical review of the manuscript; and Craig Gill, editor in chief of the University Press of Mississippi, for his continuing and enthusiastic support; and Stephen E. Ambrose, whose writings of the courage and sacrifices of America's fighting men are a continuing inspiration to me.

Finally, I would like to note that I made minor editorial changes to the interviews in the interest of readability and clarity, including providing brief explanations of unfamiliar terms and adding other supplementary information.

Wolfgang W. E. Samuel
Colonel, U.S. Air Force (Retired)
Fairfax Station, Virginia

Part 1

The Berlin Airlift, 1948

You must remember that the military people [in Washington] were thinking about this in terms of military decisions. And, militarily speaking, we were in no position to hold our own against the Russians in Germany. They had twenty divisions. Including the British and French, we could only muster three.

Lucius D. Clay

We frequently flew two to three missions a day. Our greatest enemy was fatigue and boredom, flying day after day, night after night, often in grueling weather conditions.

Sam Myers, Berlin Airlift pilot

On July 16, 1945, President Harry S. Truman decided to take a look around Berlin when Stalin did not show as scheduled for the Potsdam Conference because of his slight heart attack, a carefully kept secret at the time. "I took advantage of this unscheduled delay," wrote President Truman in his memoir. "About halfway to the city we found the entire American 2nd Armored Division deployed along one side of the highway for my inspection. In an open half-track, I passed down the long line of men and vehicles, which comprised what was at that time the largest armored division in the world. Men and tanks were arrayed down the highway in front of me as far as the eye could see. The line was so long it took twenty-two minutes to ride from the beginning to the end of it" (1:341).

In 1948 there was no 2nd Armored Division to check Soviet ambitions. There was no meaningful American combat power west of the Elbe River. American ground forces in Germany were constabulatory and occupational in nature, neither equipped nor organized to fight the three hundred thousand–man Red Army to the east. American airpower was equally weak. Nothing remained of the once mighty Eighth Air Force. Air Force commander Lieutenant General Curtis E. LeMay characterized the situation: "At a cursory glance it looked like USAFE would be stupid to get mixed up in anything bigger than a cat-fight at a pet show. We had one Fighter group, and some transports, and some radar people, and that was about the story" (LeMay 411).

In a mad disarmament scramble soon after World War II, the U.S. armed forces declined from 12 million men to a mere 1.5 million. Those remaining on active duty in 1947 were not the hardened combat veterans of 1945. Military spending dropped from ninety billion dollars to eleven billion dollars. Although many people saw the need for rebuilding the U.S. military, it was not a popular political issue. Under the decisive leadership of President Truman, however, supported by a remarkably capable team of men including Dean Acheson, Clark Clifford, George Kennan, and General George Marshall, the nation soon reorganized its military and put in place a viable postwar foreign policy. The National Security Act of 1947 passed Congress in July, establishing a much-needed Department of Defense, headed by the secretary of defense with three civilian service secretaries. President Truman's foreign policy was surprisingly proactive and showed signs of success. The Truman Doctrine was enunciated as a direct response to Soviet pressure on Greece and Turkey. Aid was made available to these and other nations to resist communist encroachment. And what eventually became known as the Marshall Plan was set in motion in June 1947, when

Secretary of State Marshall outlined a European recovery program in a speech at Harvard University.

But a new U.S. defense organization and aid to nations in need could not stop determined aggression by a militarily powerful foe. In February 1948 Czechoslovakia came under Soviet control through a communist-inspired coup. The political and military stage was set for an attempt to bring a vulnerable Berlin under Soviet control as well. With Berlin, Stalin could reasonably expect much of Western Europe to follow and fall under the Red Army's "protective" umbrella. American military weakness was readily apparent, and communist political movements in France and Italy were strong and seemingly on the verge of ascending to power. Soviet planners must have reasoned that the British and Americans might be able to supply their own garrisons in Berlin by air but would not be able to supply Berlin's civilian population. An airlift supplying even the minimum needs of a city of more than two million inhabitants was too big a task to even contemplate. The Soviets knew for sure that they could not do it. A similar attempt by the Luftwaffe to supply the much smaller 6th Army at Stalingrad had failed miserably. Another strong factor in Stalin's favor appeared to be the suffering of the vanquished German population, which was cold, hungry, and living mostly in ruins and makeshift buildings, with threadbare clothing and without hope for a better future. Stalin knew that such suffering, combined with the absence of hope, made people pliable tools for exploitation. The stage clearly was set for a Soviet blockade of Berlin.

In the spring of 1948 Stalin must have thought that the moment was almost right to oust the Allies from Berlin, although winter would have been a better time to begin such an undertaking. The American and British initiative to revive West Germany's stagnant economy by introducing a new currency forced Stalin's hand. On the positive side of the ledger, both the United States and Britain, although militarily weak, had experienced and resolute political and military leaders at their helms. The principal players in the unfolding Berlin drama were:

United States

Harry S. Truman	President
General George C. Marshall	Secretary of State
Kenneth C. Royall	Secretary of the Army
General Lucius D. Clay	Military Governor of Germany (the three western zones of occupation) and Commander, U.S. Forces in Europe

United Kingdom

Clement Attlee	Prime Minister
Ernest Bevin	Foreign Secretary
General Sir Brian Robertson	Clay's British Military Counterpart

France

Georges Bidault	Premier
General Pierre Koenig	Clay's French Military Counterpart

Soviet Union

Marshal Joseph Stalin	Premier
Marshal Vassily Sokolovsky	Clay's Soviet Military Counterpart

To some, the Berlin Airlift may appear to be an interesting but minor operation, overshadowed by subsequent Cold War events. It was anything but. The stakes were exceedingly high for the West—a continued Allied presence in Berlin, the survival of its people, and the political survival of Western Europe in the face of open aggression should the Soviets succeed. Events began to look a lot like 1937. Because of the West's military weakness, some senior politicians and some senior military officers as well publicly expressed their fears that American and British military measures would cause the Soviets to react militarily. Would it not be better to let them have Berlin? was a question asked aloud in high places in Washington. Truman, Bevin, and Clay remained unimpressed, however, and were determined not to take their counsel from the barrel of a gun. From January 1948 onward, events moved rapidly toward confrontation.

January 1948—Soviet soldiers stopped a British military train en route to Hamburg from Berlin, holding the train for eleven hours. Soviet harassment of Allied military train traffic became a recurring experience.

February 1948—The communists staged a coup d'état in Czechoslovakia, adding that nation to the growing list of Soviet satellites.

March 1948—Senator Henry Cabot Lodge wrote to General Clay, "Is it safe for Americans to remain in Berlin?" Clay optimistically replied, "I believe American personnel are as secure here as they would be at home" (Smith 466). The members of the ongoing Six-Power Conference in London (the United States, United Kingdom, France, and the Benelux countries) preliminarily agreed to the formation of a West German government and for its association in the European Recovery Program (the Marshall Plan). The Western shift away from viewing Germany as an enemy had begun. On **March 20** Marshal Sokolovsky walked out of the Allied Control Council in Berlin, short-circuiting the council's attempt to formulate quadripartite policy for Germany. On **March 31** the Soviets—abrogating earlier agreements—announced a new set of traffic regulations for Berlin. There were to be no freight shipments from Berlin to the West without Soviet approval, and all military passengers and their baggage would be inspected. Generals Clay and Robertson responded by using airlift resources under their control to start what later became known as the Baby Airlift. The EATS pilots would be the first to fly supplies into an increasingly beleaguered Berlin.

April 1948—The U.S. Army prepared contingency plans to evacuate Berlin. On **April 2** Army Secretary Royall suggested the evacuation of American dependents from Berlin. And on **April 10**, in a teleconference with General Clay, General of the Army Omar N. Bradley expressed his belief that Berlin was untenable and that the United States should withdraw to minimize the loss of prestige. Clay viewed such proposals as alarmist and politically ruinous: "If we had started moving our dependents out we would never have had the people of Berlin stand firm" (Smith 474). Clay responded to Bradley that the United States should stay in Berlin unless driven out by force.

May 1948—British Foreign Secretary Bevin, remembering Munich, urged a steady course to the British Parliament. In a foreign policy address to the House of Commons he declared, "We are in Berlin as of right and it is our intention to stay there." (Smith 477).

June 1948—On **June 10** the Soviets attempted to remove locomotives and rolling stock from the American sector of Berlin. Clay posted guards, and the Soviets backed off. The following day the Soviets halted rail traffic into Berlin for two days. On **June 16** the Soviets, anticipating Western currency reform, walked out of the quadripartite government of Berlin, the *Kommandatura*. Both the Allied Control Council and the *Kommandatura* were now defunct: no medium remained for the Soviets and the Western powers to interact. Berlin was about to be split both economically and politically. On **June 20** the three Western occupying powers announced currency reform for western Germany. The deutsche mark replaced the hopelessly inflated reichsmark. Currency reform now divided Germany economically and forced the Soviets' hand. On **June 22** Marshal Sokolovsky announced that as of June 26 the new Soviet-issued reichsmark would be the only valid currency in Berlin. In response, the Western allies promptly introduced the deutsche mark in the western sectors. Firmly convinced that the Soviets were bluffing, General Clay directed his military deputy at Headquarters, U.S. Army Europe, Lieutenant General Clarence Huebner, to put together a regimental combat team of about six thousand men, including armor, artillery, and bridging equipment, to proceed on the autobahn from Helmstedt to Berlin. General LeMay, Clay's air commander, was directed to provide air support. When acquainted with Clay's proposal, however, President Truman rejected the idea outright, and usually supportive British friends also were not enchanted with Clay's approach. The idea was finally dropped in July for lack of political support (Smith 495).

On **June 24** the Soviets cut the last rail links to Berlin as well as electricity to the city's western sectors. Within two days, highways and canals to Berlin were blocked. British Secretary Bevin was annoyed with developments and sought a practical solution. He asked Robertson if

Berlin could be supplied by air and received a qualified "yes" for an answer. On **June 25** Robertson acquainted Clay with the airlift proposal that Air Commodore Reginald "Rex" Waite, one of Robertson's staff officers, had worked out and that he had previously presented to Bevin. In Robertson's presence, Clay called LeMay at his headquarters in Wiesbaden. In *Mission with LeMay*, the General recalled the conversation:

> So, I had only been on the job for six or seven months when there came that all-important telephone call from General Lucius B. Clay . . . could we haul some coal up to Berlin?
> "Sure. We can haul anything. How much coal do you want us to haul?"
> "All you can haul." (LeMay 415)

Clay recalled telling LeMay, "I want you to take every airplane you have and make it available for the movement of coal and food to Berlin." Furthermore, according to Clay, "I never asked permission or approval to begin the airlift. I asked permission to go in on the ground with the combat team, because if we were stopped we'd have to start shooting. . . . But we didn't have to start fighting to get through in the air, so I never asked permission" (Smith 500, 502–3).

On **June 26** the Berlin Airlift formally began, and the first C-47 aircraft delivered its cargo to Berlin's Tempelhof Airport. In Britain, Secretary Bevin told the press, "His Majesty's Government intends to stay in Berlin come what may." In a message to General Marshall, Bevin requested the immediate dispatch of American B-29 bombers to be based in Britain (Smith 507). And on **June 28** President Truman ordered a full-scale airlift to supply West Berlin. Two squadrons of B-29s, thought to be nuclear capable (they were not), were dispatched to Germany. One squadron was already at Fürstenfeldbruck Air Base near Munich on an unrelated training exercise. Other groups of B-29s were ordered to bases in England, including the bomb group that had dropped the two atomic bombs on Japan. Finally, Undersecretary of State Robert A. Lovett again mentioned the possibility of withdrawal from Berlin to President Truman, who replied, "We stay in Berlin, period" (Smith 508).

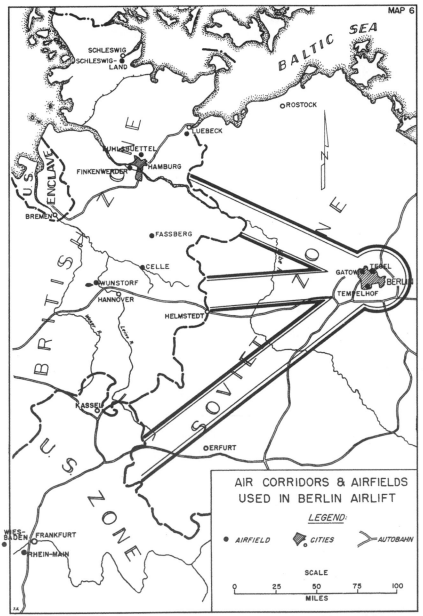

MAP 6

Air corridors and airfields used during the 1948–49 Berlin Airlift. Frederiksen
141.

July 1948—High-level doubt about the airlift persisted in Washington. Assistant Secretary of the Air Force for Matériel Cornelius V. Whitney told the National Security Council that "the Air Staff was firmly convinced that the airlift was doomed to failure." Lovett continued to dismiss the airlift as unsatisfactory and a temporary expedient, and Secretary Royall predicted its demise that coming winter. Truman's response to his doubting staff was to expand the airlift as quickly as possible and to commit the required number of C-54 transports to ensure success. In London, Secretary Bevin ran into similar pessimism when General Robertson, who had proposed the airlift as an option, suddenly began to doubt its efficacy. Bevin's expressed view was that he would rather hold Berlin to the bitter end and be driven out by force than give way voluntarily (Smith 514).

May 1949—Truman, Bevin, and Clay's unshakable commitment not to surrender Berlin to Soviet blackmail resonated with the air crews who had to make the airlift work. The crews flew their hearts out and made the naysayers eat their words, and on **May 12, 1949,** the Soviets formally ended the blockade. Three days later, General Clay, who was greatly respected and admired by Germans, returned to the United States and retired from the army. General Clay not only saved Berlin with his vision and steadfastness but in the process of doing so successfully transitioned Germany from an occupied enemy country to one that would one day rejoin the free nations of the world.

August 1949—On **August 24** the North Atlantic Treaty went into effect, and the North Atlantic Treaty Organization (NATO) was born. NATO's creation was a direct result of the Soviet-imposed blockade of Berlin and would in time contribute to the demise of the Soviet Union.

September 1949—The Federal Republic of Germany was established. Operation Vittles, the American name for the Berlin Airlift (the British called it Operation Plain Fare) officially ended on **September 30.**

The airlift's achievements are described in many publications. One of the most authoritative, *Berlin Airlift A USAFE Summary,* states that American and British aircraft flew 2.3 million tons of cargo into Berlin on 277,569 flights and that American aircraft sustained seventy major accidents. General Clay summed up the airlift's accomplishments: "If we had withdrawn from Berlin, which we would have had to do without the airlift, I don't think we could have stayed in Europe. I doubt if there would have been a Marshall Plan. I doubt if there would have been a NATO. How can you prove these things? I don't know. But I'm convinced that if we had left Berlin, we would never have had the confidence of the West Germans, or of any of the Western Europeans. I think that if we had pulled out and the Russians had moved in, we would have lost confidence in ourselves. If they had succeeded in that, it would have started a whole chain of events. The airlift prevented them from doing that" (Smith 505).

The C-47 and C-54 flyers who made the airlift a success were a hodgepodge of men with varied skills and experience levels. The only thing they had in common was that they were pilots or flight engineers. The lucky ones received C-54 training in Montana's blue-sky country; the others learned in the often treacherous German skies. For at least six months of the year, Central European flying meant battling freezing rain, fog, violent thunderstorms, and frequent marginal visibility. Landings at Tempelhof Airport with a maximum load onto short runways were more closely comparable to aircraft-carrier landings than to those on the up to ten thousand feet of concrete common at American air bases. The airlift was a "come as you are" operation, with no plans or procedures for handling the massive flow of diverse aircraft types into the restricted geography of West Berlin. In the early days, some people referred to the airlift as a cowboy operation, reflecting the chaos in the sky. The pilots had to learn to fly in narrow air corridors in all kinds of weather, making straight-in-one-try-only approaches into fog-shrouded fields. There were no sophisticated landing aids, just a world of ball and needle—compass, altimeter, attitude and airspeed indicators. That there were not more accidents is a tribute to the adaptive skills of the American and British flyers. Skills or not, they could not have done the job without ground control approach (GCA) radar, rudimentary radars by contemporary standards. The men who stared into the flickering green tubes hour after hour, as well as the pilots who had to put their trust in the GCA controllers' judgment, made GCA landings in zero visibility the system of the future.

The airplanes used in the airlift were severely punished in the "heavy load–frequent landing" environment. Maintenance focused on keeping the props turning. Fatigue combined with boredom became a real problem for many, as echoed in the stories that follow. The Berlin Airlift flyers conquered their unique challenges with skill

German schoolgirls in Celle, soup pails in hand, watch a coal-laden C-54 on its way to Berlin, 1949. C. Vaughn.

and imagination. They did not disappoint the leadership that put its trust in them, nor the American and British people, or the people of Berlin.

Chapter 1

Men of the Airlift

One of the greatest feats of flying in history.

Stephen E. Ambrose, historian and author

There wasn't one pilot who thought it wasn't going to work. Maybe there were some higher up in command who thought we weren't going to cut it, but the pilots thought what they were doing was going to succeed.

Joe Laufer, Berlin Airlift pilot

Colonel Howard S. "Sam" Myers Jr.

Sam became interested in flying early in life. His father was a World War I navy aviator who flew a twin-engine Curtis NC-4 seaplane on antisubmarine patrol out of Queenstown, Ireland. "They would see the submarine out there, pick up a bomb from the cockpit, and lean over the side," said Sam, with pride in his voice as he spoke of his father's experiences during World War I. "When they got to the release point, they dropped it." His father's stories fascinated Sam, and there was little doubt in his mind that once he grew up he would fly airplanes. "I was born in Boston, Massachusetts, in 1923, but I grew up in Virginia Beach, Virginia. In 1943, at age nineteen, I was called to active duty. I graduated from twin-engine school at Lubbock, Texas, the following year. Then I was sent to Tarrant Field, now Carswell Air Reserve Base, for B-24 transition training and then on to March Field, in Riverside, California, where I made my home after retiring from the air force. I was getting my crew ready to go to the Pacific. But in August of '45 they dropped the A-bomb. The war ended, and everything came to a halt. I opted to stay in the air force and was transferred to Bremen, Germany. I arrived in Bremen in August 1946 and was assigned to EATS, the European Air Transport Service, flying C-47 and C-45 aircraft. EATS was formed to provide the European theater commander with airlift for his far-flung troops from the United Kingdom to Turkey. I flew embassy runs and diplomatic missions throughout Europe, northern Africa, and the Middle East and made ammunition runs for the Greek government forces in 1947 during the communist attempt at a takeover. EATS really started the Berlin Airlift. We were in place. Eventually, we were absorbed into the larger Berlin Airlift operation and provided a cadre of trained and experienced pilots. It was not just our flying skills which were important to the Berlin Airlift, but also our experience in the sometimes unpredictable, often treacherous European weather.

"In April 1948 I was transferred from Bremen to Wiesbaden, still a first lieutenant, and assigned to the 71st Headquarters Command. My family lived in town on Galileo Strasse in requisitioned German housing. I remember July 1, 1948, when the Armed Forces Radio broadcast, 'Attention all United States military personnel. You are to immediately report back to your duty stations. This is not a practice. All leaves have been canceled. Military pilots will report to their commanding officers without delay for further instructions.' From then on I was a perpetual pilot. I flew from Rhein-Main Air Base in Frankfurt and nearby Wiesbaden Air Base. For the next twelve months I logged over two hundred airlift missions to and from Berlin in C-47 and C-54 aircraft."

Lieutenant Sam Myers in the cockpit of his EATS C-47 at Bremen, 1947. H. Myers.

At the start of the airlift there existed a lot of goodwill but little real knowledge of what it would take to supply a city of more than two million people with its minimum daily needs. The first thing that had to be determined was exactly what was needed and how much. Then a determination could be made of what types and how many aircraft would be required to provide the minimum food and fuel to keep Berlin from going communist. According to *A Special Study of Operation "Vittles"* by Aviation Operations Magazine, the minimum food requirements for Berlin for one day were:

646 tons flour and wheat
125 tons cereals
64 tons fats
109 tons meat and fish
180 tons dehydrated potatoes
85 tons sugar
11 tons coffee
19 tons powdered milk
5 tons whole milk for infants
3 tons fresh baking yeast
144 tons dehydrated vegetables
38 tons salt
10 tons cheese

Strict rationing was implemented for various categories of people, ranging from 2,609 calories for heavy workers, such as those unloading the arriving aircraft, to 1,633 calories for six- to nine-year-olds. The nearly 1,500 ton daily requirement of food, when added together with coal and miscellaneous supplies, came to a total of 4,500 tons to be moved to Berlin every day. This led to the determination that 225 C-54 aircraft were needed to move the U.S. portion of the daily tonnage. Initially, 102 C-47s were used from two airfields—Rhein-Main, near Frankfurt, and Wiesbaden Air Base. Eventually, on the U.S. side, two additional bases were added in the British zone—RAF Celle and RAF Fassberg—to fly coal to Berlin. A total of 201 air force C-54s and 24 navy C-54s, drawn from squadrons throughout the world, were assembled at these four air bases by the end of December 1948. The C-47, with its limited capacity of 2.5 tons, was phased out by mid-September and was replaced by the 10-ton-carrying C-54. Having one type of aircraft simplified the scheduling and control problems that the mix of 150-mph C-47s and 170-mph C-54s had created. To keep 225 C-54s flying, an additional 100 aircraft were in the maintenance pipeline, either at Burtonwood in England, for 200-hour inspections, or back in the zone of interior (as the United States was referred to at the time), for major 1000-hour inspections and overhaul. Replacement crews were trained on other C-54s at Great Falls Air Base in Montana. Nearly the entire inventory of C-54 aircraft was committed to the support of the Berlin Airlift.

The command and control arrangements, the fourth important leg for a successful airlift (the other three being aircraft, crews, and ground facilities) were soon in place. Since the United States provided the bulk of the aircraft, the British readily agreed to American leadership, and on October 15, 1948, the Combined Airlift Task Force, headed by U.S. Major General William H. Tunner, began to operate from Wiesbaden. Lieutenant General LeMay, then the commander in chief of U.S. Air Forces Europe (USAFE), first brought in Brigadier General Joseph Smith, who immediately set to work establishing procedures to fly the Berlin air corridors. Prior to his departure from Germany in October, LeMay arranged for Tunner to run the airlift operation. As LeMay wrote in *Mission with LeMay*, "Tunner was the transportation expert

The first pilots to fly the Berlin Airlift were from EATS. Here, EATS pilots are lined up in front of one of their aging C-47 aircraft at Bremen, 1947. Lieutenants Hal Hendler and Sam Myers stand third and fourth from left. H. Myers.

to end transportation experts. . . . It was rather like appointing John Ringling to get the circus on the road" (LeMay 416). Tunner had been responsible for the operation of the famed World War II China-Burma airlift from air bases in India, also known as "flying the hump" for the perilous crossing of the Himalayas.

"Tragedy struck quickly," Sam Myers recalled. "While making an instrument approach to Tempelhof, one of our EATS C-47s crashed in the Friedenau section of Berlin, killing both pilots. The accident served to bring forth an outpouring of sympathy and gratitude by Berliners for the American flyers. They erected a plaque to honor the dead pilots, and for months thereafter, flowers were placed at the spot where the two Americans died. It seemed this tragedy brought an end to the lingering animosity toward the American occupiers.

"A typical flight for me began at 5:30 in the afternoon when I reported for duty for a scheduled 7 P.M. take-off from Rhein-Main. I met my copilot at the briefing. It was unusual to schedule the same crew members to fly together regularly. We were assigned tail number forty-two. Forty-two was its hardstand number painted in large black letters across both sides of the vertical stabilizer and the rudder. We would be tracked into and out of Berlin by air-traffic control using that number. Our cargo was eight hundred two-liter bottles of milk, intended for the infants of Berlin. The prior day we carried 5,500 pounds of macaroni and dehydrated potatoes. What a mess that turned out to be. I was at seven thousand feet when the carburetors iced up. Nothing much I could do about that. I couldn't fly lower without endangering others flying below me. I was also falling behind, and the aircraft behind me was gaining on me. To maintain my altitude and airspeed, I had no choice but to turn to my copilot and ask him to jettison our cargo. Out went 5,500 pounds of macaroni and dehydrated potatoes, littering the Soviet zone below. I regained my assigned altitude and airspeed, continued on to Berlin, and flew straight back to Frankfurt without first landing in Berlin—I was empty already.

"On the next flight I hoped to do better. I picked up our maps, letdown charts, radio frequencies, and other assorted information—and of course a thermos of hot coffee to stay awake. The weather at Rhein-Main was a two hundred–foot ceiling and light blowing snow. The temperature was thirty-three degrees, visibility half a mile, wind south-southwest at fifteen miles per hour. The minimum takeoff ceiling at Rhein-Main was one hundred feet, so we were OK to go. The en route weather had a cold front lying across the Fulda beacon, with occasional thunderstorms reported by other aircraft. It would be a bit bumpy, to be sure, so we had to make certain our glass milk bottles were tied down securely. My copilot and I grabbed a shuttle, and we went out to hardstand forty-two. After a walk around the aircraft to ensure that the milk bottles were properly secured, we cranked up the engines. Over the radio I received takeoff clearance from the tower: 'Baker Easy Forty-two (Wiesbaden was Able Easy) proceed to Tempel-hof Airport via standard Darmstadt departure as published. Climb to assigned cruising altitude of 7,500 feet with a departure brake release time of 1900 hours.' I taxied out, following twelve other twin-engined

C-47s, with as many behind me. We were scheduled to depart at three-minute intervals. The tower cleared us to take active runway twenty-five (the magnetic heading for that runway was 250 degrees) at 1858 hours after the aircraft ahead of us released his brakes for his takeoff roll. Fifteen seconds prior to 1900 hours, I released my brakes and accelerated down the runway. I started my climb to nine hundred feet and turned toward the Darmstadt beacon. As soon as the gear was up, the aircraft disappeared in the clouds, and we were flying on instruments. 'Baker Easy Forty-two level at 7,500 feet,' I called into Frankfurt control. My copilot tuned in the Fulda beacon, hard up against the border of the Soviet zone. I listened to the aircraft ahead of me. If he was too fast or too slow, I needed to speed up or slow down to maintain our three-minute interval. At Fulda, this critical spacing was reestablished for everyone flying the corridor.

"Ice formed on the props and the leading edges of the wings. I actuated the wing boots, rubberized leading-edge devices to dislodge the ice, and I surged the engines to throw the ice off the props. The ice sounded like machine-gun bullets when it struck the fuselage. Then the carburetor of number two engine (the right engine) began to backfire. Again icing. Scenes of the previous day's macaroni dump ran through my mind. I didn't want that to happen again. I was able to maintain my altitude. I tracked steadily on a heading of fifty-seven degrees for the 211 miles to Berlin. About halfway down the corridor, I tuned in Tempelhof radio range. I heard a steady hum, meaning that I was flying down the centerline of the corridor. Had I been right, of course, I would have heard a strong *N* in Morse code; left, of course, an *A* of dots and dashes. The approach to Tempelhof Airfield was above a cemetery flanked by five-story apartment buildings. I initiated my approach at two thousand feet and was picked up by the Berlin area GCA controller: 'Baker Forty-two, Tempelhof GCA, turn left to heading 337, maintain two thousand feet, landing on runway twenty-seven, altimeter 29.73, ceiling two hundred feet, visibility half a mile. Advise when passing Tempelhof Range and when over Wedding Beacon. Over.' The GCA controller's radio transmission was crisp and to the point. When I was over the Wedding Beacon, I called Jigsaw Control, which was the Tempelhof final GCA which took me down onto the runway. 'Jigsaw Control, Baker Forty-two over Wedding Beacon at two thousand feet.' From then on, GCA guided me down a narrow radar beam to the end of the runway. There are three runways at Tempelhof. I landed on the center runway. Upon landing, I taxied behind the follow-me jeep toward the terminal. In a line of many others, I cut the left engine while my copilot opened the cargo door on the left side of the airplane, and within minutes a German labor crew backed a truck against the open door and unloaded the milk. From the time I shut down the engine until I restarted, no more than fifteen minutes elapsed.

"Once my copilot and I got back to Rhein-Main, we got ready for another flight. We frequently flew two to three times a day. Our greatest enemy was fatigue and boredom, flying day after day, night after night, often in grueling weather conditions. No pilot wanted to be known as a quitter. It really had to be an emergency before most pilots would consider aborting a mission. Many flew aircraft with malfunctioning or inoperative instrumentation, inoperable windshield wipers, or any other failed auxiliary equipment which they thought they could do without."

An example of this can-do spirit was provided by retired Lieutenant Colonel George H. Nelson, now living in Aberdeen, Washington, a C-54 pilot who flew coal from RAF Fassberg to Berlin. "When reviewing the aircraft maintenance log during my routine preflight inspection, I noticed a curious entry made by two pilots on the previous day. After their return from Berlin the pilots wrote, 'Number four (right outboard engine) fire warning light burns in flight.' The next pilot to accept the airplane for a flight to Berlin had cleared the write-up by entering in the log 'Bulb removed.'"

Although food and coal were the principal cargo of flights to Berlin, Lieutenant Harold Hendler, who like Sam Myers had been flying EATS C-47 aircraft from Bremen before transferring to Wiesbaden, flew some rather unusual cargo. On June 23, 1948, three days before the formal start of the Berlin Airlift, Hendler flew boxes of the new German currency into Berlin. The currency reform for the western sectors of Berlin was to occur two days later. Hal had an air policeman on board armed with a .45-caliber pistol. In addition, he was given three incendiary grenades to use in case he crashed his aircraft in the Soviet zone. "I was instructed to put one grenade on each wing over the fuel tanks and the third grenade on the boxes with the money. I was to make certain that none of the new money fell into Soviet hands. Fortunately, I didn't have to go through that exercise. My second unusual cargo was dynamite. At the newly built Tegel Airport in the French sector of Berlin, the landing approach was over a radio tower used by the Russians. The tower represented a major impediment to flight safety. I recall hearing that the French Berlin garrison commander sent a memo to Marshal Sokolovsky requesting the removal of the tower. The answer was as expected—*nyet*. I flew the dynamite into Berlin and the French used it to blow up the tower. Marshal Sokolovsky is supposed to have asked his French counterpart, 'How could you do such a thing?' The French commander's reply, 'With dynamite.' "

Lieutenant Hendler was another of the many children in the 1930s who became mesmerized by airplanes and the visions of adventure they brought forth. Born in New York on September 26, 1921, an only child, Hal used to go to nearby LaGuardia Airport every chance he got and stand for hours at the perimeter fence, watching airplanes take off and land. "I never got tired watching. In my spare time I carved balsa wood models from memory, replicas of the airplanes I longingly watched taking off and landing at LaGuardia. With the outbreak of World War II, I volunteered for pilot training, but it took until late in 1943 before I was given a slot in the aviation cadet program. By the time I graduated in 1945, the war was over. To be a pilot was a dream come true. In 1946 I was posted to Bremen, Germany. Of the nearly two hundred missions I flew into Berlin during the airlift, I remember one most vividly. It was a sunny day in July 1948 when I landed at Tempelhof. A RIAS (Radio in the American Sector of Berlin) announcer accompanied by a German woman and her two-year-old daughter met me at the aircraft. The woman wanted to say thank you to an American pilot for saving her city from the Russians. She presented me with several gifts she had made from the few materials available to her—handmade writing paper embossed with the seal of the city of Berlin, a stationery folder to go along with the paper, and a small unicorn toy for my children. I found it very touching." Hal Hendler, like his friend Sam Myers, settled in Riverside, California, after he retired from the air force.

First Lieutenant Leonard W. Sweet
Bronze Star, Air Medal (2)

Len Sweet is a New Hampshire farm boy to whom flying was something birds did. He had no interest or inclination in that particular direction, or so he thought. In 1940, a year after graduating from high school, Len joined the Massachusetts National Guard at the urging of a school friend. A few months later his unit was federalized, and Len found himself on active duty in the 104th Infantry Regiment at Camp Edwards. In the summer of 1941 the 104th participated in what Len recalled as "very strenuous maneuvers in the field." Upon his return that August, he and five others "went to the air corps recruiter at division headquarters and applied for transfers to the air corps to get out of the infantry. We were approved. At Scott Field, Illinois, where I was going through radio school, word got around that the air corps was accepting enlisted men without a college education for pilot training. Upon graduation pilots would be promoted to the rank of staff sergeant. I applied. In November 1942 I received my pilot wings and, as promised, I was promoted to the rank of staff sergeant. In early 1943 I was promoted to the newly created rank of flight officer. By November 1943 I was given a reserve commission as second lieutenant in the Army Air Force.

"Upon graduation from pilot training I was assigned to the 479th Antisubmarine Group at Mitchell Field on Long Island. We flew patrols up and down the East Coast, first in twin-engine B-18 bombers, later in four-engine B-24s. In the spring of 1943 we were sent to England.

21

Our mission was to catch German submarines going in and out of the Bay of Biscay to and from their pens along the coast of France. We sank one submarine. In November 1943 my group was disbanded, and we returned to the States for training in the new B-29 bomber. I checked out in the B-29 and remained behind as an instructor pilot at a base in Kansas until the war ended. At the end of the war I was discharged, but I stayed in the inactive reserve.

"In October 1948, quite unexpectedly, I received a letter from the U.S. Air Force recalling me to active duty as a first lieutenant to fly the Berlin Airlift. I liked the idea of going back into the military. I missed flying. The middle of November I received orders to report to Great Falls AFB, Montana, for transition training into the C-54. When I arrived, three feet of snow lay on the ground. It was so cold it practically took my breath away. The training I received duplicated the Rhein-Main–to–Tempelhof flight pattern, including takeoff and letdown procedures. Our approaches were GCA-radar controlled, and the landing simulated the short five thousand–foot runways at Tempelhof. The training aircraft were loaded with ten tons of bagged sand to simulate the weight we would be hauling once we got to Germany. I finished my training in December and was home for Christmas. The first week in January 1949 I reported to Westover AFB in Massachusetts, which was the main jumping-off base for high-priority Berlin Airlift support flights to Germany. I was about to start on one of the greatest adventures of my life.

"My destination was Wiesbaden, in the American zone. They didn't waste time getting me in the air once I arrived. Us newcomers were required to fly nine trips as copilots, and then we took three check rides as first pilot before being turned loose. I accomplished this in my first week.

"The procedure they had established to ensure proper spacing between planes was ingenious. There were three air corridors to Berlin. We flew the southern corridor and landed at Tempelhof. The English and our aircraft from Celle and Fassberg flew the northern corridor and landed at Gatow and Tegel. Everyone returned through the central corridor. Precise spacing was essential because we had a steady line of planes going to Berlin three minutes apart. To maintain this spacing we had three radio beacons we passed over before entering the corridor. Each pilot, when passing over a beacon, called out his hardstand number and the exact time over the beacon. Since I knew the number of the plane ahead of me, I could tell how far behind I was when I crossed the beacon. If I was more than three minutes behind, I sped up a little. If I was less than three minutes behind, I slowed down.

"We also kept a five hundred–foot altitude difference between airplanes. One airplane would fly at 5,500 feet, the next at 5,000 feet, and the third at 4,500 feet. Then the stagger would start over again, with the following aircraft flying at 5,500 feet, and so on. The corridors were only twenty miles wide, so I had to maintain a pretty accurate heading. When I was fifty miles from Berlin, I was picked up by long-range radar, and if anyone was too close or too far behind the plane ahead, the radar controller would have us make corrections to get back to the three-minute spacing as we approached Tempelhof. After flying once or twice a day, seven days a week, and most of the time at night or in solid instrument weather, things began to get a little monotonous. We were getting tired and bored. To relieve the boredom, to keep us awake, some pilots made wisecracks over the radio. Of course, that was strictly prohibited, but it was overlooked and tolerated under the circumstances. On one occasion a plane reached the fifty-mile point out of Berlin, and I overheard the long-range radar controller directing him to make a 360-degree turn to lose one minute. The pilot responded, 'If I make a whole 360-degree turn, I'll lose two minutes.' There was momentary silence, then the radar controller came back on the air and said, 'Do a 180 and back in.' Dialogue such as this continued through the winter and helped us to relieve the tension and pressure of continuous precision flying at night and in bad weather.

"On each of our flights we carried ten tons of cargo. A large flatbed truck with a ten-ton load backed up to the plane as soon as we landed in Wiesbaden. The cargo to go in the front of the plane (we carried only food from Wiesbaden) was put on the back of the truck to ensure the proper weight distribution throughout the aircraft. After loading, a GI would get in and attach the tie-down straps so the cargo would not shift in flight—a potentially fatal event. To do this loading and unloading, the air force hired thousands of Germans and DPs, men who came from all over Europe, men who had lost their homes and families during the war and had no place to go. They were grateful for the job, and they worked hard. The Germans got so good they could load and unload ten tons of cargo in ten to twelve minutes. In Berlin the German load crews had another interest. As soon as they pulled up to the plane, the first thing they did was run to the cockpit and empty the ashtrays. They would take the cigarette butts home and roll new cigarettes out of the remaining tobacco and sell them to Russian soldiers in the eastern sector of Berlin. Cigarettes were rationed in our PX to two cartons a week. Sometimes we brought one or two cartons to sell for thirty-five dollars each. The Germans still made money by selling the cigarettes one at a time.

"Tempelhof was located in the heart of Berlin, almost completely surrounded by five-story apartment buildings. There was one area where a cemetery was located between two apartment blocks, and it was over this cemetery that we made our approach, even though the buildings were only a few hundred feet apart. At times the weather was so bad, we would make the landing without ever seeing the buildings on either side. I can't say enough about the GCA radar operators, who were really fantastic in guiding us in safely every time. Later in 1949 the runway we were using required extensive repairs. We had to land on a runway beside the first one. This meant we had to come in over the top of one of the apartment buildings and then practically dive toward the end of the runway. To help us see the top of the building at night or in bad weather, strobe lights were installed on the roof. This was the first time flashing strobe lights were used to guide airplanes. After every trip we had to fill out a questionnaire asking us how we liked the lights, how effective they were, and if they blinded us. The lights were a great help. Today strobe lights are used on the approaches at nearly every major airport in the country. It began in Berlin.

C-54 being unloaded at Tempelhof, 1949. The large tail number was key to air-traffic control into and out of Berlin. M. Balfe.

"The pressure to keep flying was unbelievable, but I guess it was necessary to accomplish what had to be done. On one flight I lost an engine. It stopped dead and I had to feather the propeller to keep it from windmilling and continue the rest of the flight on three engines. The C-54 was a great airplane and flew well on three engines with a full load. I landed at Tempelhof and naturally assumed I would have to stay there until the engine was fixed. While the aircraft was being unloaded, the operations officer drove up in a jeep and asked, 'Do you want to stay here or fly back to Wiesbaden?' He didn't wait for an answer but quickly added, 'If you stay, it will probably take several days to get the parts flown in.' I looked at the copilot and flight engineer, and we agreed we didn't want to stay at Tempelhof. They cleared us to take off on three engines, over the five-story apartment houses, over the cemetery.

"Most of our loads to Berlin were made up of milk or other foods, but sometimes we had unusual cargo. On one trip I had a load of wine for the French garrison. When it was unloaded, a French officer checked the load. He became disturbed when he discovered one of the cases had been opened and three bottles of wine were missing. He didn't want to leave the plane until he found the missing bottles. I told him I had no idea where they were and that he would either have to leave the plane or ride back to Wiesbaden with us. He finally did get off the plane, but as I taxied to the runway, I could still see him waving his arms and shouting at me. When we arrived back at Wiesbaden, to our amazement we found three bottles of French wine under my seat.

"As spring arrived and the German weather improved, things eased up considerably. We were no longer required to fly seven days a week, and we got a little time off. By that time even the Russians had to admit the airlift was a success. We had accomplished the impossible. Over two million people had been supplied by air through a hard German winter. The West Berliners even started to do some manufacturing, and we carried some of their goods out on our return trips. In July 1949 my tour was up, and I was given orders to return to the States. I was assigned to Carswell AFB at Fort Worth, Texas, to fly B-36 bombers. When the Korean War ended in 1953, the military again had a sharp downsizing, and most of the reserve officers like myself called up for the Berlin Airlift and Korea were released from active duty. I was one of them. I reenlisted in the air force and spent the rest of my career as an enlisted man. Unfortunately, this ended my flying career, since enlisted men were no longer allowed to fly as pilots." When Len Sweet finally retired he chose not the sun of California, Florida, or Nevada but rather the area where he was born and raised. "It has taken me a while," he wrote, "but I have finally come home and am getting settled up here in New Hampshire."

First Lieutenant Marshall M. Balfe

Air Medal

Born in Newburgh, New York, in 1921, Marshall confessed to being interested in airplanes since he was a small boy. "I always wanted to fly.

I built model airplanes, rubber-band powered, until I left high school. I was a member of the Model Airplane Club. I read constantly about the great fighter pilots of the First World War. I knew the names of all the famous pilots in the Allied air services and the German pilots, as well as the names of most of the airplanes used by both sides. Before World War II broke out, I got involved in the Civilian Pilot Training Program. I went to night school to learn the things I would need to get a private pilot certificate. There were fifty-two people in the class, some of them high school teachers. The first ten with the highest grades were to get a scholarship to take flying lessons in a light plane. I came in number ten. I was the first in my class to solo.

"In 1942 I was accepted into aviation cadet training. About three hundred of us cadets started the course, and about one hundred finished. We trained in BT-13 and BT-15 aircraft, which we called vibrators. When we stalled the aircraft and went into a spin, the engine cowling would rattle loudly. The entire aircraft seemed to make noises as if it was coming apart. There was a delay in my finishing the course because I had to get my teeth repaired before the army would commission me. In February 1944 I finally received my wings as a fighter pilot and was commissioned a second lieutenant. I was twenty-three years old. Upon graduation I was assigned to Shaw Field near Sumter, South Carolina, as a flight instructor. We flew AT-6 advanced trainers. During the year I instructed at Shaw, fifty flight instructors were killed in accidents, and each instructor had a student in the plane with him. I had graduated as a fighter pilot. I had no trouble. I was declared surplus in 1945 along with many other pilots and separated from the Army Air Force.

"In 1948 I asked to be recalled to active duty. I missed being around airplanes. I reported to Great Falls, Montana, on December 24, 1948, for C-54 training. We didn't do any training until January 1, 1949. After two months of training, I joined the Berlin Airlift at Rhein-Main and flew from there to Tempelhof Airport in Berlin until September 1949. My cargo was coal, except for one load—ten tons of chocolate bars. The inside of the plane looked like a coal mine. The coal was moved in barracks bags, ten tons, 120 pounds per bag. The bags were stacked on the floor the length of the airplane and tied down with rope. There was a narrow lane along the left side of the plane so we could get to the cockpit. Coal dust lay on the seats and covered our flight suits. We flew night and day, on holidays and weekends. The planes never stopped flying except for maintenance. After twelve hours on duty, we were relieved to get some rest. Normally, if all went well, we could make two round-trips in a twelve-hour period. From Frankfurt to Berlin usually took one hour and forty-five minutes with an airspeed of 170 knots.

"Russian fighter planes flew around Berlin, but they didn't come near us. We heard rumors that during bad weather the Russians would release balloons on a long cable in hopes one of our planes would snag the cable and crash. It was only a rumor. My flights were mostly routine. Once in a while I would have to feather a propeller because of engine trouble, but that was not too serious. Nearly everyone experienced that more than once. When there was a serious problem, though, it usually happened unannounced and with catastrophic speed. One of our C-54s flared out at the end of the Tempelhof runway to land; at that instant a section of wing outboard of the engines broke off upward. The plane turned upside down, landing on its top, and skidded down the runway to a stop. The three crew members were seen to exit the plane at high speed.

"I recall one of our C-54 pilots who upon landing thought he had damaged the landing gear. He never stopped rolling and took off again to return to Frankfurt. The procedure at the time was one approach, land. Missed approach, go back to where you came from. He got rid of his load of coal on the way to lighten the aircraft. The flight engineer and the copilot, a small fellow, went back and removed the escape hatch over the wing. The hatch was about three feet square. The two men picked up the sacks of coal and threw them out the hatch one at a time. They threw the whole ten tons of coal out over eastern Germany. The copilot suffered a strained back. When the plane landed, it was discovered the landing gear was fine.

28

"It was our custom during landing to place a Coke bottle upside down on the glare shield over the instrument panel. If the Coke bottle fell over on touchdown, the pilot making the landing had to buy lunch for the other two crew members at the mobile snack truck. The number of times the bottle fell over was surprisingly small. Tempelhof Airport was ringed with five-story apartment buildings. The airport runways could not be extended. They were at their maximum length of five thousand feet. We had to make sure we landed on the end or close to the end of the runway to be able to stop.

"Flying the airlift was a job I was assigned to do, and I did my best to do it right. As for the German people, I felt they were victims of Hitler and his gang and suffered a lot during the war. I liked Germany.

"After the airlift I was assigned to an air weather squadron at Hickam Field, Hawaii, flying B-29 weather reconnaissance aircraft. The assignment sounded like paradise. It wasn't. My squadron was sent to Kwajalein Island, one of the islands in the Marshall group, to participate in atomic bomb testing. I was there for six months. Twelve B-29s and one C-54. I saw two atomic bombs explode. My job was to pick up airborne samples of the bomb debris after each detonation. A large scoop had been installed on the rear top of my aircraft's fuselage, and the hot stuff was piped to large holding tanks in the bomb bay. We flew several times in and out of the radioactive cloud to gather sufficient samples of the explosion. This was Operation Ivy in 1952. I left the air force in 1953 and then went to work for the FAA as a flight examiner at what is now Bradley Airport near Hartford, Connecticut." Marshall Balfe, now retired, resides in Gualala, California.

Colonel David M. Taylor's experience flying into and out of Tempelhof echoes Lieutenant Balfe's contention that Tempelhof could be a difficult place to land: "I started flying into Tempelhof in January 1949. Since I didn't have my family along, I wanted to fly as much as possible. I flew about 132 missions, probably more. I didn't keep a log. The weather was lousy much of the time, but since we flew strictly instruments, and we had good GCA, it didn't really interfere too much with our operations. I remember one particularly foggy day sitting at the

C-54 wreckage off the end of the Fassberg runway, 1949. One pilot died in the accident. W. Samuel.

end of the runway at Tempelhof waiting for clearance to take off. A C-54 broke out of the fog just before touchdown. He flared late and touched down hard. As the gear collapsed and the aircraft hit the runway, the wings came off. The fuselage continued to shoot down the runway, heading for the GCA shack. The GCA crew immediately abandoned their perilous position and watched as the fuselage of the C-54 stopped just short of impacting their shack. No one on board the aircraft was hurt. I carried a movie camera with me. When I saw the plane was in trouble, I filmed the crash. Only minutes after the crash, I took off from Tempelhof for Rhein-Main. The runway had no debris on it and was declared open. The airlift didn't stop for anything, not even for a crashed airplane."

Colonel Harold R. Austin

Born on a farm near Sweetwater, Oklahoma, and raised in Brownfield, Texas, thirty-five miles south of Lubbock, Hal Austin was fascinated by airplanes as long as he could remember. On the rare occasions when an airplane passed overhead, he would run out of the house to watch until the plane passed from sight. On a warm summer day in 1934, at the age of ten, his uncle came by and drove him to the edge of town, where a group of barnstormers had landed their biplanes on a farmer's meadow. They were giving fifteen-minute rides to anyone who could come up with five dollars. "Five dollars was a lot of money then," Hal recalled. "I didn't have five dollars and was content to watch them perform their tight turns, dangerous looking loops, and come skimming low and fast across the ground. I walked around each plane and touched it gently as if it had a soul. Then, totally unexpected, my uncle bought me a five-dollar ride. It was the most exciting thing that had ever happened to me. After that ride I dreamed of flying airplanes someday. It changed my life."

In 1943, at the age of nineteen, when the Eighth Air Force experienced terrible losses over Europe, the aviation cadet program was opened to teens with only a high school education. When Hal learned of that opportunity, he immediately joined the Army Air Force. In April 1945, after passing through a number of training bases, he received his pilot wings and a commission as second lieutenant. By then the war was nearly over in Europe, and after the Japanese surrendered later that year, Hal was declared surplus, along with many other young pilots, and released. "To make a living, I accepted a post office job in a small town in New Mexico, Deming. My mail route proved to be less of a challenge than I expected. I really missed flying. One day in January 1947 I stepped into the office of the local air force recruiter and volunteered to return to active duty in any capacity. I was offered a position at Luke Field in Arizona as a tower operator with the rank of master sergeant. As a tower operator I would control the takeoff and landing of aircraft. I took the job."

"It felt good to be back in uniform," Hal confessed, sitting in his comfortable home in Riverside, California, a popular retirement location for air force flyers. "Soon after reporting to Luke Field, I was assigned to attend communications school at Scott AFB in Illinois.

Once I graduated, in January 1948, I regained my former rank of lieutenant. As a trained communications officer, I was assigned to McChord AFB in Washington state. There I was promptly put in the right seat of a C-82 transport as copilot, flying support missions for the U.S. Army. I never got a chance to work as a communicator. Six months later I received orders to report to Hamilton AFB, near San Francisco, to await shipment to somewhere in the Pacific. I sat around at Hamilton for several days, waiting for my orders to arrive. When they finally arrived, I didn't go to the Pacific; instead, I was sent to Great Falls, Montana, to check out in the C-54 to fly the Berlin Airlift. On November 30 I arrived at Rhein-Main Air Base. On December 1 I flew my first mission to Berlin in the right seat. After that it was fly, fly, fly—ease the power back, ease the nose up, touch down. Unload. Back to Rhein-Main for more coal.

"We flew Christmas and New Year's Eve. Of course, we acted up when we arrived at Tempelhof on Christmas Eve. We announced our arrival as Santa and his reindeers. We were promptly told to shut up. The C-54 was a fantastic airplane to fly. They only fixed the engines, things which we absolutely had to have to fly. Other malfunctions were ignored. I had a working autopilot on only one aircraft I flew, but that time I nearly got into big trouble. It was night, and we were on our second run to Berlin, me and my copilot, Darrel Lamb. We had taken off at two in the morning. Both of us were sleepy. We didn't call in over the Berlin beacon. When I awoke I saw Darrel was sound asleep. The bird dog, our radio compass, was pointing toward the tail. There were not many lights on the ground below us—everything was pitch black. I really got scared. I awoke Darrel, who was as startled as I was. He cranked in Berlin radio. It was weak. We had no idea how long we had been asleep, but we promptly did a 180. It took us thirty minutes to get back to Berlin, about ninety or so miles. We were probably near Stettin, somewhere over the Baltic Sea, when we made our turn. The corridor wasn't always full of aircraft, so we waited until we heard someone call in over the Berlin beacon. Six minutes later, someone else called in his hardstand number. We waited three minutes and then called in our own number and rejoined the stream of aircraft into Berlin. We sweated blood for a couple of days, expecting the hammer to come down on us at any time. Nothing ever happened."

Fatigue was one of the greatest hazards during the Berlin Airlift. Hal Austin's dangerous incursion into Poland, although rare, is an example. Fatigue combined with a night, zero-visibility landing could be a deadly combination. Ice on wings, propellers, and on the runway also did not help. As a result of the frequent landings while loaded to maximum capacity, many of the aircraft badly needed maintenance before their scheduled two hundred–hour inspections. In such an assembly-line flying environment, where crews flew day and night regardless of weather conditions with marginally maintained aircraft, a price had to be paid: thirty-one Americans died carrying food and coal to a hungry and cold Berlin. In addition, thirty-nine Royal Air Force personnel and British civilian employees performing airlift duties lost their lives, as did thirteen Germans.

While Hal Austin still looked over his shoulder after his inadvertent penetration into Poland, he was hatching another way to get himself into trouble. He had met Rosemary, the stepdaughter of an army warrant officer who was stationed near Frankfurt. Hal thought he could impress the young lady if he took her on a flight to Berlin. Rosemary agreed to go, thinking it would be fun. "Hal told me I would have to come on short notice," Rosemary, who later became his wife, said, "and it would be at night. He found a parka for me, with a hood that had a fur lining to hide my face, and a pair of men's overalls. When he called, I put that on. 'Keep your hands in your pockets,' he said to me when he picked me up. 'Your hands will give you away, not being a man.' Well, to get into the GI truck, a weapons carrier, to take us out to the plane, I swear, the stairs into the truck were this high." Rosemary held her left hand up to the middle of her waist. "All the guys were yelling, 'Hurry up. Hurry up.' Hal whispered to me, 'Look down and go to the end of the truck and sit in a corner.' No way could I get on that truck on my own. The guy in front of me finally turned around and held out his hand. I had to take my hands out of my pocket and take his. He had this expression on his face, like, what am I holding? He pulled me up and kept watching me. He didn't say a word. But he kept watching me as I sat in the far corner of the truck. Hal in the meantime acted like I wasn't there. We got on the plane. It was supposed to be ready. And lo and behold, two GIs were working on something in the cockpit. Hal quickly grabbed me and shoved me into one of two bunks behind the cockpit and shut the curtains. 'How much longer?' I heard him say to the maintenance men. 'I have a window to make.' The maintenance men responded in the usual colorful language, followed by a "Sir," and suggested to Hal he take the blankety-blank spare on the next hardstand. Hal didn't want to do that because the plane was loaded and the rear door was already closed. He kept stalling. Finally, when he realized the maintenance men were not about to move, he opened the curtains, said, 'Come on Honey,' and reached in and grabbed me. Off we went out the door behind the copilot's seat. The two maintenance men stood there looking like, what have we got here?"

"That was the first time after three months of flying that I had an airplane that wasn't ready to take off," Hal interrupted Rosemary. "The next airplane we went to was ready."

"Some airplanes were crashing," Rosemary continued her story. "They didn't publicize it. But after his first plane wasn't ready, Hal thought it wise to give me a safety briefing. 'If anything happens, crawl away from the airplane as far as you can,' he said." Rosemary laughed loudly, recalling the incident. "I would probably be dead by then. How could I crawl then? In Berlin they unloaded the plane. I stayed in the bunk behind the curtain. Once we got back to Rhein-Main, it was light, and Hal worried the entire time someone would see me and recognize I was a woman."

Hal Austin apparently was not a fast learner when it came to taking young women along for rides. Two weeks later he took not only Rosemary but also her friend to Berlin. "On the way back from Berlin the girlfriend sat between and behind us, in the flight engineer's position," Hal recalled. "It's night, and the weather is rough. Her eyes are as big as saucers. I tell her not to worry, but if she should get scared, please, not to scream. St. Elmo's fire was on the props and the wings, and number four engine suddenly began to cough, and I had to shut it down. Rosemary's girlfriend started to scream like a wounded banshee and wouldn't quit. She thought we were going to crash. That was the last time I took any of them along."

Hal and Rosemary were married on July 2, 1949, in Frankfurt am Main, Germany. With the end of the airlift in September 1949, Hal and Rosemary Austin transferred to Barksdale AFB, Louisiana, near Shreveport, where Hal would learn to fly the new and fast RB-45C Tornado reconnaissance jet.

Lieutenant Colonel Edward Gorski

Air Medal

Any pilot who flew in Germany through the terrible winter months of 1948–49 will readily acknowledge that without the competence and professionalism of the ground controllers, the airlift would not have succeeded. Ed Gorski, who in retirement lives in Riverside, California, like many of his fellow airlifters, was one of the ground controllers at Frankfurt Airport during the airlift. Ed's parents immigrated to the United States from Poland and settled in Milwaukee, where Ed was born in 1921. He was one day from being drafted in 1942 when he looked at the newspaper and saw ads reading, "Join the Navy," "Join the Marines," "Join the Army Air Corps." He went to the Army Air Corps recruiting office, took the exam, passed, and got his name taken off the next day's draft list. Ed went through aviation cadet training at various bases and in 1944 received his wings as a multiengine pilot at Stockton, California. He was assigned to B-17s. Upon completion of B-17 training and crew formation at Lincoln, Nebraska, he expected to leave for England as part of a replacement crew. Ed and his fellow fliers knew what the term *replacement crew* meant. "Then a miracle happened, I was not assigned to the Eighth Air Force but instead went to Salina, Kansas, to train B-17 Mickey Operators. *Mickey Operators* were airborne radar operators.

"After the war I chose to stay in the air force. I liked flying. It grew on me. They didn't need pilots at the time, so I attended air-traffic-control school in Oklahoma City—that way I stayed around airplanes. In late 1945 I got on an airplane at Langley AFB in Virginia and with several other controllers headed for Europe. The plane stopped in Munich, then Prague, and finally in Frankfurt, dropping off controllers in each place. In Frankfurt I set up a traffic control center for Germany, located on top of the IG Farben Building. I prepared the flight plans, and a radio operator talked to the pilots giving them their air-traffic-control (ATC) clearances. I then helped establish ATC centers in Munich and Berlin. The ATC center in Berlin was manned by members of the four occupying powers—Americans, English, French, and Russians. Throughout the airlift, the center functioned, and its members continued to cooperate. The Americans, English, and French controlled aircraft and coordinated with the Russians if there was a need for it. The Russians always thought we might be doing something funny in the corridors, and on occasion aircraft deviated and the Russians scrambled their fighters. But they cooperated. Aircraft in the corridors at all times were controlled by American GCA radar at either end of the trip.

"I was sitting at the control board when the airlift started in June 1948. I sat there for a number of hours straight without interruption. My relief man didn't understand what was going on when he showed up, because we had airplanes coming and going. Until then, it was unusual to have that much traffic. Initially it was a real close thing, hit and miss. When the generals came over to set up the airlift system, General Smith at first, then Tunner, they wanted five altitudes out of Rhein-Main at three thousand, four thousand, five thousand, six thousand, seven thousand, and eight thousand feet. Well, after a number of days we found because of wind conditions the aircraft at the top would overtake the aircraft at the bottom. Things were out of sequence sometimes when the aircraft arrived in Berlin. Fulda was the checkpoint when coming out of Berlin. That was where the aircraft were picked up

Joint Air Traffic Control Center in Berlin, 1948. H. Myers.

by air-traffic control in Frankfurt. We would have to hold out-of-sequence aircraft at that point if the wind at the lower or higher altitudes differed substantially. At Fulda we ended up with stacks of airplanes. Of course, the same thing happened on the other end in Berlin."

C-47 pilot Lieutenant Harold Hendler knew about stacking up over Fulda. "I usually only had thirty minutes of fuel remaining at that point. To avoid declaring an emergency, although I was still in IFR conditions, I would declare VFR. In other words, I was saying I could see where I was flying when I really couldn't, at least not much. I could see the lights of Frankfurt shining through the undercast, and that was enough for me to proceed on my own to Rhein-Main or Wiesbaden and land. Risks were taken by everyone to make the airlift work. We just didn't talk about it."

"The problem over Fulda got so bad," Ed Gorski recalled, "that some of us convinced our bosses to talk to General Tunner to go to three altitudes. Five altitudes made things too problematic, especially for the C-47s—they overtook each other or fell behind. It was a mess, a cowboy operation. With three altitudes approved, we flew at three thousand, four thousand, and five thousand feet. From then on things worked out beautifully. Once the C-54s came, everything worked smoothly. It ran like clockwork. But initially it was a scary thing, no question about it. We also had a lot of people flying out of a desk. When they got into weather, they weren't really qualified. They did the job, but it was scary. I was one of them. When I got off my shift, I flew one up and back. That was my indoctrination to understand what was going on. Overall, it was panicky initially with the C-47s. After a while it got organized as the pilots got more experience.

"I had one interesting flight to Berlin. My copilot and I wondered why we couldn't get to our assigned altitude. We finally got there after an hour's laborious flight time. We were hauling perforated-steel planks to Tempelhof on our C-47. These perforated steel planks also came in a lightweight aluminum version. Our log said that's what we were hauling. But they had loaded the steel planks instead, which were of course nearly twice as heavy as the aluminum planks. It is a wonder that we made it to Berlin at all.

"We had a lot of people at USAFE headquarters who had airlift experience flying the hump in World War II, and we incorporated their knowledge into our operation. We also mimicked the FAA. We had attended their school in Oklahoma City, and they came over and watched us. They were amazed how we had managed to pick it up as junior officers. At that time our traffic load was the highest anywhere in the world. After a week of watching, the FAA representatives offered us jobs when we got out of the service. Everyone stayed. No one took an FAA job. Flying was still glamorous."

An article in the November 16, 1948, *Airways and Air Communications Service* newspaper features a picture of Lieutenant Gorski sitting behind a large traffic-control board in the Frankfurt center. The article mentions that in November 1948, Berlin ATC controllers averaged a radio contact with an aircraft every fifteen seconds. At Tempelhof, then the busiest airport in the world, the tower averaged better than one radio contact per minute. The air-traffic controllers were not unappreciated by the flyers. Lieutenant Leonard Sweet wrote, "I'm proud of the 176 trips I flew from Wiesbaden to Tempelhof. We often read of the accomplishments of the pilots, ground crew, logistics folks and even the thousands of DPs who could load and unload ten tons of cargo in ten or twelve minutes. There's no doubt that all of these people working together did a tremendous job. But there was one group of men that was absolutely essential to our success, the GCA radar operators who guided us to the runway. During winter in Germany the days are pretty short. Much of our flying was done at night. Also, my first impression when I got to Wiesbaden was that no one paid any attention to the weather. Rain, snow, sleet or fog, everybody kept on flying. I found it hard to believe at first, but it didn't take me long to learn. The cool, confident voice of the GCA final controller would guide us in every time. If we happened to drift a little off the glide path, he would calmly give us the correction needed to get us back on course. Then, as soon as we were safely on the ground, he would almost immediately pick up the next plane turning on final approach. This was because the next plane was only three minutes behind me.

"I remember one day that brought home to me how really great these men were. If it hadn't happened to me I would probably find it hard to believe. Sometime during the month of February 1949 a dense fog settled over most of Germany. This was too much even for the airlift. The fog became so dense that in the afternoon they stopped vehicular traffic on the base. All flights were grounded. But many of us were in the air, somewhere between Berlin and our home bases. There were no alternate bases open within reach of our fuel reserves. We had no choice but to return to our home base and put our faith in the GCA controllers. When I started my approach to Wiesbaden it was 7 P.M. and the fog was incredibly thick. About halfway down the final approach, I made the biggest mistake I could possibly have made. I called to the copilot to turn on the landing lights. As soon as they came on, I realized my mistake and told him to turn them off. The damage was done. The brilliant glare of the lights reflecting off the fog destroyed my night vision and temporarily blinded me. About that time I heard the GCA controller come on the air: 'You are now over the end of the runway. Take over visually and land.' Although I couldn't see anything, I flared back, and the next thing I knew I was on the ground. My first thought was to find out where we were. If we had one set of runway lights on each side, we were OK. If we had two sets on one side, we were in trouble. We were right in the middle of the runway, and GCA had landed us safely before I had seen the ground or any lights. All I had to do was bring the plane to a stop and try to find my way through the fog to the parking area. The fog lasted for three days. When it cleared, we went right back to flying every day. Looking back, I wonder how many other lives were saved by these dedicated men who sat in front of those little radar screens for hours at a time and served as the eyes for those of us doing the flying. Without them there could never have been a Berlin Airlift."

Lieutenant Colonel Joseph F. Laufer
Air Medal

Like most pilots who flew the airlift, Joe Laufer received his training during World War II. Joe was born in Chicago in 1923, an only child. He was four years old when Lindbergh flew across the Atlantic, and that experience captured him for life. His mother read the Lindbergh newspaper coverage to him at the breakfast table, and from then on he wanted to be a pilot. Joe read every aviation book he could lay his hands on. He knew about the Lafayette Escadrille, about Richthofen, and of course about Lindbergh. At his first opportunity, in 1942, Joe joined the Army Air Corps, with his parents having to sign their consent because he was only nineteen. The army kept him in limbo because there were not enough slots available, but finally in 1943 he was assigned to a pilot training class. One day while in training at Kelly Field near San Antonio, Texas, Joe was asked to report to headquarters. "It scared the living daylights out of me. I put on my uniform and made sure I looked perfect. Sitting quietly and apprehensively in a room with several others, a colonel finally entered to tell us we had been selected to train with the Royal Air Force. Yippee! I immediately departed for Terrel, Texas, a British pilot training base, where instead of flying aging Stearmans I flew the new and hot T-6 Texan. Upon graduation I hoped to go into fighters but instead ended up ferrying airplanes from the United States to North Africa, England, and Italy—B-26s from the Martin plant in Omaha, B-24s from Willow Run in Michigan, Douglas A-26s and B-25s from plants throughout the United States to wherever they were needed."

Joe recalled one of those "milk runs" from the United States to North Africa. "We left Morrison Field, Florida, for Puerto Rico, British Guyana, Brazil, Ascension Islands, and then on to Monrovia on the African continent. We were three lonely aircraft over a big ocean, always looking out for each other. From Monrovia we flew to Dakar, and then we intended to go on to Marrakech. To get to Marrakech we had to cross the Atlas Mountains. The weather forecast called for only high clouds. We were tooling along for about an hour when, looking ahead, I saw big cumulus clouds shrouding the Atlas. I couldn't climb over the clouds, so before we knew it, we were in the soup. I had picked up an excellent navigator in Philly. His name was Lash. Odd, how we never forget certain names. I said, 'Lash, we have to go through that mountain pass.' He gave me a heading, and I flew it. I don't remember any more how long we flew, but then I got scared, and I said, 'Lash, if we don't break out pretty soon I'm going to make a 180 and get out of here.' Suddenly we were in the clear. You could see the mountains on either side. He was a good navigator. Several planes were behind us. They didn't make it through the pass. They flew parallel to the mountains westward to the coast and then doubled back. Of course, Lash and I were long on the ground having a drink in the club when they landed. They said in astonishment, 'You came through the pass?' I boasted, 'Hell, it was wide open.'

"I got out at the end of the war for the sake of my mother. But I joined the reserves at O'Hare Field, and in 1947 the War Department recalled me and sent me to armaments school at Lowry Field, Colorado. After graduation I ended up at Pope AFB, near Fayetteville, North

Carolina. I was assigned to a P-51 photo-recce outfit—with no guns. Never saw a gun again. Pope was the pits. The 82nd Airborne colocated with us was a really wild bunch. I went to Personnel to get out of there. They put me on the overseas list, and I ended up at Hamilton Field, near San Francisco, awaiting shipment to the Pacific. It was August 1948. Instead, they sent me to Great Falls, Montana, for six weeks of C-54 training. From there I flew a C-54 to Frankfurt. In Frankfurt I was put on a military train to Fassberg. I had no idea where I was when I got there. I arrived in Fassberg at midnight. After a couple of hours of standing around and waiting, someone came and called my name. I was assigned to the 48th Troop Carrier Squadron. I grabbed my bag, and a weapons carrier took me to a barracks and a cold room. That night I was flying. It was two weeks before I saw the ground I was flying over because of the weather. I flew coal into Tegel. We shared Tegel with the Brits. Timing was always critical, so we were assigned block times. Fassberg planes would take off between sixteen minutes after the hour to forty-nine minutes after the hour, at three-minute intervals. If you got to the end of the runway at fifty minutes after the hour, you could not take off. Then you waited thirty minutes until the next block opened up. It happened to me a couple of times. If you had a block time of forty-nine, for instance, often you had to play beat the clock because of some problem. We'd jump in the plane, start the engines, and while we were taxiing, we would run through the engine checks, pressures, and temperatures. Normally we'd do this while sitting at the end of the runway. We'd taxi at high speed and check all four engines, and after that we'd run the before-takeoff checklist, hoping that by the time we did this and we got to the end of the runway, say at forty-nine, the tower would let us go. And if we weren't quick enough, they'd say, 'Hold position and wait.' Then we sat there cooling our heels.

"I had the usual maintenance problems. One time at Tegel on one of the engines the starter wouldn't work. They had a shoelike contraption that fit over the propeller blades and was attached to a rope. The rope was wrapped around the propeller hub; in turn, it was tied to a jeep. When the jeep gave the rope a pull, you had to have the ignition

Block-time board at RAF Fassberg, 1949. Simple aids such as block-time boards controlled a complex operation. J. Laufer.

on and be ready to hit the mixture controls. It worked on the first try. One incident scared the crap out of me one night. As we went down the runway I discovered that the more speed we gained, the more aileron I had to crank in. Finally I broke ground. I flew to Berlin with the wheel cranked all the way to one side. The landing was tricky. As we decreased speed, I had to gradually decrease aileron control. It turned out that we had two hundred gallons of gas in the right-wing tank. It was supposed to be empty. We had nothing in the left. And we didn't know it. Often the fuel gauges didn't work properly in an airplane, and just as often we didn't write them up. If we did, it grounded the plane. We were reluctant to red X an airplane. The airlift had to go on. As a result, many airplanes were in poor condition at the two hundred–hour point when we took them to Burtonwood for overhaul.

"Visibility was our major problem. One time the visibility was so poor I could not taxi to the unloading area. The plane behind me was sent back to Fassberg. There was a Russian airfield in the takeoff zone at Tegel. At about four hundred feet you had to make a steep turn to

43

C-54 pilots standing in front of Operation Vittles HOWGOZIT board, 1949. The 61st Group was number one when this picture was taken at Fassberg. J. Laufer.

avoid flying over the Russian field. On one flight I saw Yaks lined up on the field. Later they were gone. They had these Yaks dispersing on different airdromes. Only two or three times was I buzzed by Russians. I could see them coming in the distance making a head-on approach, and then they would break off. I was never really concerned about them. After takeoff from Fassberg, it was our practice to check in over Dannenberg beacon with our time and altitude. I listened to the aircraft ahead of me to adjust my airspeed to maintain the three-minute interval between us. At the Berlin beacon, approach control would pick us up—Corkscrew and Zigzag. Corkscrew took us to near the field, and Zigzag took us in. Those radar guys were the best in the world. They could bring you in through the eye of a needle."

Over a period of eight months, Joe Laufer thinks he flew 150 missions, "maybe a few more. I didn't keep a log, nor did most of the pilots, to the best of my knowledge. We just did the job we were trained to do—fly airplanes. There wasn't one pilot who thought it wasn't going to work. Maybe there were some higher up in command who thought we weren't going to cut it, but the pilots thought what they were doing was going to succeed." In eight months of flying, Joe had three days of leave. He spent that time walking around Berlin. The city was mostly in ruins—block after block of crumbling walls and empty holes that once had been windows to a gentler world. "I never met any Berliners. I hardly ever saw any of them, except when they were unloading my plane, or the girls at the snack truck. I thought of them as ordinary people who needed our help, not as former enemies." At RAF Fassberg, Joe's home base, he experienced culture shock. "The German maids when they came to clean my room would open the windows, regardless of the temperature outside. They were the original fresh-air fiends. I would be trying to get some sleep after a night of flying, and they would come in, throw the windows open wide, and go about their business as if I wasn't there. In time, I learned to sleep through it all." After retirement from the Air Force, Joe went to work for the Civil Aeronautics Board in Washington. Today he resides in Annandale, Virginia.

Colonel Robert S. Hamill

Distinguished Flying Cross, Air Medal (11), Purple Heart

"I was born in 1918 in Hamill, South Dakota. My father, Gail Madison Hamill, after whom the small community was named, ran a trading post on the Rosebud Sioux Indian Reservation. In 1925 my family moved to southern California. I had a talent for football and qualified for the San Jose football team under Coach Dudley DeGroot, who later coached the Washington Redskins. By 1941 my coach was Glenn S. Warner, better known as "Pop" to us players. I didn't come from a wealthy family. To be able to attend college, I had to cash in on my football skills. In addition I served as campus policeman, male model (with my clothes on), cleaned the stadium after games, and had my

Lieutenant Laufer picked up this C-54 at the Burtonwood maintenance depot in England. It was the one thousandth aircraft to go through a two hundred–flying–hour inspection and repair process. J. Laufer.

own Coke machines in fraternity, sorority, and other campus houses. There wasn't anything I wouldn't do to earn an extra nickel to stay in school. My mother taught me the value of education and never let me forget it.

"In 1939 San Jose was the highest-scoring college football team in the nation. I was a sophomore. By 1941 I was a two-way lineman and cocaptained the team. I was voted Little All-American. On December 3, 1941, accompanied by our coach, Pop Warner, I led the San Jose Spartans to Honolulu, Hawaii, to participate in a series of charity games. Ben Winkleman was officially listed as our coach, but Pop Warner did all the coaching. We were having breakfast in the Moana Hotel on Waikiki Beach, the morning of December 7, when we saw a lot of stuff happening in the water. The Filipino waiters were yelling, 'Whales! Whales!'—that's what they thought it was. It must have been bombs or antiaircraft fire. We kept on eating. The night before, we had been told the army would be conducting maneuvers off the beaches and we

46

would see tow targets. We kept looking for tow targets. It took a while to realize what was going on.

"Three weeks later we returned to the mainland aboard the *President Coolidge*. During the voyage, two players each were assigned a stateroom to tend to the wounded. It was horrible. They were burned all over their bodies and stank from the burned flesh and disinfectant. Every night bodies were taken on deck to the fantail and buried at sea. I never thought about going into the military before that, but as soon as we landed in San Francisco I led my football team to the navy recruiting office. They had a program which let you finish college before you went into flight training, and we all wanted to fly. I was the first in line. A dentist looked at my teeth and told me that I couldn't fly for the navy. I had an underbite, and that wouldn't do. I sat dejectedly on a bench, watching my teammates go through their exams. One finally came over and asked, 'What's the matter, Moe? You look down.' I told him. Within five minutes, my team walked out of the navy recruiting office and we went next door to the air corps office, where we signed up. The navy lost a hell of good pilot," Moe concluded with a twinkle in his eyes. "When I returned to the Varsity House, my home at the time, I found eight draft notices waiting for me. One notice was from the Chicago Bears offering me $150 a game. That was a fortune then. Another notice informed me that I had made Little All-American. The last notice I opened was from Uncle Sam. It was the most important.

"In early 1942 I reported for active duty and started air-crew training. I was sluiced through a number of bases. At Merced Field in advanced training I got to the point of my check ride. The commander of the squadron was Captain Edwards, he gave me my ride. After we landed, he got out and looked up at me and said, 'Where did you learn to play football?' I started telling him my whole life story. He walked away. I found out later that I was so rough on the controls that he thought I must have been a football player. He was trying to tell me how much I overcontrolled the airplane when he asked that question. He had no idea I ever played football. He made his point and walked away. At Williams Field in Arizona, in advanced twin-engined training,

I flew plywood AT-10s. The Arizona heat made the AT-10s fall apart, and the planes were grounded. It was decided that anyone with over one hundred hours flying time would graduate. I graduated without a check ride and was appointed a second lieutenant. B-25 training followed at Columbia, South Carolina. I got checked out ahead of my class. My first solo mission was at night. I tried to be an eager pilot, being the first one checked out. At the end of the runway, my instrument lights didn't come on. I was not about to abort my first solo mission and get the stigma pilots get for aborting. I was going to be a hotshot pilot. I had the engineer run his flashlight across the instrument panel, and we did the run up. As I started down the runway, I had runway lights, so I had no problem. When we got to the end of the runway, I pulled back on the stick, and it turned pitch black in the cockpit. I couldn't see the instruments. I told the engineer to give me some light. He did, and that blinded me. From the seat of my pants I kept flying. Pretty soon I felt a slap on my face. The flight engineer was shaking a pine branch at me, 'Sir,' he said, 'I think you went through the trees.'

"The plane was pretty badly beaten up. The bombardier's hatch was torn off, and the wind was rushing through the airplane. As I am making my approach to land I yelled to my copilot, 'Flaps.' He either didn't hear me or was too scared to move, but I didn't have flaps, I realized, as I was going down the runway like a son-of-a-bitch. I went around, got the flaps down, and made the landing. Two days later I met a flying evaluation board headed by the group commander. He read me the riot act. Then he grounded me. They made me a second lieutenant squadron commander of a processing squadron of active-duty people who had been accepted for pilot training. I didn't even know how to set up a morning report. But the sergeants took care of me and made me look good. One Sunday the local Columbia paper did a story on my squadron. The group commander read about this second lieutenant and his great squadron and promptly called me into his office. He gave me two choices—be a permanent ground pounder squadron commander, or go overseas flying B-25s. I went back to flying.

"I was at Walterboro, South Carolina, for advanced training. One morning we were going on the range for bomb training. We had to go to Myrtle Beach to pick up the bombs first, real early in the morning. There had been a party at the club the night before, and my bombardier was a happy drunk. I couldn't take him, but I wasn't going to abort the mission. I took my bombardier to his room and told him to stay there. He went right to sleep. Six of us were flying formation up to Myrtle Beach to get the bombs. One by one, the guys dropped out, buzzing people in the cotton fields below. Finally there was only lead and me. I wanted to go down and buzz like the rest of them. Then I saw a fairly big river. It was wider than a B-25, with steep banks. In those days the epitome of being the greatest pilot was to fly close enough over the water to get water in the lower turret. Here I went. The guys in back were yelling, 'We're getting water, we're getting water.' I didn't realize two things. First, the river wasn't going to stay straight forever. Second, the migration of ducks in February. There was a major turn in the river, and thousands of ducks were on the near side, out of the wind, where I couldn't see them. I thought, 'Do I pull up, or shall I carefully turn and not hit my wing in the water?' The banks looked pretty high to pull up, so I decided to turn. Well, the ducks heard the roar of that noisy B-25, and thousands of them came up right through me. The bombardier's hatch was completely busted in. The rocker boxes were broken and dangling. The leading edges of the wings were dented. I didn't land at Myrtle Beach. I knew that airplane wasn't going to fly again.

"I was the only one landing at Walterboro. Everyone was there to meet me. We dropped the hatch and four of us got out. It was a five-man crew. They looked into the bombardier's compartment, and all they could see was blood and guts and feathers. The compartment was full of dead ducks. They thought the bombardier had been killed and was lying under that bunch of dead ducks. Well, the Lord was looking out for me that day and for my bombardier, Frank Snow, for if he had been along he would have been killed for sure. There went my flying career again, I thought. The only thing that saved me, I believe, was that at this period of the war in 1943 they desperately needed pilots. I completed the remainder of my training, and my crew and I went by train up to Kellogg Field, Michigan, where we picked up a new B-25 at the factory. Then we flew the long circuitous route from Michigan to Florida to South America to Ascension Island and on to North Africa.

"At a rear base near Cairo, Egypt, we were assigned to the 12th Bomb Group. We went into town to look around. Only the copilot stayed behind. Soon a half-track came after us, picked us up, and took us directly to our aircraft. The engines were running. The operations officer said to me, 'The copilot has been briefed. Just don't fly above four hundred feet.' I taxied out into an open spot to take off—I didn't know where the runway was—when all at once they flagged me down. I had taxied into a minefield at the forward base. Then, carefully, they led us out of there, and I took off. The following day I checked the mission board in front of the operations tent and found that I was on the schedule to fly a night mission. I confronted the operations officer and said to him, 'There must be some mistake. I just got here, and I am listed on the mission board to fly at night. I am not checked out yet.' The ops officer turned to me and said, 'Are you the pilot?'

"I responded, 'Yes, Major. I haven't been checked out day or night.'

" 'Didn't you fly yesterday?'

" 'Yes, sir.'

" 'Was it daylight when you took off?'

" 'Yes, sir.'

" 'Did you land after dark?'

" 'Yes, sir.'

" 'You are checked out, Lieutenant.' And with that comment I was dismissed.

"I remember that first mission against the Afrika Korps. The flak—it sounded like gravel hitting the aircraft. A couple weeks later, on May 6, 1943, just before the Germans surrendered, I was flying my sixth mission. The aircraft in front of me received a direct hit. It was the new group commander on his first mission. The airplane disintegrated. I was busy dodging debris. When I got back to base, I was pretty well shot up. We couldn't get the gear down. I gave the crew the opportunity to bail out, but they opted to stay with me. I was going to belly in. The procedure was for the copilot to back up his seat and get out, then the pilot. Then there is room for the bombardier to exit, and so on. I was still sliding down the desert, props throwing up dust, when I felt a foot on my ear. My bombardier was standing on my shoulders, trying to get out. I don't remember who got out first. Later on we tried to get out the way he did, but without that adrenaline we couldn't do it. I popped three disks in my back. Otherwise, no one was hurt. After my muscle spasms died down, I went back to flying.

"The next day the army captured Cape Bon. In the German hospital tents, they found two of the crew of the plane that had blown up in front of me the day before. I had told them that no one could have survived. The pilot's leg had been amputated. The medical records were there. Everything the German doctors had done was perfectly recorded. The other survivor was the bombardier. I asked him how he got out. He didn't know.

"As the weeks passed, I worked my way up to Sicily. I was bombing on the other side of Mount Aetna when an 88mm shell went through my right wing and exploded above the aircraft, killing the gunner in the upper turret, knocking out the intercom. I finished the bomb run before returning to base. After we landed we counted over five hundred holes in the plane. The dead man got the Purple Heart. The rest of us got nothing. When I returned home, I had flown forty-two combat missions.

"After the war was over, I was operated on for my crushed disks. I spent considerable time in the hospital. I got out in 1947 with the rank of major, but my football career was over. Instead, I opened a little fast-food restaurant in Santa Ana, California. One day an air force major came into the restaurant and asked, 'How would you like to fly airplanes again? I can get you an airplane so you can go anywhere you want.' The major said, 'I can check you out over here in Long Beach. All you have to do is sign up in the reserve.' I signed up. I was bored. This was in 1948. I had not even checked out yet when I got a letter:

'Welcome to the air force,' it read, 'We need you for the Berlin Airlift.' That's how I got back in. I went to Montana for C-54 training. They checked us out, and then they sent us over to Germany. I ended up in the 29th Squadron at Fassberg. My first flight was on April 13, 1949, my last on August 24, 1949. I flew 205 missions in seventeen weeks. I flew more than what my records show. On Tunner's Easter Parade I flew five missions which are not recorded in my records, but I know I flew them. I flew whenever I could.

"Most of the flying was boring, boring, boring, with the exception of one mission. We landed at the French base of Tegel. We carried coal, and the British carried fuel. We'd sit there waiting to take off and watched the Brits land. The fuel baffles weren't too good on the Brit airplanes. When they'd land, the fuel went one way, and they bounced. The fuel went the other way, and they bounced again. Of course we were supposed to observe radio silence, but every Yank out there said, 'One, two, three—' The Brits called back, 'OK, Yanks, shut up.' Every once in a while they'd have an accident landing. One mission I remember well was when Tegel was closed because one of the British fuel tankers had crashed. They diverted us to Tempelhof. On this mission I flew through my first really big thunderstorm. I remember going from two thousand to eight thousand feet and back down again. We put on the lights in the cockpit, and the copilot worked the throttles. All I could do was keep the airplane level. First it was solid black in the cockpit, then with the lightning around us it would turn brighter than daylight. By the time I got to my GCA run into Tempelhof, I probably lost ten pounds. Well, we were coming out of the clouds on final approach. I had never been to Tempelhof before. We were breaking out of the overcast. I looked to my left and saw that I was right in between these apartment houses. The windows were lit up. I became really frightened, because I just knew I was going to crash. I added power. I was ready to pull up and go back. Then I saw the runway. I had already added power. I was trying to get the power off. I landed so fast. I recall yelling for the copilot to help me on the brakes—we didn't have reverse props in those days. I used up the entire runway. It was that approach

Wreckage of a crashed British fuel tanker at Tegel, 1949. R. Hamill.

in between those apartment houses that frightened me to death. That thunderstorm made me forget everything.

"Fassberg was a good base. We never missed a mission, and I never aborted. Everything I remember was 'Mach Schnell. Mach Schnell.' I would get out there with the German crews and help them unload the coal from their trucks. That's how I got my exercise. Then we'd go down to the wagon and get a coffee and a donut. All I did was fly and sleep. Three days off, ten days flying. Some days off I flew for guys who wanted time off to play poker."

But all was not work for the airlift flyers. The spring and summer of 1949 were beautiful. Off-duty American airmen strolled through the streets of Fassberg, a town untouched by war, looking for something to do. They crowded the few bars, sitting outside on sunny days, drinking German beer, smoking, and whistling at German girls passing by. Master Sergeant Chester J. "Jim" Vaughn is probably representative of many of the young single men who served in Germany at the time. Jim was an Indiana boy, born in 1927, growing up in the depression years.

"Those were tough times for us," Jim recalled. "I learned firsthand what sacrifice was all about, so when I arrived in Germany in 1948 I could empathize with the plight of the German people. As a twenty-one-year-old airman, I did the job I was required to do as an aircraft mechanic." Jim was stationed at RAF Fassberg with Moe Hamill: Moe flew the planes Jim fixed. According to Jim, "When I was not on the job, I took the time to explore the local sights, keeping on the lookout for beautiful German girls. I found one, a lovely young lady, Ursula, who lived in the town of Lüneburg. After a fast and furious courtship, we were married in the Fassberg base chapel on August 17, 1949, and then spent a short honeymoon on the island of Sylt in the North Sea. In late September 1949 I brought my new German bride to the United States."

Jim and Ursula's marriage must have been one of the first airlift weddings, but many more airmen were to marry German girls in the weeks to follow. Other relationships were more casual. "Easy girls" drifted to American military bases, and the associated problems were a headache for squadron commanders. The commander of the 29th Troop Carrier Squadron, Lieutenant Colonel Elmer E. McTaggart, was faced with the age-old problem of what to do about it. He finally wrote a letter to his men, appealing to them to mend their ways:

Again during the month of June, the 29th Squadron proved it was the best unit on the station. As we did in May, we carried more coal to Berlin in the greatest number of flights. We had the greatest number of aircraft in commission and the least amount of turn-around maintenance. As a matter of interest, let me enumerate what the 29th Squadron was leading in for the month of June:

    a. Greatest number of flights to Berlin.
    b. Greatest amount of coal to Berlin.
    c. Largest number of aircraft in commission.
    d. Greatest number of discrepancy reports.
    e. Greatest number of VD cases.

There can be no doubt from the above that we are the workingest, fightingest . . . outfit on the field. It is nice to deal in superlatives when speaking of our squadron. However, I wonder if it is possible to eliminate discrepancy reports and VD from our list? Each one of you is certainly entitled to a "well done." Let's keep up the good work.

I have no idea how successful Colonel McTaggart was in his appeal, but three months later the airlift ended, and RAF Fassberg reverted to its former quiet self.

After the Berlin Airlift, Moe Hamill piloted Boeing KC-97 tankers and commanded a KC-97 squadron before transferring to SAC headquarters in Omaha, Nebraska. He retired after thirty years of air force service to pursue a successful career as a financial securities broker in Newport Beach, California. Master Sergeant Jim Vaughn retired from the air force in 1966 and went to work for United Airlines as an aircraft mechanic. Today Jim lives near Las Vegas, Nevada.

Chapter 2

The Bomber Boys

On Monday, June 28, Truman ordered a full-scale airlift. The same day he sent two squadrons of B-29s to Germany, the giant planes known to the world as the kind that dropped the atomic bombs on Japan. But in fact, these had not been modified to carry atomic bombs, a detail the Russians were not to know.

David McCullough, *Truman*

R. J. made a recording for the BBC. It was broadcast every thirty minutes, I believe, on the BBC for the rest of the day, announcing "The Yanks are back!"

Joe Gyulavics, B-29 navigator

Although the Berlin Airlift was fought by air crews flying unarmed C-47 and C-54 transports, behind them towered a big stick, the B-29s of the newly created Strategic Air Command, better known as SAC. Little has been said about the men who manned these bombers and their contribution to the airlift's success, but without their presence, no American or British combat capability in Europe could have checked the territorial ambitions of Marshal Joseph Stalin. In late June 1948, one B-29 squadron of the 301st Bomb Group was on rotational training at Fürstenfeldbruck Air Base near Munich. With the Soviet implementation of the Berlin blockade on June 26, General George C. Kenney, the first commander of the still-forming Strategic Air Command, ordered the other two B-29 squadrons of the 301st Bomb Group to deploy to Goose Bay, Labrador, and then proceed to Fürstenfeldbruck, where they arrived in early July. The 307th Bomb Wing at MacDill AFB, near Tampa, Florida, was put on three-hour notice for deployment, and the 28th Bomb Wing at Rapid City AFB, South Dakota, was tasked to be ready to deploy on twelve hours notice. Later that July, both wings arrived in the United Kingdom. All other SAC bomber units were put on twenty-four-hour alert. None of the deployed or deploying B-29s had nuclear capabilities.

Colonel Joseph J. Gyulavics

Distinguished Flying Cross (3), Air Medal (5)

"My father immigrated from a small village in Hungary, Taliandorogd, in 1912," Joe Gyulavics recalled. "He came alone to the United States to get rich. His plan was to eventually return to Hungary, buy a farm with the money he made in America, and live comfortably ever after. After years of working in coal mines in Pennsylvania, he saved enough money to buy a farm, but it was outside Buffalo, New York, not in Hungary. He sent for my mother and older brother. For several years my parents tried desperately to make the farm pay, but eventually they lost it. My father then went to work in a steel mill in Buffalo, which had a close-knit Hungarian community nearby. I was born in 1925. Everything in my life was Hungarian, including the language I spoke, until we moved to a house across from a public school and I got to play with other kids. By the time I was in the first grade, I could speak English well.

"I always wanted to fly. As a little boy, when I heard the roar of airplanes, I ran outside to watch them fly over our house. I built models out of balsa wood but could never afford to buy paint for them. There was a little airport about five miles out of town. I peddled out there on my bicycle to watch the small Taylor Cubs land and take off. I went around the back side of the field, near the runway, and hid in the tall grass so I could see the planes close-up. Once one pilot saw me hiding in the grass and taxied over and chewed me out. Eventually I got a ride in an open-cockpit plane. It was a dream come true. My older brother paid the pilot three or four dollars to take me up, which was a lot of money at the time. In 1941, at age sixteen, I graduated from high school. When the war broke out in 1941, I wanted to join the army and fly. Many of my older classmates were joining the services and going to war, but I was still too young. I went to Syracuse University for a year, but I had little money, and it was a constant struggle. As soon as I turned seventeen I tried to join the navy. They flunked me on my physical. They said I had a heart murmur. 'I'm a healthy kid,' I thought. 'I don't have a heart murmur.' I went home, and my family physician examined me. He found no heart murmur. I asked him to put it in writing. I intended to go back to the navy examiner with the letter in hand, but then I got a job as a draftsman at the Curtis-Wright Aircraft Company, where they built P-40s and C-46s, and I was making good money. So I waited until I turned eighteen and then tried to join the Army Air Force before the draft board got to me. The army also flunked me on my physical, but this time it was a deviated septum. 'You can't fly with that obstruction in your nose,' the doctor said to me, 'but you can be a ground crewman.' 'What do I have to do to fly?' I asked him. 'Get an operation,' he said.

"I found a doctor who operated on my nose. He took out a couple of bones, and I paid him twenty-five dollars. The Army Air Force accepted me in the aviation cadet program. I spent the next two years from 1943 to 1945 being bounced around as a buck private waiting for a flying-school slot to open up. None ever did. For those two years I served as assistant crew chief on a P-40 at Aloe Field in Texas; as a butcher in a mess hall in Smyrna, Tennessee; drove a fuel truck on the flight line in Stuttgart, Arkansas; and did every odd job you can think of. When the war ended, I was sitting there as a buck private and hadn't done one damn thing. 'If you want out, you can get out,' I was told. 'No,' I said, 'I haven't achieved anything yet.'

" 'If you want to stay, you can go to navigator school at Ellington Field, near Houston,' the army personnel people told me. So I went to navigator school. Talk about being snakebit. On graduation from Ellington my entire class went up on the stage in the base theater and received their commissions as second lieutenants—everyone except me. Personnel lost my physical somewhere, misspelled my name on the records, and now couldn't find them. I graduated as a navigator but not as a lieutenant. My classmates went overseas while I sat at Ellington waiting for the paperwork to come through. Ten days later I got my commission, went home, and got married. I was sent to Las Vegas Army Air Field as a celestial-navigation instructor. We had a nice honeymoon in the early days of Vegas. In November 1946 I was discharged. They gave me three hundred dollars mustering-out pay, and I was on my own. When I finally got back to Buffalo, it was too late to get into school. My wife was due with our first child in a few months, and I didn't have a job. Things looked bleak. I went to see the army recruiter and he told me I could enlist as a master sergeant for eighteen months, but I couldn't choose my branch of service. They put me in the signal corps—sent me to New Rochelle, New York, and put me in charge of a platoon of telephone-pole climbers. I knew nothing about the telephone business, but I was the senior NCO in charge. I wrote a letter to the adjutant general of the Army Air Force and asked him, 'What am I doing here? I am a qualified navigator, and I should be in the air force.'

"Lo and behold, I soon got orders to go to Rapid City Army Airfield in South Dakota as a celestial-navigation instructor. When I got there, they were still sweeping the wheat out of the hangars the farmers had used for storage while the base was closed. The base was being reopened for a B-29 bomber outfit coming in from Alaska. As soon as the planes hit the ramp, most of the crews said, 'We've had enough. We want out.' They got out, and the 28th Bombardment Group didn't have enough crews to fly all of its airplanes. I saw an opportunity and approached my squadron operations officer. 'Hey, I'm available,' I said to him. 'I'm a navigator. I know you're short. I'll be happy to fly.' 'But you're a master sergeant,' he said. His facial expression told me to get lost and leave him alone. I didn't. 'I can fly,' I said to him firmly. 'I was commissioned a second lieutenant. I have my navigator wings.' I showed him my orders. After taking a look at my orders, he said, 'OK, you're back on flying status, but only for one month at a time.' I said reluctantly, 'I've never flown in a B-29 before.'

"He looked at me, exasperation showing in his eyes. Then he turned to a navigator sitting at a desk nearby and said, 'Lieutenant Curtis, go and check the master sergeant out.'

" 'Come along,' Lieutenant Curtis said to me in a friendly voice. We went to a B-29 parked out on the ramp and climbed in. 'This is where you sit,' he said. 'This is the airspeed indicator,' and he pointed to it, 'and this is the altimeter. There is the compass. The drift meter is over here.' That was it. A week later I was heading across the Atlantic for Germany navigating a 77th Bombardment Squadron B-29 of the 28th Bombardment Group. I was a last-minute replacement for a crew which didn't have a navigator. On the way out to the airplane, the operations officer told me, 'Oh, by the way, on your way down to MacDill, air swing the fluxgate compass.' Air swing the fluxgate compass? My God! How do I do that? I looked into my old aviation cadet textbook, which I carried with me in my navigator bag. Sure enough, there was a chapter on how to swing a fluxgate compass. It was supposed to be done on the ground on a surveyed compass rose, but we didn't have time to do that. Prior to takeoff, one of the other navigators suggested to me, 'Why don't you fly over Tallahassee. There's a good radio beacon there. Have the pilot take up a cardinal heading into the beacon while you take a sun shot with your astro compass, compare them, and then interpolate. You can work it out.'

"I said, 'Yeah, yeah,' like I knew what he was talking about. I was stunned. The rest of the squadron landed at MacDill while I had my pilot flying headings into Tallahassee radio. Even over the roar of the engines I heard the pilot, Lieutenant Gale Cummings, yell to the co-pilot, 'Go see what that navigator is doing back there. He's only a master sergeant. I don't even know him. I have never seen him before.' I didn't know any of them either. We landed at about six o'clock that evening. Everybody went to the chow hall and ate and then went to the transient barracks for crew rest. I hadn't finished compensating the compass yet, and I was afraid to admit that to anybody. That night I went out to the airplane. I had a hard time finding it in the dark, parked on a strange airfield on a remote hardstand. When I finally found the plane, I climbed aboard. Of course, there was no power. I used my flashlight. It was a lot hotter in Florida than in South Dakota, and I was sweating, tired, and starting to panic. I was in my winter flying suit. I got out my old cadet manual and followed the instructions. It's a bezel ring you adjust on the fluxgate compass. I didn't have a screwdriver to make the adjustments, so I used my pocketknife. I was not too confident that the adjustments I made were correct. We took off the next afternoon for Germany via the Azores.

"I got a few drift readings over the Atlantic before it got dark. I tried a celestial fix with the old A-10 sextant. I centered the bubble on a star, made little marks on the ring covered with wax paper, and then averaged out the pencil marks I had made. Supposedly that was the altitude of the star. After shooting three stars I went into the books and calculated a line of position for each of the stars, which I then plotted on my chart. Of course, my fix was where we had been when I started the procedure an hour earlier. Come dawn the next morning, we flew in a broken overcast and undercast. No drift readings were possible. No way to shoot the sun. I was flying dead reckoning most of the time. The pilot turned around in the cockpit and yelled back at me, 'Hey, when are we supposed to hit the Azores?' Straight ahead, forty-five minutes, I said, with as much confidence as I could muster. Pretty soon the pilot yelled, 'Hey, pretty good, pretty good, Nav!' I crawled into the nose of the aircraft and there, sticking through the undercast, silhouetted against the rising sun, was Pico Alto. We were heading right for it. From then on I could do no wrong. I almost got lost going from the

Azores to the coast of France. I was about fifty miles off. It didn't matter to the crew.

"In October 1947 we finally found our way into Giebelstadt, Germany. There hadn't been much recovery. The hangars were still bombed out. The runway was in good shape, though. They had a GCA radar at Giebelstadt, but they were still practicing. We had a few hairy GCA-controlled approaches in bad weather, which I would just as soon forget. Both pilots and GCA operators needed much more practice. When we had good weather, which wasn't often, the squadron flew in formation, nine or ten aircraft, over the capitals of Europe as a show of force. It was an education for me to see places I had only read about. We flew low, at about three thousand to four thousand feet. My crew was selected to fly to Dhahran, Saudi Arabia, to demonstrate the reach of the B-29. Flying over the Arabian Desert was much like flying over the Atlantic: no landmarks, no navigational aids, no nothing. We got back to Rapid City in December 1947. I was assigned to my own crew, piloted by Lieutenant J. R. Wright. Our B-29s had the letter *R* in a black circle painted on their tails—the same letter that was painted on the tail of the *Enola Gay* in 1945, although she didn't belong to the 28th Bomb Group. We had three squadrons in the group—the 77th, the 717th, and the 718th. In the months after returning from Giebelstadt, I checked myself out on the APQ-7 radar, which was installed in our B-29s. The radar had a sixty-degree sector scan over a range of two hundred miles. I also checked myself out on the Norden bombsight. We didn't have a bombardier on the crew.

"The air force became a separate service in 1947, and with that the Rapid City Army Airfield became Rapid City Air Force Base. We also changed our unit designation from 28th Bombardment Group to 28th Bombardment Wing. Names changed, but little else. We still didn't have a bombardier on the crew. One Sunday afternoon in July 1948 I got a call to report to squadron operations immediately. When I got there, everybody was filling out papers. 'We're going on TDY,' I was told. 'Go home and pack a bag for a couple of weeks and come back and you'll get briefed.' When I did, however, things didn't seem right.

People were filling out forms like powers of attorney and last will and testament. I packed, and when I got back to the squadron, we were briefed that we were going to Goose Bay, Labrador, and then on to an undisclosed location. The navigators got together to discuss the route. Master Sergeant Nestor Velasco and I were the only enlisted navigators—the rest were lieutenants or captains. Naturally, we two didn't have much to say about the route. Takeoff was scheduled for the following day.

"The base was a flurry of activity. Engineers were running up aircraft engines, trucks full of equipment were crisscrossing the ramp. When I got to my airplane, I saw the maintenance men loading ammo in the gun turrets and filling extra ammo cans. What impressed me most was a bomb-bay kit that had been uploaded. I had never seen it before. I asked our crew chief, Master Sergeant Joe Pellerin, 'What is that stuff?' 'Flak suits,' he said, grinning knowingly. Flak suits! Well, I said goodbye to my wife and young daughter, and off we went to Goose Bay—all three of our squadrons, ten aircraft each. At Goose Bay, after crew rest, they briefed us that the wing was going to RAF Scampton in England. Evidently, the Russians were blockading Berlin, and we were going over in case something happened. The thing that amazed me most as a navigator was that the air force didn't have any charts for us. We were given WAC charts (world aeronautical charts) of England, nearly useless for our purposes. The whole of England was on one of these charts. The briefers gave us the coordinates of RAF Scampton, near the little town of Lincoln. There was a small circle on the chart which was the base. But there were circles all over England. The place was covered with airfields. We were advised that the best way to find the base was to fly up the River Thames until we could see the big cathedral on the hill in the center of town, then turn north for five miles, and that was RAF Scampton.

"We took off at night, flying at four thousand feet. Clouds below us, clouds above. No stars, no drift readings possible. Nothing. We were number five. The wing commander, Colonel John B. Henry, flying ship number 6-308, was first. He was flying with the top navigator in the wing, a captain. We were flying in a bomber stream. I did a lot of dead reckoning on the way over, and a lot of praying. After several hours I cranked up the APQ-7 sector scan radar with its two hundred–mile extended range and good land-water contrast. At about our estimated time of arrival for landfall, I picked up land. The land-water contrast was so stark I thought there were high mountains ahead of us. 'Oh my God,' was my next thought—we were heading into Norway, because I didn't know of any sizable mountains in England. As we got closer, I realized it was just land-water contrast, not mountains. I breathed a deep sigh of relief. I tried to pick out the coastline, but with my little WAC chart, everything looked the same. There was nothing I could identify to help me determine precisely where we were. The pilots kept saying, 'Where in the hell are we, Joe?' I put them off and put them off until we came across what I thought was a distinctive bay and river just south of Scotland. 'I must have drifted north,' I thought. Authoritatively I said to the pilot, 'Turn south.' He turned south. I recognized the Wash on the radar, a prominent inlet off the coast of Norfolk, and I knew London had to be straight ahead. I picked up London. On the radar, London was a huge return. When we got near London, I told the pilot to start letting down. No clearance, no nothing. We flew at whatever altitude and wherever we wanted. We were down to about five hundred feet when we spotted a river running in the right direction and began following it. The pilot tried calling the control tower at Scampton but got no response. Sure enough, up ahead there was the cathedral. OK, turn north five miles, I told Lieutenant Wright when we got over the cathedral. 'OK,' he said, 'we're heading north. Now, which one of these fields is Scampton?'

"I looked out the nose of the aircraft, and there was one airfield after another. Well, it had to be the airfield with the B-29s on it, I told R. J. We were number five on takeoff. There should be four B-29s lined up on one of those fields. We flew all over and saw no B-29s on any of those airfields. The briefers at Goose had told us there was a signal square in front of the control tower at Scampton, a square with painted white rocks in it which spelled out the letters *SA*. The other fields had other letters to identify them. From our altitude we couldn't make out anything. R. J. Wright finally made contact with Scampton tower and told them we couldn't locate the field.

"The tower operator replied, 'You just flew over us.'

" 'But there are no B-29s on the ground,' R. J. said.

" 'No. No one else has arrived yet.'

" 'Well, we'll wait,' R. J. replied. We circled and circled. Finally, the control tower called, 'There are important people here waiting for you. You better land.'

"R. J. Wright was a first lieutenant and strictly military. He wanted to do things right, and doing things right meant that the wing commander should be the first one to land. But he had little choice in the matter and prepared to land. He tried to make a perfect landing for the occasion; instead, he slammed our bomber into the runway. He inadvertently depressed the mike button on the steering column when we hit the runway and said out loud, 'Oh shit,' a comment which was monitored by not only the tower but also the waiting guests. The tower operator made a curt remark about us using proper English while in the United Kingdom. We taxied in. There was the BBC, a big welcoming crowd, the air marshal of the Royal Air Force. All the big wheels had assembled for the occasion—the arrival of the first American B-29 bomber in England. Nobody else was there yet. R. J. Wright got out first. I finally got out, sweaty and dirty. I stayed out of the way while the pilot, the copilot and the bombardier, the only three officers on the crew, gave their interviews. R. J. was making a recording for the BBC. It was broadcast every thirty minutes, I believe, on the BBC for the rest of the day, announcing 'The Yanks are back!'

"It must have been an hour later when the next airplane came in. The wing commander, Colonel Henry, led by the wing navigator, had ended up several hundred miles too far north. Nobody mentioned anything about it. But R. J. was peeved at me because he was put in an embarrassing position by our early arrival. When Colonel Henry landed, the show was over. The brass had departed. Colonel Henry was met by the base commander and a few low-ranking types. R. J. got the publicity.

"No one had made provisions for our arrival, and the RAF was a bit overwhelmed by such a large group of personnel and aircraft. As a senior noncommissioned officer I got to sleep in the NCO Club, which had little rooms upstairs. They put four of us in one room in double-decker bunks. The other enlisted men slept in Quonset huts. We ate in a common mess. The British fare was not great by our standards—stewed tomatoes for breakfast and meat pie for dinner. Every day was pretty much the same. We couldn't buy anything because there was no base exchange. There were no stores on an English air base. The RAF did the best they could to provide for us, but the men complained continually about the food. After several weeks a C-54 arrived loaded with rations. I remember bully beef, fresh beef, chicken, butter, and eggs. But then what really embarrassed me and made me feel bad, they split the mess hall in half. We had gotten acquainted with many of the RAF troops by then and formed friendships. The RAF ate their standard fare on their side, while we ate fresh beef, chicken, and eggs on our side, and the RAF didn't have any of that.

"Because of our sudden departure, a lot of problems were cropping up at our home base. Nobody had allotments in those days. We got paid in cash and paid our bills as we got money in hand. We weren't there, so there were no provisions made to pay the wives. The wives were running out of food, had no money to pay the rent or buy the necessities of life. There was a lot of complaining, and the morale of the troops was suffering. The problem was serious enough that one day we were called together in a hangar and were addressed by the senator from South Dakota, the Honorable Chan Gurney, and the 15th Air Force commander, Major General Leon Johnson. They gave a pep talk and assured us that every effort would be made to solve our problems. And they really did help. When they got back to the States the word was put out on the base for the wives to meet. Partial payments were made, and groups were formed in town for the wives to help each other. We didn't have any clothes either because most of the guys packed only enough clothes for two weeks. They got a C-54 and put the word out to the women that they could send things to their husbands. My wife sent me cans of chicken, tuna, candy bars, and extra clothes.

"Our B-29 bombers flew formation missions into Germany, something we had never done before at Rapid City. We also flew the Berlin corridors. We had never flown in a controlled situation such as this, but to fly in the Berlin corridors we had to file a flight plan and stay within this narrow, twenty-mile-wide corridor. It was something new to us. There were radio beacons, which were helpful, but we were warned that the Russians could distort the beams. As a navigator I had to put my skills to use. Our mission was to show ourselves to the Russians. I remember flying single ship into the southern corridor to Berlin and flying out the northern corridor and then back to England. Some other guy would do the same thing flying in on the northern corridor and out the southern corridor. I did that two or three times while I was there. We flew above the transports. They probably didn't even know we were there. We were pressurized and could fly higher, while the heavily loaded transports flew below us, unpressurized. We encountered Russian fighters only once. Two Yak-9s came alongside and looked us over. Our gunners swung their gun turrets around. The Yaks sat out there a few minutes and then peeled off.

"Something else scared us more than any Russian Yaks could have. We heard that somebody had proposed the use of B-29s to deliver coal to Berlin. The thought of loading up the bomb bay with bags of coal drove the maintenance people out of their minds. They heard that in the cargo airplanes the coal dust got into everything. The rumor was that since we couldn't land on the runways in Berlin, we would jettison the coal bags into the Berlin Olympic Stadium. I heard the bombardiers talking about using their bombsights and worrying about the trajectory of a bag of coal. People actually came around and looked at our aircraft to see how they could load things into the bomb bays, but fortunately it never came to that.

"The morale of the enlisted men in the wing remained shaky. They

Crew 603 at RAF Scampton, August 1948. Lieutenant R. J. Wright is standing at left with wheel hat; Master Sergeant Joe Gyulavics is third from left, standing. J. Gyulavics.

28th Bomb Wing B-29s over the English Channel, passing the white cliffs of Dover, 1948. J. Gyulavics.

were probably getting letters from home saying that their families were hurting. The men would resort to nearly anything to get home. We had more high-level visitors to Scampton—General Hoyt S. Vandenberg accompanied the new secretary of the air force, Stuart Symington. I was really impressed by the young, handsome four-star who had recently taken over from General Carl "Tooey" Spaatz as air force chief of staff. Secretary Symington and General Vandenberg seemed genuinely concerned. General Vandenberg told the assembled enlisted men, 'Don't worry about things back home. We're going to take care of your families. Your replacements back in the States are getting ready to relieve you. You are doing a fine job. Stick it out for a few more weeks, and you'll be on your way home.' It was late October 1948 when we came back to Rapid City. We had been at Scampton a little over three months. When we returned, the local community gave us a big welcome, including a picnic to show their appreciation. A B-29 outfit from Salina, Kansas, came over to England to replace us. They had three months to get ready; we had less than three days.

"In 1949 I went to B-36 upgrade training. The 28th Wing got its first B-36 that August, and we were checking out in it when I applied for pilot training. My pilot at the time was a Captain Steffes, a West Pointer. He encouraged me to go to pilot training and gave me the push I needed to apply. It was a major decision because I had to give up my rank as master sergeant and revert back to cadet status. In January 1950 I left the 28th Bomb Wing to begin a new life. I sent my wife and daughter home to live with my mother. As an aviation cadet I had to live on seventy-five dollars a month, and I couldn't support my family on that. I went to Goodfellow AFB first, then to Reese at Lubbock, both in Texas. When I graduated as a pilot, I was commissioned a second lieutenant in the U.S. Air Force—for the second time."

Colonel Richard Schulz, a young lieutenant bombardier, was a member of MacDill's 307th Bomb Wing, the other B-29 wing that was shifted to England on short notice. "One afternoon in June 1948, the wing was on a flying training exercise when we were ordered to land immediately. We assembled in the wing briefing room and were told that we were on twelve-hour-alert status and would be departing shortly for RAF stations Marham and Waddington in the United Kingdom. Our mission was to provide support for the Berlin Airlift. We were to plan on a two-week deployment but to pack as if we were going away for six. The mission was classified secret, and we were counseled that if we revealed our destination to anyone, including our wives, we would be subject to courts-martial. We headed out of MacDill for England the following week, stopping in the Azores for refueling and crew rest. In England we were quartered in World War II Quonset huts once occupied by air crews of the Eighth Air Force. Each of us had a small private room, in contrast to the open-bay arrangement the Eighth Air Force crews had to put up with. Each morning our batman, an RAF enlisted man assigned to take care of our needs, would bring us hot tea in bed. To say the least, this was much different from our customs."

Dick Schulz had applied for pilot training before leaving for England. While at RAF Marham his application for training was approved, and in early October 1948 he returned to the United States. At this time, SAC had little of the vaunted precision and power that it later acquired under the driving leadership of General LeMay. But SAC had the atomic bomb, or "gizmo," as the air crews called it. And the gizmo counted for something. A fourth B-29 bomb wing, the 509th, was deployed to England. The 509th was the wing that dropped the atomic bombs on Japan. It had the reputation of having the gizmo, while the other bomb wings didn't. The 509th came from Walker AFB in New Mexico. The wing consisted not only of the usual three squadrons of bombers but also its own squadron of KB-29 refueling tankers. Air refueling significantly extended the bombers' range and was an important asset in creating the global reach to which SAC aspired. The KB-29 tankers put the Soviets on notice that no place in the Soviet Union was unreachable.

Lieutenant Colonel Joseph Studak, then a lieutenant and now a resident of Austin, Texas, was assigned to RAF Fassberg in 1948. He was the ramp control officer, responsible for knowing the status of every aircraft on the ramp—if it was empty or loaded, ready to go or down for maintenance. "I had to ensure that aircraft were in commission and loaded, and I maintained the squadron rotation for takeoff order to even out the flying load on a weekly schedule. I directed the engine start times to provide a steady flow of aircraft ready to take off in three-minute intervals. It was a twelve-hour shift with plenty of overtime. I left Fassberg in early March 1949 and reported for duty as a navigator with the 509th Bombardment Wing at Walker. (The 509th Bomb Wing, with its thirty silverplate B-29s, was the only B-29 unit whose aircraft were modified to carry the atomic bomb.) In April, only four weeks after leaving Fassberg, I left with my new unit for 120 days in England. My squadron was based at RAF Lakenheath, while the other two squadrons of our group were at RAF Marham. The 307th Bomb Wing, which deployed to Marham in 1948, had by that time returned to MacDill. While in England we dropped a lot of practice bombs in the Wash, the tidal flats off the Norfolk coast. I finally left England in September 1949 when the Berlin Airlift was officially declared ended."

The Strategic Air Command publicized its global reach in ways other than deploying B-29 bombers to Germany and England. In July 1948 three B-29s of the 43rd Bomb Group—some units were called "wings," others were still called "groups"—attempted an around-the-world flight. Two of the aircraft completed the fifteen-day flight, but the third crashed into the Arabian Sea. Soon newer B-50 and B-36 bombers made nonstop flights from the U.S. mainland to Hawaii. The message to the Soviets was clear—the United States could reach any place at any time. SAC still had a long way to go to make good on that promise, but it would get there in a short time.

Chapter 3

"Ramp Rats"
The Men Who
Kept Them Flying

German mechanics were extensively used to balance airmen shortages. The incentives for German aircraft workers were one free meal per day, inexpensive clothing and free billets.

Berlin Airlift: A USAFE Summary

Things were different then. If a man said he could do the job, the retort from the boss was, "Have at it." I really think that all of us believed we could do anything.

Tom Etherson, Berlin Airlift C-54 maintenance man and flight engineer

The first things that come to mind when speaking of the Berlin Airlift are the airplanes and their pilots. In the final analysis, they made the airlift happen. Thoughts then turn to the vast tonnages of food and coal delivered and to the number of missions flown. Finally, one recalls the men who died to save Berlin. Often forgotten are the men who kept those airplanes flying—who sealed leaking fuel tanks, busted their knuckles trying to change recalcitrant sparkplugs, swept snow off wings with push brooms, and changed lightbulbs in two-story-high vertical stabilizers. These men worked twenty-four hours a day in rain, sunshine, and snow to keep the airplanes flying, to make the Berlin Airlift a success. Rarely did anyone think to run hot coffee and donuts out to the men on the line. Rarely did anyone ask if they were warm enough out on the open-air engine dock. Rarely did anyone wonder how they could change an engine in the rain and driving snow. But the sergeants and airmen kept working—grousing, yes, even fighting back when the opportunity presented itself. The men on the line, the "ramp rats" of Rhein-Main, Wiesbaden, Celle, and Fassberg, never neglected to keep the airplanes flying.

Master Sergeant Thomas W. Etherson

Tom Etherson was a ramp rat at RAF Celle. Tom was born in 1927 in Blissville, New York, a place, he insists, that no longer exists. He was a less than enthusiastic student, and with the war going on, he was looking for an opportunity to escape into the real world. His opportunity came when he turned sixteen. The Merchant Marine accepted young men at age sixteen, while the army and navy required youngsters to be at least seventeen years old. After learning how to launch and steer a lifeboat, Tom shipped out for the Mediterranean in May 1944, just short of his seventeenth birthday. He found it a long and boring trip. He made one more trip to Sicily and the south of France in 1945, and upon turning seventeen, he jumped ship and joined the army. Tom recalls being among a thousand or so basic trainees ordered to fall out on a parade ground. A sergeant walked down the line of recruits, counting off ranks and ordering men to the left and right. Those on the right, including Tom, were assigned to the Army Air Force. He wound up at Keesler Field near Biloxi, Mississippi, where he acquired the skills of an aircraft mechanic. From there he shipped out to Panama, and in February 1947 he elected to get out of the Army Air Force and went off to New York City. New York was cold and gray when he got there, the streets covered in snow and slush. Tom soon discovered he preferred a warmer climate and promptly reenlisted to escape the cold of New York. Some place warmer turned out to be Tachikawa Air Base, Japan.

"Duty in Japan wasn't bad. I worked on the C-54 aircraft engine maintenance docks. We had two men per engine plus the people needed for the general maintenance inspections, about fifteen men total per aircraft. We worked an eight-hour day, five days a week. The aircraft and engines were run through the wash rack before being towed into the covered docks. We used the checklists of Pan American Airlines. Our working conditions weren't bad. Living conditions weren't bad either. A Japanese houseboy took care of the barracks for a pack of cigarettes a week. He made my bed and ran a rag over my shoes. The chow was plenty good, and there was lots of it. The vegetables were grown on a hydroponic farm since the local produce was grown using human waste, called "honey." Most of the meat came frozen from the States, and the milk was made from powder. Our recreational facilities were great. A round of golf cost a quarter, with a nickel tip for the caddie, who, by the way, was female. The train into Tokyo was free. Although we had firebombed the city during the war, there was little evidence of it in 1947. The Ginza was a shopper's heaven. You could get anything from oil paintings to good copies of American money. One of the canteens had been an exclusive club before the war, the Bankers Club. I felt pretty smoked strutting through the place. Not far from the Bankers Club was a bathhouse. Little girls with short slips led us into a huge tub made of marble. Once they got you into the tub, any thought of what might be under that slip soon faded. The heat made my entire body go as limp as a wet noodle. After that, one of the sweet things would give me a cup of hot sake. That's all she wrote. It took two of the girls to get me out of the tub. I couldn't even stand up. What did they do then but shower me with cold water, which caused my brain to think I felt great, although a little wobbly in the legs. Right about that time the army MPs would show up and write us up for not wearing a tie—professional jealousy, of course, because the air force wasn't required to wear a tie with a summer uniform, but the army was. After the MPs wrote us up, we'd get a couple of rickshaws and head for the railroad station to get back to the base.

"I think I got the word that my outfit was going to Germany the end of September. The leisure life came to a screeching halt. One hundred–hour inspections had to be pulled on thirteen airplanes. I started to put in long hours. No longer was I free to take it easy when my engine was done. I had to help in other areas that still needed work. I turned twenty-one and celebrated my birthday at the Enlisted Men's Club. The Japanese beer came in large bottles, and I must admit I don't remember how many I drank and how I got back to the barracks that night. When I awoke my mouth tasted like someone had dumped a honey bucket in it. I didn't see anybody in the barracks, so I thought I was late for work. I hustled down to the maintenance area. No one was around. So I thought I must be early. I went to the maintenance dock to wait until everybody showed up. I dozed off. When I woke up, I saw a guy pulling guard duty. I called out, 'Hey, where the hell is everybody?' He was so startled, he almost fainted. 'What the hell are you doing here?' he said. 'This is Sunday and no one is working today. Get your butt out of here.'

"The day came when we said goodbye to Nippon. I heard if you saw Mount Fuji when you left, you would return. I tried to look out the other side of the airplane so I wouldn't see it, but the plane turned, and there Fuji was. Since I owed the barracks boy a couple of cartons of cigarettes, I wondered if this was an omen. Our first stop was Kwajalein atoll. The natives evacuated from Bikini lived on one end of the island in a tent city. They lived a sad life, and I don't think they really knew what was happening to them. Our next stop was Guam, North Field. As the plane approached the airfield, it looked like we were flying into a cliff—a little scary. There were no facilities on Guam, so we slept in the aircraft. The mosquitoes buzzed around inside that C-54 sounding like the engines were running. Our next stop was Hickam Field,

Hawaii. After we serviced the aircraft in the rain, we found the NCO club. It must have shocked the waitress because all of us wanted fresh milk. Most of us hadn't tasted fresh milk in a year or two.

"We got our first glimpse of the land of the big PX as the sun was setting. The sunset made the Golden Gate Bridge look red. We landed at Fairfield-Suisun (later renamed Travis Air Force Base). We had a briefing by the commanding officer about what not to do in the land of plenty. I was shocked to find that the beer bottles were only one-third the size of the Nippon bottles. Also, the girls were not impressed with how many cigarettes I had. At roll call the next morning, we were a sorry-looking lot. Someone unfolded a large banner. It read, 'Golden Gate in '48, Salt Mine in '49.' I guess this didn't impress the old man very much, because I never saw the banner again. From California we went to Kelly Field in Texas, where the aircraft were winterized. We had four days in San Antonio. Those living close by were allowed to go home for a couple of days. I didn't go, because New York City wasn't considered close by.

"Next stop was Westover Field in Massachusetts. We were not allowed to go into town because our transfer from Japan to Germany was supposed to be a secret movement. The military police would look the other way when we walked out the gate. I was in a bar at Chicopee Falls when the radio announcer said the 317th Troop Carrier was passing through on the way from Japan to Germany to join the Berlin Airlift. He went on to say that you could recognize the troops by the 5th Air Force patch they wore. Then the beer really started to flow. So much for a secret movement. After Westover, we went to Newfoundland, the Azores, and then to Wiesbaden, Germany. In Wiesbaden I started pulling fifty-hour inspections. The maintenance docks were ready. I had chow and went to work. The maintenance area was set up between the runway and the taxi strips. When it rained, which it did for a week, we got wet—the maintenance docks had no overhead shelters. So we worked in the rain and slopped around in the mud for about two weeks until the inspections were completed. Although the docks were waiting, there was no room in the barracks. My buddies and I found space in the attics of an old German barracks. It didn't matter much since we were tired at the end of our shift. The food made up for it. The chow was great. The fact that it was served by pretty German girls made it seem that much better.

"One morning we were replacing an oil cooler, a messy job, when a man walked up with no hat, no insignia on his flight jacket, and a stub of a cigar in his mouth. One of the NCOs said, 'Hey, you can't smoke here.' The stranger replied, 'Don't sweat it.' He questioned us on how we were doing and what we needed most to keep the airplanes flying. Everyone had his own wish list, but no one thought to tell him that we had no winter clothing. When the stranger left the line, the chief came out of his tent, where he kept a huge potbellied stove going at all times. He asked us if we had seen a general. We asked him what the general looked like. It turned out that the cigar smoker was General LeMay.

"A plane caught on fire in the nose dock one night. Since we didn't have the luxury of the wash racks as we had in Japan, an airman tried to improvise by squirting gasoline on the engine to clean off some of the muck. The docks were equipped with explosion-proof lights, but unfortunately the explosion-proof light cover in this dock was cracked. Poof. The dock burned. The engine and the deicer boots close to the engine burned. When the fire was put out, the aircraft was towed to one side of the dock. The next night the plane was still sitting there. I was told by the guy who sat by the potbellied stove to get the navigation taillight off the burned aircraft. I was standing on the back of a weapons carrier when the expediter and aircraft scheduler drove up—an officer. He was the one who checked on the status of each aircraft. He called out, 'Hey you. Will that aircraft be ready for the next block?' Now, 'Hey you' is not the proper way to address anyone who has been out in the cold all night, especially when the questioner was sitting in a heated vehicle. I told him it sure would be.

"The expediter said, 'Say, *sir*.'

"I said, 'Sir!'

"He called in the tail number and drove off, never giving me another look. I have a feeling that both the expediter and the guy who set the engine on fire disappeared forever, because I never heard or saw either one of them again.

"That night we got our first snowstorm. In the morning everything looked grand. When we reported for work to the guy who sat by the potbellied stove, he sent one of his clerks out to tell us to sweep the snow off the wings. We got some rope, tied it around our waists, and with a man on each end to keep us from slipping off the wings, we swept off the snow. We were moving along fine and having fun dodging the snow that flew over the wings when we saw this fellow walking toward us. It was a navy chief. He looked like he had stepped right out of a recruiting poster—creased blue pants, leather flying jacket, scarf, visored cap. Next to him we looked like the Germans loading the coal on the C-54s. He told us to clean the snow off his airplane. I told him we would as soon as we got finished with ours. In the meantime, he should get back into base operations and stay warm. When we finished our last aircraft, we went back to our maintenance dock and went to work. A little later a guy came running up, saying, 'Look at the navy.' Out on the wing was the well-dressed chief, trying to sweep the snow off his plane and trying to keep from slipping off the wing at the same time. There were two or three officers standing around mumbling and snarling that they were late for takeoff because the chief had not cleaned the snow off the wings.

"That evening when we had buttoned up the engines and I was washing my hands in gasoline, I felt a sharp pain in the knuckle of my right hand. I noticed a tip of metal sticking out of it. With my dirty fingernails, I scratched it out. I didn't think anything about it because my knuckles were scratched and scabby anyway. A few days later the most ugly sore I've ever seen appeared on my hand. The entire hand blew up like a balloon. I went in to see the guy who sat by the potbellied stove and told him I needed to see the medics. He asked me what was wrong. I showed him my hand. He said, 'You wise guys from New York will do anything to get out of work.' When I slipped away to the medics, the medic looked at my hand and said, 'We have to show it to the doc.' The doctor said that the hand was infected from the lead in the gasoline. Lead could cause blood poisoning. He gave me a bottle of sulfa pills and told me to keep an eye on my arm. If a blue streak appeared, I was to get right back to him. He also said I was to report to the first sergeant for light duty. He didn't want me to go back to the flight line until the hand was completely healed—heartbreaking news. The first sergeant, the guy who sat by the potbellied stove, and I were not the best of friends, and when I told him I was restricted to light duty, he said, 'Go hit the sack and see me in the morning for duty.'

"That afternoon I tried to guess what sort of duty he would have me do, probably cleaning latrines. I couldn't do clerical work. More guys worked in the orderly room than on the flight line. The first sergeant told me to get out of my filthy fatigues because I was getting grease all over his orderly room. I changed into a class-A uniform. It was ten in the morning. I was told to go to the headquarters on a bike and pick up distribution and leave it with the mail-room corporal. I didn't ask what else, and he didn't say anything else. After I dropped off the distribution, I took off for chow. Went to a *Gasthaus* where the night crew hung out and started to enjoy Wiesbaden. The hand healed up a little too quickly, but I kept the bandage on anyway.

"After a while, I saw myself back on the flight line. We were preparing to move the outfit to Celle. My job was to park and service aircraft when they returned from Berlin. Not a bad job—at least I wasn't anyplace near the guy with the potbellied stove. We left for Celle on December 22, 1948, a day I'll never forget. We were rousted out about five in the morning, had chow, and loaded our possessions—one barracks bag for each man. Our tools and other equipment were loaded up the night before. In fact, we loaded up anything that was not bolted to the floor. But it turned into the usual SNAFU, hurry up and wait. I think we were waiting for the guy's stove to cool off.

"Just before we could get noon chow they decided to load our aircraft. The flight to Celle was only to last about an hour. The plane was colder than a grave digger's ass in Alaska. The heaters required a sparkplug to generate heat, but no one ordered any. The one-hour flight lasted five hours. The copilot was TDY from Washington, D.C., and must have needed the flight time. It was dark when we got to Celle. The potbellied stove was radiating, but first we had to unload the aircraft and service them to continue their round-trips to Berlin. We got to our barracks about one in the morning. We had beds, but the mattresses were still in Wiesbaden. We slept the best we could, thanks to our heavy GI overcoats. About six in the morning, I got up and made for the latrine. It was dark, and the barracks had no power. I found a commode by the light of a Zippo lighter. I was wearing one-piece fatigues, and when I dropped them I was damn near naked. When I sat down I noticed this cold air, like standing outside in the wind. I sat down and then jumped three feet into the air. The toilet seat was gone. I sat there in the wind on the cold porcelain seat. The windows in the latrine were broken. I cursed the damn Krauts.

"On the way back to my bunk, I ran into a couple of other airmen. We hadn't eaten for twenty-four hours. When we got into the chow line, we discovered why the British were so thin. We had a cold piece of fish and a slice of burnt toast. That was it. No seconds. The Brits said it was because of the rationing. We learned that the Brits separated the messing by ranks. The privates, PFCs, lance corporals, and corporals ate in the cellar. The sergeants, the staff sergeants, and some technical sergeants ate upstairs. Master sergeants and the Crown's sergeants ate in the NCO club. I was a corporal—the second time around. I wished I hadn't been a wise guy, or I'd be a sergeant and wouldn't have to eat in the cellar. Our first job that day was cleaning the hangar floor. Someone, probably the same crowd that had broken the windows and stolen the toilet seats, had chopped open fifty-five-gallon oil drums and rolled them across the hangar floor. In the couple of years the hangar was closed, bird shit and feathers, dead mice, and bugs had settled in the oil, which then turned to tar. We took a break for chow. The noon meal, supper, and midnight chow were the same—mutton with some sort of heavy flour and water mixture on top, plus tea. Those meals never varied for all the time I was in Celle. On Christmas Day at noon, I was standing in the chow line when the little Brit in front of me turned around and said, 'We're in luck today, Yank.'

"I said, 'How's that?'

"He replied, 'It's Christmas. We get double rations.' For a moment I saw a picture of turkey with all the trimmings. The dream only lasted for a moment. As soon as I stepped inside, I knew what they were doubling up on, only this time most of the sheep still had their coats on.

"Instead of working on the engines, I was assigned to the airplane general crew—checking hydraulic leaks, cleaning coal dust off the control cables, and because I was a wise guy from New York City, the guy who sat by the potbellied stove designated me as the number-one man for fuel-tank repairs. The C-54 was a wet-wing airplane, meaning the wing itself was a gas tank. When a leak exceeded a number of drips per minute, we had to open up the wing and find the leak. Dropping a wing-access plate was no easy task. I had to put a jack under the wings and take the studs off the access plates. Once the plate was removed, it had to be cleaned so it could be put back on. Also, before I could put the plate back I had to prepare a mixture of two compounds called stoner's smudge. This required kneading these two compounds until they had the consistency of bread dough. The more I kneaded, the blacker it got, and the mixture stuck to my hands like another skin. If I was still stationed in Japan I could have gone to the hot baths, and maybe the stuff would come off. But there was only cold water in Celle.

"Before I could put the goop inside the fuel tank, any residual fuel had to be removed with a garden hose, and someone, usually the German helpers, sucked on the hose to siphon it out. My man Rudi said, 'It will ruin my teeth.' I thought he could die from a mouth full of gas. But no ill effects were ever apparent in either of us. When we got to town, many of the girls didn't want to have anything to do with the guys with the black hands. A lot of German civilians came by our table in the *Gasthaus* and asked us what kind of secret weapon we were working on. Then they walked away laughing. The German civilians who worked with us were great mechanics as well as great friends. They used our American tools. One wrench used to install sparkplug leads was a real knuckle buster. It took the Germans to figure out how to work the thing so it wouldn't bust your hands. Every time I went to tighten a sparkplug, the front end of the wrench would slip. The Germans manufactured their own. I kept one for years and guarded it like it was gold. Another reason I will never forget our German workers was that they shared their food with me. In the evenings they were served at a soup kitchen as part of their pay. One man would pick up the soup cans for the entire crew and get the soup. They gave me a can, and I drew rations with them. Certainly it was better food than the slop served by the Brits. The poor Brits couldn't help it—they had so little themselves. Overall, I must say we got along pretty well with the Brits.

"Fassberg was up and running a couple of months by that time. Someone in the headquarters building decided that Celle should haul more tonnage than Fassberg. 'Beat Fassberg' was the battle cry around headquarters and other warm places where the coat holders hung out. Work, work, and more work for us guys out in the cold places. There was an eleven o'clock curfew for those of us under the rank of staff sergeant. The Brit MPs would come into the *Gasthaus* and say, 'We'll be back in ten minutes.' The damn American MPs would start rounding us up immediately. There was no one to complain to. We worked a minimum of fourteen hours a day, seven days a week. By the time we got to town and settled down to a tall beer, it was time to pack it in. I still wonder today what kind of people came up with those curfew ideas. Some clown who was a reservist came over from New York and said there were werewolf gangs of German teenage kids who would attack GIs, and that's why we had the curfew. The only teenage kids we ever saw were nice, and we gave them cigarettes, candy bars, or chewing gum.

"I had fun tormenting the sergeant who never left his stove. We worked the entire winter in nothing heavier than a field jacket and a sweater. It was a cold winter. About the time of the Easter Parade— Easter Sunday, April 16, 1949, 1,398 flights delivered 12,940 tons of coal and food to Berlin, a one-day record—we were issued fleece-lined leather coats and jackets. A lot of German girls were walking around in them the next winter. The guy who sat behind the potbellied stove and a couple of other clowns at headquarters came outside and patted each other on the back for the great job they did. Originally, we went over to Germany for thirty days TDY from Japan. It wound up being sixty days, then ninety days. It didn't bother any of us single men. But a lot of the flight engineers had families at Tachikawa. The morale got pretty bad. So they sent most of those guys home, and greasy mechanics like me who were supposed to know everything about the airplanes were suddenly made flight engineers. While we sat up there between the pilot and the copilot, we had no idea what to look for. I wouldn't look out the window because it was too scary. If the instruments were in the green, I just sat back and smiled. Come to find out that most of the new guys flying the airplanes were TDY from the States and hadn't had much time in the airplane either. What a crew we were. Things were different then. If a man said he could do the job, the retort from the boss was, 'Have at it.' I really think that all of us believed we could do anything."

Master Sergeant Martin Allin, who made his home in Tennessee after retirement, had previously served as a flight engineer, but he had not flown on the C-54. His experiences resembled Sergeant Etherson's. "The standard crew configuration for a C-54 was two pilots, a navigator, and a crew chief/flight engineer. During the airlift there was no need for navigators, so the crew was reduced to three. I arrived at Rhein-Main Air Base on November 30, 1948. I was a so-called crew chief/flight engineer in the States. I was debriefed in the base operations building at Rhein-Main. They asked if I wanted to fly. I said yes. I was immediately assigned to a flight, and a check engineer was to check me out. Get this: I had never flown before on a C-54 except once as a passenger. Away I went to Berlin. The checker showed me this and that on my way there and back. When we got near Rhein-Main coming back, he said, 'Sarge, you better hit the technical orders for the C-54 aircraft, 'cause I am going stateside tomorrow.'

" 'OK, who will take your place?' I asked.

Budding C-54 flight engineers at RAF Celle, spring 1949. Tom Etherson is far right. T. Etherson.

"He laughed and said, 'You!' So I became a flight engineer on the C-54. I slept the first three nights on a first-aid stretcher in the operations building. The weather was the worst in a century. A total fog bank across Germany. We flew anyway. We were covered with coal dust. The wings dripped aviation gas all the time. Our beards grew. We looked like rejects from hell. But what we did was outstanding and we saved the United States from World War III. It was the most important achievement of my twenty-five-year military career. Those 130 flights from Rhein-Main to Berlin made me proud to be a part of that great operation."

In the spring of 1989 long-retired Master Sergeant Thomas Etherson and his wife, now residing in Las Vegas, Nevada, made a nostalgic visit to Celle, where forty years earlier he had served as aircraft mechanic and flight engineer. "I got to talking to a girl who was showing us around the castle in Celle, which was all painted and beautiful. I told her what Celle looked like when I first arrived in 1948. The castle was gray and the beautiful park that now surrounds it wasn't there. I told her about the broken windows and the missing toilet seats in my barracks at the base. She laughed and said, 'You have to have lunch with my husband.' The next day we had lunch, and I met her husband, Dieter. Dieter was ten years old in 1945. After the Luftwaffe abandoned the base, he and his friends went out there and removed the toilet seats and anything else they thought they could trade on the black market. Because they were kids, they busted all the windows. And anything they couldn't carry away, like the fifty-five-gallon drums filled with fuel oil, they broke and spilled over the floors of the hangars. There I'd been, back in '48, cursing the Germans, and it was just a bunch of kids. Dieter and I had a good laugh."

Part 2

Korea, 1950

The outbreak of that war came to me as a complete surprise, as it did to all our military men—from Seoul to Washington.

Matthew B. Ridgway

Our combat aircraft losses for both the squadron and the wing were high. This was due primarily to the low-level mission we were flying. Out of the twenty flying-school classmates that went to Japan with me, only a handful returned home.

Dick Schulz, B-26 pilot

In early 1950, Americans were concerned with making a living and achieving their dreams of owning their own homes and cars. There was plenty of work, and the lean years before World War II were a fast-fading memory. The U.S. military was still downsizing, and the defense budget for the year was a mere $13.5 billion. Although the McCarthy hearings (accusations of communist penetration at the highest levels of government) troubled some, there was no war. Times were good.

To those entrusted with national security, however, things looked much more worrisome. The Soviets exploded an atomic device in 1949, and Chiang Kai-shek fled the Chinese mainland for sanctuary on Formosa (Taiwan). The National Security Council issued NSC-68, a lengthy but seminal document that defined the communist world threat and recommended to President Harry S. Truman the end of demobilization and a significant strengthening of both armed forces and international alliances. NSC-68 reflected the deep concerns of a group of American policy makers led by the bright young political analyst Paul Nitze. But NSC-68 did not reach President Truman's desk until April 1950, too late to affect the outcome of the North Korean People's Army's invasion of South Korea only ten weeks later, in June 1950. The invasion transformed NSC-68 into a national-planning document with immediate budget implications for the administration. To get to where the NSC-68 planners thought the United States needed to be to combat and contain the communist threat would take "about fifty billion dollars per annum. This was a very rough guess," according to Secretary of State Dean Acheson (*Present* 377).

The North Korean armed forces' **June 25, 1950**, attack on South Korea was unexpected and quickly threatened to overwhelm the smaller and less well equipped South Korean army. The United Nations Security Council, acting quickly in the absence of the Soviet delegate, expressed its concern in a resolution calling for a cease-fire and the withdrawal of the North Korean Army (NKA) to north of the thirty-eighth parallel. It was absolutely clear that the North Korean attack was "an open, and undisguised challenge to our internationally accepted position as the protector of South Korea," recalled Acheson in his memoir (*Present* 405).

On **June 26** President Truman directed U.S. air and naval forces to support the hard-pressed South Korean army south of the thirty-eighth parallel. The following day the United Nations Security Council adopted a U.S. resolution calling for U.N. members to provide help in repelling the North Korean attack and restoring peace. Seoul, the South Korean capital, fell to the NKA on **June 28**, and President Truman responded by authorizing U.S. air and naval forces to attack targets in North Korea. On **June 30** General Douglas MacArthur, commander of the Far East Command, reported to Washington that the intervention of U.S. ground forces would be necessary to prevent a total rout of the South Korean army. President Truman concurred with the request for ground troops, and on **July 5** Task Force Smith, the first American ground combat unit hastily assembled and rushed into South Korea to stem the North Korean advance, made initial contact with the enemy near Osan. General MacArthur became commander of United Nations troops in South Korea on **July 8**. In just two weeks the United States had gone from a comfortable state of peace to war. The fast and furious tempo of military operations in Korea continued, and American ground forces were thrown into the fray as quickly as they arrived. American airpower slowed the invaders' pace, bought precious time for the U.S. Army to build up a defensive perimeter around Pusan, and kept the invaders from quickly reaching their objective, the incorporation of the south into a greater Korea.

On **July 3** Major General William F. Dean, commander of the 24th Infantry Division, landed at Taejon and proceeded to hold the city against superior forces until July 20, giving Lieutenant General Walton H. Walker, commander of the 8th U.S. Army, time to disembark and deploy arriving troops for the defense of the Naktong perimeter, protecting the port of Pusan. Walker told his troops to stand or die: there was to be no more retreat. (General Dean was captured by the North Koreans and subsequently was awarded the Medal of Honor for his defense of Taejon.) On **September 15** the 1st Marine Division, under the leadership of the seventy-year-old MacArthur, threatened to cut off the North Korean invaders in a daring amphibious landing on the rocky tidal coast near Inchon. The Eighth Army initiated a near simultaneous counterattack, breaking out of the Pusan perimeter and driving back the weakened North Korean forces. After the U.S. trap was sprung, little remained of the North Korean attacking force: "Perhaps thirty thousand stragglers out of an army of approximately four hun-

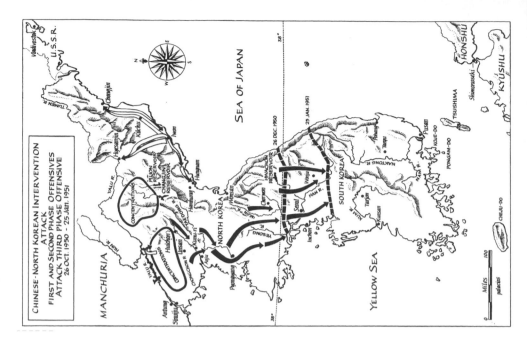

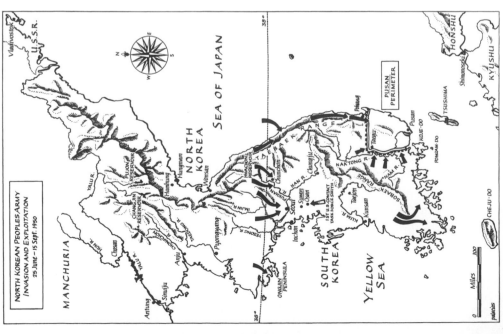

North Korean penetration of South Korea, June–September 1950, and the results of Chinese intervention, October 1950–January 1951. Acheson, *Present* 403, 470.

dred thousand men made their escape without equipment across the parallel," wrote Acheson (*Present* 447).

On **September 27** Seoul was recaptured. The Joint Chiefs of Staff instructed General MacArthur that "your military objective is the destruction of the North Korean Armed Forces. In attaining this objective you are authorized to conduct military operations, including amphibious and airborne landings or ground operations north of the 38th parallel in Korea, . . . support of your operations north or south of the 38th parallel will not include Air or Naval action against Manchuria or against USSR territory." In line with his instructions, MacArthur drove north to destroy what remained of the North Korean People's Army in a sweeping envelopment up the east and west coasts of North Korea. The U.S. Eighth Army, commanded by Lieutenant General Walton H. Walker, spearheaded the drive in the west toward Pyongyang and beyond. The U.S. X Corps, commanded by Lieutenant General Edward M. Almond, was sea lifted to Wonsan on the east coast of North Korea and began to drive north. Each attacking force split into several columns as it progressed into ever more mountainous terrain. MacArthur's envelopment strategy was bold but risky—when viewed from another perspective, it represented a perilous division of his limited forces should the power equation change. A Chinese message delivered on **October 3** to the Indian ambassador warning that China would send troops to defend North Korea seemed to gain no-one's attention. To the contrary, General MacArthur at a meeting with President Truman on Wake Island on **October 15**, predicted the war would be over by Christmas and that China would not intervene.

On **October 26** a regiment of the Republic of Korea (ROK) 6th Division reached the Yalu River near Chosan. Chinese forces engaged the regiment the same day and destroyed it. The ROK II Corps near Unsan and the 5th and 8th U.S. Cavalry Regiments were attacked by Chinese forces the following day. The battles lasted several days, inflicting heavy casualties on both sides. Then the Chinese ground forces seemed to vanish from the scene as quickly as they had appeared. On **November 1** the first Chinese MiG-15 jet fighters appeared over North

Korea. The military situation had changed drastically. To Secretary of State Acheson, close adviser to the president, the gnawing question was, "What were the facts about [the] Chinese military presence in North Korea and what were their intentions?" (*Present* 466).

The appearance of the Chinese should have given pause to General MacArthur, but instead he ordered a general offensive on **November 24**, but it stalled within twenty-four hours when Chinese forces reappeared and counterattacked on **November 25**. As November came to a close, both the Eighth Army in the west and X Corps in the east were in retreat. In the bitter cold of a Korean winter, many isolated U.S. Army and Marine Corps units fought stubbornly for their survival over treacherous mountain terrain. General Walker was killed in a jeep accident on an icy road on **December 23, 1950**, and Lieutenant General Ridgway assumed command of the U.S. Eighth Army three days later. The Chinese entry into the war had surprised both MacArthur and those in Washington. The military power equation had changed totally. MacArthur's strategy to split his forces and attack in the cold of winter over difficult terrain had been a major miscalculation.

The Chinese offensive took communist forces back to Seoul by **January 4, 1951**, but then the offensive stalled. Ridgway quickly repositioned his forces to take advantage of the terrain as well as the increased length of Chinese communist lines of communication. By skillfully trading real estate for enemy attrition, he turned his forces into a killing machine: Chinese troops died by the tens of thousands. By **March 15, 1951**, Ridgway's forces retook Seoul, and the morale of the Eighth Army was restored. On **April 12, 1951**, Ridgway succeeded MacArthur as commander of United Nations forces in Korea. Until the armistice was signed on **July 27, 1953**, the opposing armies struggled in a narrow mountainous corridor north and south of the thirty-eighth parallel. The final cease-fire line ran from north of the thirty-eighth parallel on the east coast of the Korean peninsula to a point south of the thirty-eighth parallel on the west coast. The United States suffered 33,629 combat-related deaths and 105,785 wounded, and more than 10,000

Americans were missing or prisoners of war at the time of the cease-fire.

Korea, of course, was an alliance war. In addition to the United States and South Korea, twenty other nations contributed troops, ships, planes, and medical units. U.S. allies, fighting under the flag of the United Nations, sustained their share of casualties, with the great majority of those battle deaths South Koreans. However, the South Korean civilian population suffered the greatest number of deaths, as nearly three million perished.

What did Korea mean to the airmen who fought the war, mostly in aging World War II aircraft? Initially, the air war emphasized close air support of hard-pressed American and ROK ground forces and the maintenance of air superiority over the battlefield. The North Korean air force was quickly destroyed, and close air support was expanded to include interdiction of North Korean forces. With the Chinese communists entry into the war and the appearance of the MiG-15 as an offensive air element, "it appeared that air power would have to be employed much more broadly to reduce the numerical superiority of the Chinese," wrote General William Momyer. "We had to shift from an air strategy oriented primarily toward close support of our ground forces to a new strategy featuring (1) offensive fighter patrols along the Yalu, (2) attacks against forward staging bases from which MIGs might strike 5th Air Force airfields and the 8th Army, and (3) intensive attacks against the main supply lines of the advancing Chinese army" (Momyer 5). In three years of war, the Far East Air Forces destroyed 950 enemy aircraft, including 792 MiG-15 fighters. The Far East Air Forces lost 1,986 aircraft, the majority of them American.

What lessons did Korea provide for future conflicts? In stark contrast to the terms of unconditional surrender thrust upon Nazi Germany and Imperial Japan only eight years earlier, the Korean War ended in what many perceived as a stalemate, with no clear-cut winner. But, stated Secretary of State Acheson, "From the very start of hostilities in Korea, President Truman intended to fight a limited engagement there" (*Present* 416). What evolved was a national policy of containment of communism, a policy which by its nature precluded old-fashioned wars with old-fashioned outcomes. Furthermore, the Soviet explosion of an atomic device in 1949 had made the country a potential threat to U.S. survival. At the time, there was no other nation with a comparable hostile ideology and the added potential of sufficient military power to threaten U.S. national survival. As a historic first, this threat had to be dealt with intelligently and with restraint. Although the Korean experience could have provided many lessons useful to airmen twelve years later in Southeast Asia, the immediate focus was and for years remained on the Soviet Union and its offensive nuclear arsenal. In response to the Soviet threat, the Strategic Air Command evolved into an immensely powerful, nuclear-armed air force to checkmate the Soviet nuclear potential and political ambitions. Air defense of North America against potential Soviet intruders became the second well-funded issue. As a result, tactical air forces atrophied, switching to nuclear armaments to ensure a modicum of funding and participation in the role of defending the United States in a nuclear world. For the U.S. Army, *readiness* became its mantra, so that it would never again let itself get caught unprepared by an aggressor.

Korea was destined to become known as the forgotten war, as the late Colonel Harry Summers referred to it, with few obvious lessons for the immediate future. To many the war appeared to be an anomaly, out of place in a time of jet planes and the atomic bomb.

Chapter 4

The F-51 Mustangs
from Dogpatch

Headquarters Twelfth Air Force, APO #650, General Orders Number 65, 13 October 1943.

Section II—Awards of the Distinguished Flying Cross. Under the provisions of AR 600-45, . . . the Distinguished Flying Cross is awarded to . . . Charles E. Schreffler, 0-734000, First Lieutenant, Anderson, Indiana. For extraordinary achievement while participating in aerial flight in the North African, Sicilian and Italian Theatres of Operations as a Pilot of a P-38 type aircraft. On 30 August 1943, while escorting a B-26 type bombardment group over Lago di Patria, Italy, Lt. Schreffler's flight of 4 P-38's were attacked by thirty ME-109's. Observing a lagging comrade in grave danger he unhesitatingly led his flight in an aggressive assault on the threatening enemy aircraft, destroying one ME-109 and probably destroying another. Lt. Schreffler so expertly maneuvered his small flight, despite one engine being disabled by hostile fire, that the flight safely rejoined his squadron. His outstanding ability as a flight leader and combat pilot has reflected great credit upon himself and the armed forces of the United States.

By Command of Major General Doolittle

Colonel Charles E. Schreffler

Distinguished Flying Cross, Air Medal (10)

In the sunshine of southern California, where Charlie Schreffler settled after an eventful air force career, he recalled one particular June afternoon in 1950. "While sitting on the porch of my quarters at Clark Air Base in the Philippines, I saw innocent-looking puffs of smoke seeping out of the jungle foliage. It was an artillery duel between the communist Huks and the local constabulary, just beyond the Clark Air Base perimeter. A flight of four Philippine F-51 Mustangs passed overhead in echelon formation to join the fray. My unit, the 18th Fighter Bomber Group, had converted to the F-80 jet only recently, giving our World War II–vintage Mustang fighters to the Philippine air force. Maybe one of those attacking planes was mine, *Sally Flat Foot*. I could see the Mustangs descending one at a time, strafing what they thought were guerrilla positions. In the jungle it was hard to tell where anything was—I knew that from experience. The Mustangs pulled up sharply at the end of their high-angle strafing passes. I saw them reforming for a second run at the Huks. A feeling of nostalgia overcame me as I watched them. I missed flying the 'Stang, as we affectionately called the Mustang. But then I couldn't remember any plane I flew I didn't like.

"I remember one of my last flights in the F-51, a routine training flight just before I transitioned into the F-80 jet. My wingman and I were on our initial approach to Clark when without warning we were jumped by a couple of F-51s from our sister squadron, the 12th. I flew with the 67th squadron. We maintained our flying skills by engaging each other in mock air battles, but this wasn't quite the way it was supposed to happen, and the resulting midair collision bent *Sally Flat Foot*'s props and put a few dents in her nose. The other Mustang had its tail chewed up. We landed safely. It's trite to say that flying is hours of boredom and moments of stark terror, but it is true.

"That June my wife was making arrangements for our move back to the States. I was reading the paper and having a beer on our porch. I hated everything associated with moving. The packers were coming on

Sally Flat Foot V, Charlie Schreffler's F-51, as it looked after a midair collision with another F-51 over Clark Air Base, the Philippines, 1950. C. Schreffler.

Friday June 24. Our household goods were to be picked up on Monday, the 27th. That day I intended to clear the base and stay out of the way. After they picked up our stuff, we would spend a night in the base hotel and then embark on a boat at the nearby Subic Bay Navy Base for a leisurely trip back to San Francisco. I was looking forward to going home. I tried to go back to reading the paper, but I was still too distracted by idle thoughts as a result of the Philippine F-51s, who by then were on their second strafing run. I put down my paper and decided to watch them instead. *My war* was behind me, I thought smugly, and I was glad.

"I'll never forget December 10, 1941, three days after the Japanese attacked Pearl Harbor. My friends and I, in a patriotic fervor, went to the army recruiting office in Fort Wayne, Indiana, and signed up for the Army Air Corps. I was born in 1921 in Coshocton, Ohio. When I was still very young, my parents had moved to Indiana. I always wanted to fly, ever since the barnstormers came by when I was seven and gave me a five-minute ride. I passed my physical and became an aviation cadet. I went through preflight and primary training in the PT-13 and BT-13. The BT had flaps and a sophisticated set of instruments, none of which the PT had. In advanced training I got to fly the fighterlike AT-6 Texan at Luke Field, Arizona. I graduated in December 1942 and that same day was put on a train to transition into P-38 fighters at Glendale, California. In March 1943 I crossed the country by train. I processed through Fort Dix in New Jersey and embarked on a ship which joined a large convoy across the Atlantic, bound for Oran, Algeria. From there I shipped to a dusty base outside Casablanca for P-38 refresher training. Finally I got to fly my first combat mission. It was against a small harbor in Sardinia. I had never dropped a bomb before. I felt a little foolish not knowing how to aim my bomb or even when I was to drop it. I watched my flight leader closely and did exactly what he did. When he released his bomb, I let go of mine. I don't know where the bomb went or if it hit anything other than water.

"On my next mission over Sicily, we ran into some German Me-109s. In the ensuing melee one of our own aircraft shot up my leader, and we both returned to base. Up until then everything seemed sort of unreal, even comical at times. After all, I was a fighter pilot, not a bomber pilot, and I didn't expect our own planes to fire on us. But then everything in battle is confusing. My perceptions of war changed drastically on my next mission, a long-range sweep by over two hundred P-38s against German and Italian air bases around Foggia on the Italian mainland. I finally got to use my guns. We came in from the Adriatic side, flying at fifty feet to avoid detection. We totally surprised the enemy and destroyed over one hundred of their aircraft on the ground. Soon after that mission, I learned about fear and how to fly through it. We were escorting a group of B-26 Marauders up the Italian boot when we were jumped by seventy-five to eighty Me-109s and FW-190s. We got all the B-26s into the target and out without losing one, but we lost eleven of our own. In the confusion of the air battle, a German Me-109 suddenly came into my sights, and I fired instinctively. The 109 burst into flames and exploded. I added one more probable enemy fighter destroyed that day before returning to my base.

"By September 1943 I had racked up fifty combat missions over Italy and was returned home to Bradley Field, Connecticut. There I stayed until April 1945 as a P-47 instructor pilot. I liked flying and wanted to stay, but I was discharged that October along with thousands of other pilots. I returned to Fort Wayne, Indiana, to my old job as a draftsman. I stayed in the Air Force Reserve, and to my great surprise, in 1947 I was offered a regular air force commission. I accepted immediately and was assigned to Andrews Air Force Base, near Washington, D.C., as a maintenance officer. In July 1948 I transferred to the 18th Fighter Group at Clark in the Philippines. World War II should have been my only war. I was wrong. In a few days I was involved in another equally brutal war. The 18th Fighter Bomber Group was quickly thrown into battle to stem the surging tide of the North Korean People's Army.

"Our household goods were picked up as scheduled. That evening my wife mentioned a curious thing to me. The household goods people had contacted her and asked if she wanted to change the destination of our shipment. When she asked them why she would want to do that, they told her that her husband wouldn't be accompanying her. 'Is that true?' she asked me. That's how I learned about the invasion of South Korea. My wife took the ship home to San Francisco, while I left for Johnson Air Base, near Tokyo, Japan, to pick up an F-51. By the time her ship docked in San Francisco harbor, some of the returning wives learned that their husbands had died in South Korea, in a war of which they knew nothing."

The situation in South Korea was desperate. The U.S. military in Japan was largely an occupational constabulatory force, poorly trained and not much better equipped. What remained of American military power was built around the jet fighter plane, just coming into the inventory, and the new super weapon, the atomic bomb. But the atomic bomb couldn't save Americans trapped in Seoul or, later on, in the tight Pusan perimeter. The available air bases in South Korea were so crude that the 18th Fighter Bomber Group's F-80 jets could not operate from them. The two hundred–mile distance from Japan to targets in South Korea gave the F-80 almost no loiter time over the target. Air force commanders had to look for quick alternatives. The F-51 was rugged enough to operate from crude airfields, carried a lethal weapons load, and was still available in large numbers. The decision was made to reequip the 18th Group with F-51 Mustangs.

"All 18th Group pilots were F-51 qualified. Many of us had extensive World War II experience. Our group had three squadrons—the 12th, the 44th, and the 67th." The pilots of the 12th Squadron were the first to convert. They were flown to Johnson Air Base, where they picked up thirty reconditioned F-51s that had been in storage. The Dallas Squadron, as they were to be called, flew their Mustangs to Ashiya in southern Japan, then moved on to K-2 near Taegu, South Korea. In the meantime, 145 F-51s assigned to the Air National Guard were rounded up and loaded on the aircraft carrier USS *Boxer,* which left the port of Alameda on July 15 with its load of Mustangs and seventy pilots. After a maximum-speed voyage, the *Boxer* arrived in Japan on July 22. Pilots of the 67th Fighter Bomber Squadron from Clark picked up a batch of the newly arrived Mustangs and became part of the 51st Fighter Group (Provisional), joining their advanced party of the Dallas Squadron at K-2 to carry the war to the enemy. By August 4 the name game ended when the two squadrons regained their original designations as the 12th and 67th Fighter Bomber Squadrons of the 18th Fighter Bomber Group. They fought under this designation for the rest of the war and accumulated an outstanding combat record. The 12th Squadron Blue Noses, the former Dallas Squadron, became known as the Flying Tigers of Korea, and their aircraft soon sported shark's teeth. The Red Noses belonged to the 67th Squadron, and Charlie Schreffler flew a red nose out of K-2 in July 1950.

"I remember leading a flight of two Mustangs on a road reconnaissance mission in the area of Hamhung, North Korea. As we turned south to return to base, the visibility began to deteriorate, and our position was not completely clear to me. As we crossed over a coastline, all hell broke loose. We had flown over Wonsan Harbor, which was loaded with North Korean ships. They let us know we were not welcome. From Taegu the 18th moved first to K-9, Pusan East; then to

K-23, Pyongyang East; then to K-13, Suwon near Seoul; and finally to Chinhae, K-10, which became our main operating base for the remainder of the war. Conditions at Chinhae were basic—dirt, rocks, and tents defined the base. But we didn't lose our sense of humor, and we called Chinhae "Dogpatch" and "Lower Slobovia." Al Capp, the guy who drew the *Li'l Abner* comic strip, somehow got wind of us and took us under his wing. He designed a patch for us. I still have mine. The patch shows Li'l Abner riding an F-51 Mus-

Captain Schreffler in front of his rocket- and bomb-laden F-51 at K-9, Pusan, 1950. C. Schreffler.

tang firing its guns, with the inscription "Dogpatchers." That's how we got our name, the Dogpatchers.

"Major Louis J. "Lou" Sebille was my squadron commander. On a routine close-air-support mission on 5 August, one of Lou's five hundred–pound bombs didn't release. He tried to shake the bomb loose on his second firing pass, but by then the enemy had his range, and he took several hits. Again, the bomb didn't release. Lou should have returned to Chinhae, had the bomb removed, and the holes patched. Instead, he chose to continue his attack. On his next firing pass, getting hit all the way in, he never pulled out and flew directly into the enemy vehicles and exploded. For that action Lou received the Medal of Honor. I can't vouch for the exact number of firing passes Lou made, but the squadron's reaction on hearing of his loss was one of great sorrow. Lou was a fine pilot!

Loaded and ready, an F-51 tank killer of the 12th Tiger Squadron at Pusan, 1950. C. Schreffler.

"My bunch, the 67th Squadron, launched its first missions in June 1950 from Ashiya, Japan. By the first week in August we were operating from K-2, at Taegu, within the Pusan defensive perimeter. It was a dusty, rock-strewn field with quick access to the bomb line, constantly moving south. One problem we soon discovered was differentiating between friend and foe. We were moving so fast and close to the ground it was difficult to determine who was who. The GIs were supposed to display colors of the day; they didn't always do so. Mistakes were made, and sometimes there were the unavoidable friendly-fire losses."

But there wasn't a GI whose heart didn't jump for joy when he heard the high-pitched whine of an F-51 engine bearing down on the enemy at thirty feet above the ground. The F-51s' killing power became legendary. Their napalm was the weapon most feared by North Korean infantry, and their rockets were the most dreaded by the North Korean tanks. The two 18th Group squadrons quickly established a tank-killing unit of ready-to-go, rocket-armed aircraft. Whenever a call came in that enemy tanks had been sighted, this unit went after them. When the Pusan perimeter really got tight, pilots flew as many as five or six

**Marilyn Monroe on a USO tour, cheering up the boys at Pusan, 1950.
C. Schreffler.**

missions a day. Almost immediately after takeoff, they found themselves over enemy lines. For a pilot to fly a hundred missions in two
months wasn't difficult—if he lived that long. Losses were high, operating so close to the ground, where every enemy weapon could reach
them. There was an aggregate loss of 351 F-51s in more than sixty
thousand combat missions. Nearly fifty thousand of those missions
were flown by the pilots of the 18th Group. The 18th's F-51s, along
with the twin-engine B-26 Invaders of the 3d and 452d Bomb Wings,
helped break the back of the initial North Korean invasion force and
gave the U.S. Army the time it needed to reconstitute itself.

Chapter 5

Night Interdiction in the B-26 Invader

During the Korean War the Far East Air Forces lost 1,986 aircraft, 1,144 air crew died, and four U.S. Air Force pilots won Medals of Honor. All four medals were awarded posthumously. One Medal of Honor pilot was Major Louis J. Sebille, flying an F-51 Mustang; another was Captain John S. Walmsley, flying a B-26 Invader.

Extracted from Harry G. Summers Jr., *Korean War Almanac*, and *The United States Military Experience in Korea, 1871–1982*

As I sit here and dream of home
and ones I love so dear,
I pray to God that some day soon
their voices I will hear.
But if God wills that I remain
to die on foreign soil,
Then comfort bring to those I love
through all of life's turmoil.

Byron Dobbs, B-26 pilot shot down over North Korea

Lieutenant Colonel Byron A. Dobbs Jr.

Silver Star, Distinguished Flying Cross, Bronze Star, Air Medal (4), Purple Heart

Barney Dobbs slowly taxied his heavily laden Douglas B-26 Invader toward the end of the runway at K-8, a desolate airstrip near Kunsan. Barney was assigned to the 8th Squadron of the 3rd Bomb Wing. It was the early-morning hours of February 19, 1952. Only four weeks earlier he had turned thirty-two. Barney applied the left brake to his swaying aircraft. Slowly the Invader turned to face down the runway. There were no lights. He didn't need any. He would steer down the center of the strip and when he reached 120 knots pull back on the yoke and lift off. He intended to hit his target hard and get out of the area quickly. To linger was a sure invitation to a Chinese rest camp—or worse.

"I always flew alone at night. You can't worry about a wingman while moving at 240 miles per hour at 250 feet above the ground. Neither in World War II in the Pacific nor in Korea did I ever fly in a formation larger than two aircraft. Mostly I flew alone. I liked it that way. I made a quick final check of the instruments dimly bathed in red light to preserve night vision. Everything looked good. RPM and manifold pressures were in the green. The engines sounded smooth, my crew chief had seen to that. I carried fourteen forward firing fifty-caliber machine guns, eight in the nose and three in each wing. At times when I fired, trucks just blew apart when they were hit by that many guns at once. On each wing I carried five five hundred–pound bombs. I intended to use every round of ordnance and every bomb I carried. We knew the Chinese were building for a big push, but without ammo and supplies they couldn't get far.

"My crew chief sat to my right. The top turret gunner sat behind and above us. It was our twenty-second mission in twenty-eight days, or nights, because I never flew during daylight hours. I had talked to the pilots who bombed my target in daylight. I knew approximately where the antiaircraft guns should be. I moved the throttles forward to full takeoff power. The engines responded smoothly. I released the

105

brakes. Then I concentrated on the dark runway ahead, our liftoff, and my first heading. There were landmarks, dimly outlined against the night sky, which served as my reference points. There was no need to worry about the good guys shooting at us as they had in World War II. The bad guys didn't have airplanes which came down low to bother the troops on the ground."

Captain Byron Alexis Dobbs Jr. was born in Phoebus, Virginia, on January 14, 1920, under the muzzles of the quiet guns of Fort Monroe. His father was a carpenter. When the depression hit, his family barely managed to stay alive, moving from one relative to another, always chasing the next dollar or the next meal. "One summer we stayed on my grandmother's forty-acre farm. My dad got a contract from the Heinz company to grow pickles. I recall riding the pickup loaded with cucumbers down to their plant. The job only lasted for the summer but that gave us enough money to make it through the winter. Eventually we settled in Birch Run, a small village in Michigan. Both of my parents were from Michigan. I graduated from high school in 1937. I tried to enlist in the navy. They wouldn't take me because the doctor said I had hammer toes. I tried again in 1939, but that time I went to the army recruiting office. The doctor who examined me asked, 'Is there anything else I should know about your health, Barney?' Well, I always tried to be honest, so I told him the navy had turned me down in '37 because I had hammer toes. 'I don't care which way your toes point,' the doctor said, 'as long as there are five on each foot.'

"I was assigned to Selfridge Field. They had P-35s there. At night I would go and sit in the cockpit of a plane and think about flying. I dreamed of being a pilot. When I sat in one of those planes, I was on top of the world. The officers were gods to me. They treated us real well, and I did everything they told me to do. By 1941 I made corporal and my pay was increased to forty-two dollars a month. A year later I was promoted to staff sergeant, and I applied for enlisted pilot training. I was accepted. Late that year I got my wings and was promoted to flight officer. I ended up at Peterson Field in Colorado Springs, where I checked out in the P-38. What a beautiful airplane! After only forty hours in the P-38, we were sent to Hamilton Field, near San Francisco, for reassignment in the Pacific Theater. On Monday morning, August 2, 1943, our group loaded on a B-24 cargo ship with secret orders and instructions not to open them until two hours into our flight. My close friend Al Blum and I speculated where we were going. When we ripped open the envelopes, we found our destination was Amberly Field, Brisbane, Australia. Once we arrived in Brisbane, we were told our final destination: the 8th Photo Reconnaissance Squadron at Port Moresby, New Guinea. We stayed in Brisbane two nights and thought they were crazy when they issued us six blankets each. But after the sun went down we discovered the reason: though it was August, it was midwinter there.

"In Moresby they were glad to see us. Their numbers were pretty well depleted. We lived in tents, and our comfort depended entirely on how hard we worked at it. Lumber was nearly impossible to get, but Al and I managed by hook and by crook to build us a little hut with a tent for a roof. At least we had a clean place to put our feet in the morning. The air was so humid our B-4 bags began molding after only a few days. Cigarettes absorbed so much moisture they were barely smokable. There were five or six landing strips in the area identified by their distance from Port Moresby—three-mile strip, five-mile strip, seven-mile strip, and so on. We were to fly the F-5, the photo version of the P-38 fighter. Al Blum and I stayed together as much as we could throughout our tour, flying missions all over that part of the world. I spent thirteen months and flew eighty-eight combat missions from Australia and New Guinea, fighting mosquitoes, malaria, jungle rot, and Japanese. Al flew one hundred combat missions. Al kept a diary of his day-by-day experiences in the Pacific. Years later, he sent a copy of his diary to me, and on the cover page he wrote, 'I occasionally reread it. I can still feel the anxieties, fears, frustrations, satisfactions, joys, memories of friends and comrades, sadness when someone didn't return, and the many other emotions of a shavetail involved in the greatest transition of his life—from farm boy to combat pilot.' I sure loved Al's diary, and I'm glad he sent me a copy. It brought back those bittersweet memories of when we were young men and thought we were indestructible.

"In 1946 my wife and I left for our new assignment in Germany. Both Al and I had gotten married in 1943 in San Francisco, two days before we shipped out for Port Moresby. I flew P-61 night fighters out of Schweinfurt for a while until the Black Widows were phased out of the Army Air Force inventory and given to allied nations. In 1948 I found myself at Oberpfaffenhofen, where I prepared fighter aircraft for turnover to allied nations. I was quickly drafted into the evolving Berlin Airlift. I was sent to Wiesbaden to fly as a copilot in C-47s. I had always flown fighters, and I knew nothing about the C-47 transport. It makes my hair stand up in back of my neck when I think of that time in the C-47. They put us fighter jocks in the right seat. I knew enough to keep the thing right side up. I flew into Tempelhof, landing between five-story apartment houses. It was awful. But the GCA radar controllers were superb. I was awfully glad when the airlift was over and I went back to the used-aircraft business.

"From Germany I was reassigned to the Military Air Transport Service at Westover AFB in Massachusetts. While there I flew C-97 Stratocruisers, the military version of the Pan American double-decker airliner. I hated every minute of it. One day while flying a huge four-engined C-97, I surreptitiously joined up with a formation of fighters coming in for a landing. I think they would have court-martialed me, but a war had broken out in Korea, and I volunteered to be an F-51 replacement pilot. That saved me. Once in Korea, I was assigned to K-8, "Kunsan by the Sea," as we referred to it, flying the twin-engine B-26 Invader. The B-26 was no fighter plane but the closest thing to it. I soon fell in love with the airplane.

"In the dark early morning hours of February 19, 1952, I skimmed across the craggy Korean countryside at five hundred feet above the ground, intending to be at no more than two hundred feet above the terrain in our target area. My crew and I had been to this target before, and we were good at identifying trucks moving on dark roads with their lights out. If there wasn't anything happening at the location, we

3rd Bomb Wing B-26s lined up for takeoff at Ashiya Air Base, Japan, 1950.
R. Schulz.

had plans for two other sites. I saw the telltale shadows of slow-moving trucks thrown up against the side of the road by residual fires from the daylight raids. I pointed the nose of the Invader down the valley and made my first pass. I dropped my bombs to bottle up the trucks. The ten bombs slammed into the lead trucks, blowing two of them off the road. Explosions lit up a string of trucks reaching back into a tunnel. As I emerged from the valley, banking to my left, I heard a call from a C-47 flare ship asking me if I wanted flares dropped. 'Roger, no flares,' I told the flare-ship pilot. I had no time to chat with the fellow. I was busy concentrating on flying my airplane down a dark mountain valley adjacent to the one I had passed through.

" 'I can't go home until I drop my flares,' the flare-ship pilot continued to badger me. I ignored him. I was lining up for my second pass. I knew I had surprised the antiaircraft gunners on my first pass, but this time they would be ready for me. I figured they'd expect me to reenter the valley the way I exited. I made a shallow, wide turn instead, flying down the adjacent valley, planning to reenter the way I came in on my first pass but from the opposite side. I was concentrating on my approach to the target with no further thought of the flare ship. I could clearly see the trucks on the winding mountain road. I was lined up, ready to fire my guns, when a bright flare lit up the valley, blinding me, destroying my night vision. To the North Korean gunners I must have looked like a target at their gunnery school. I pulled the aircraft up, cursing the flare ship. I was going to get that pilot's ass when I got home. But first I had to get out of here. Then the flak hit. I felt the impact of the shells as they ripped into the left engine. Fire was everywhere.

"Get out, I yelled and jettisoned the hatches. The crew chief exited over the right wing. I couldn't see the gunner exit, but I thought he was out when I abandoned the aircraft. My chute opened. I swung once or twice and then I was in the trees, on the ground. I was dazed, it all happened so fast. The damn flare ship, I thought. I remember unbuckling my chute and how quiet it was. I was alone. I looked around for my crew. Only silence. I knew exactly where I was and prepared to make my way back to friendly lines. A river ran below, and I toyed with the idea of crossing over to the other side to throw off any search parties which I knew were going to come looking for me. I discarded that idea and decided to move inland and south. There was a slight moon to aid my travel. I felt the cold. The snow reminded me that escape was going to be difficult. Someone surely would pick up my tracks. I could hear dogs barking in a village below me. I decided to hide and wait until daylight. I was dressed for the weather and thought I'd be able to stay fairly comfortable if I found a good hiding place. But by morning the dogs had tracked me down, and three villagers escorted me down the mountain, where they turned me over to soldiers. I didn't know if they were Korean or Chinese. My crew chief was there too. No sign of our gunner.

"We were kept for several days in a back room of a simple cottage. One day a Russian officer showed up. The Russian was friendly and spoke English well. He loaded me into the back of a truck and to my amazement drove me out to my aircraft. The damn aircraft didn't crash. It made a smooth belly landing and was barely damaged. The Russian was a ground pounder and didn't know what questions to ask. What he seemed to want to know from me was what we had in our aircraft that allowed it to belly land, nearly undamaged, without a pilot. Of course, we had nothing. I don't know how that airplane landed in a mountain valley without tearing itself to pieces. I eventually ended up in a permanent camp near the Yalu River. I thought myself lucky. I was alive. I had no broken bones. I thought of what might have happened to me, and that kept me going."

For nearly nineteen months Barney Dobbs endured torture and degradation as a prisoner of war of the Chinese People's Army. He was interrogated repeatedly. He recalled seven different interrogators who tried to convince him to admit he was using germ warfare. He was deprived of sleep, food, and water to make him compliant. He didn't break. He was repeatedly put in solitary confinement, including imprisonment in a three-by-six-foot hole in the ground for six months. Finally, his interrogators gave up and put him in an unheated shack with twelve other uncooperative prisoners. When Barney lay in the hole in the ground, he thought of something to hold onto, to keep his sanity, to be able to endure and survive. He tried to recall every hymn he ever sang in church, and in time he composed his own hymn in his mind, writing it down on paper once he was released.

> Korean Solitary
> The accusation, it was made:
> of course it was denied.
> They said on them germ bombs I'd dropped,
> and about it I had lied.
> A bomb that's filled with flies and fleas,
> dear Lord, I've never seen;
> but men for propaganda's sake
> can sure be mighty mean.
>
> Interrogators came and went,
> their lies were all the same.
> "Confess," they said, "and you'll go free,
> or here you will remain.

God can't help you, he's not real,
you're living in a dream."
"Not so!" said I, "He's real to me,
so go to your extreme."

"An execution is your fate,
since you've made up your mind
not to confess and tell the truth
about your heinous crime."
So, they threw me in a hole,
never to return.
And, I'm 'fraid their souls will rest in Hell
and burn, and burn, and burn.

The hole was deep, not very long,
and only three feet wide.
The sun and air through a window came,
six inches on each side.
The roosters woke me up at four,
the guards came round at five.
They brought me food,
'twas just enough to keep a man alive.

Fish heads and rice were all I had,
sometimes a piece of bread.
But I ate it with God's blessing
who watched from overhead.
Soap they gave me, but water none.
Tobacco, but no fire.
They called it "lenient treatment,"
but it only aroused my ire.

I've seen men come,
and I've seen men go.
But some men stayed for ever.
They paid the price for that plot of ground,
on the Yalu River.
I've seen 'em beg and scream
and yell for a doctor and some pills,
to stop the dysentery,
and drive away their ills.

The guard just laughed
for 'twas a joke to see a Yank a'dying,
they called it "lenient treatment"

and friend, I ain't a lyin.
Walls do not a prison make,
nor iron bars a cage.
For thoughts have wings and they are free
as wind across the sage.

As I sit here and dream of home
and ones I love so dear,
I pray to God that some day soon
their voices I will hear.
But if God wills that I remain
to die on foreign soil,
Then comfort bring to those I love
through all of life's turmoil.

As I look 'round me at the foe
who've never heard His name,
I wonder where their souls go
when they're through life's earthly game.
Never to have heard His word,
nor felt His saving grace,
nor seen the love of Jesus Christ
for the human race.

For they are children under God
the same as you and I.
But I wonder where their souls go
when their earthly bodies die.
For in this land of Commie rule
church bells are never heard.
And folks don't go to Sunday School
to study Jesus' Word.
4,000 years they've gotten by
with oxen and with hoe.
Seems to me that without God,
they're progressing mighty slow.

On September 15, 1953, the last day of the POW exchange, Barney Dobbs was released. "As they were getting ready to release us, they assembled us in a large camp, gave us decent food for several days and clean clothes. Then they put us on a train to our final camp. On the last day of the prisoner release, I was put on the last truck. I thought I

Barney Dobbs after his release from a Chinese POW camp, 1953. B. Dobbs.

was going to be left behind. Prior to my release, my wife, Kay, had no idea if I was alive or dead. All she knew was that I had been declared missing in action. As the POWs were released throughout September 1953, each day the names of the latest batch of prisoners to be released were announced on TV. It went on for days, and finally she saw my name. I still have the prison suit in which I returned home. My life as a prisoner, although much of it taken up by interrogation and by nine months of solitary confinement, included being harnessed to a cart like an ox and pulling it through the village. Fish heads, barley, and occasionally rice was the food I was fed. I constantly thought about meat and vowed that when I got home I would open a barbecue restaurant, Barney's Barbecue, to ensure I had a guaranteed supply of barbecued ribs for the rest of my life. Of course that didn't happen. Three months after my release, I was back flying airplanes. I retired from the U.S. Air Force in 1969 and settled in Riverside, California."

Colonel Richard G. "Dick" Schulz

Distinguished Flying Cross, Air Medal (5)

While Barney Dobbs arrived in Korea as a replacement pilot in December 1952 and flew from austere fields in South Korea, Dick Schulz, a Detroit native and one-time B-29 bombardier based in England during the Berlin Airlift, flew his combat missions over Korea from bases in Japan. Dick and twenty other pilots left San Francisco in November 1949 on the troopship USS *Darby*. In December he arrived in Yokohama and was assigned to the 13th Bomb Squadron, 3rd Bomb Wing, Light, at Yokota Air Base, near Tokyo. Each of the 3rd Bomb Wing's squadrons had sixteen assigned aircraft. In several months' time, his wife and young son joined him. Unlike Barney Dobbs, who got no training in the B-26 before flying it into combat, Dick was thoroughly checked out in the B-26 by an experienced instructor pilot. Dick Schulz was slowly introduced to his new aircraft, first flying easy local-area missions in daytime and in good weather. Next, he got plenty of time to practice takeoffs and landings. Finally, after much ground school and twenty-one hours of flying, he was declared a combat-ready pilot in the B-26.

Dick Schulz first enlisted in the Army Air Force in 1943. He didn't see combat during World War II but qualified as a gunner, bombardier, and finally as a radar observer on B-29 aircraft. In 1949 he gained his pilot rating. His first assignment was to B-26s in Japan. "Life was good in Japan. Between a not-too-strenuous flying schedule, frequent golf tournaments, and my family, I was enjoying occupation duty." The Korean War started in June 1950 as a "come as you are" war. There simply was no time to prepare, and units were thrown against the onrushing North Korean army with whatever they had available. The 3rd Bomb Wing flew its planes to Ashiya Air Base in southern Japan on June 24; they then moved to Iwakuni. On June 25 the North Koreans invaded, and on June 28 the 3rd flew its first combat mission. That mission was a brutal lesson of war. "Out of the thirty-two aircraft that flew that day, six did not return. One crashed, killing the crew. The other five damaged aircraft landed at other air bases." Only days earlier, the men had relaxed with their families in the early summer sun, played ball with their children, gone to church, done the things Americans do while working and raising a family. Suddenly they were at war. The wives read about their husbands in *Stars and Stripes*. Families occasionally were allowed to visit Iwakuni, where they could watch the men take off in their bomb- and rocket-laden aircraft and then wait, hoping and praying that they would return.

Dick's flying schedule was heavy. At first he flew low-level missions against targets of opportunity. "They wanted to stop the North Koreans wherever we found them. My targets were trucks, trains, and tanks. As the days passed, my targets shifted to ammunition-storage areas, warehouses, and bridges—lots of bridges to impede the flow of the North Korean army. Aircraft losses continued to rise, and we shifted the bulk of our effort to night operations, because that's when most of the movement was taking place. Our combat losses continued to be high, primarily due to the low-level missions we were flying but also because the B-26 at low altitude could be an unforgiving airplane if a pilot momentarily lost his concentration. For example, on a strafing run, the airplane could exceed four hundred knots. If you didn't start to pull up in time, you would fly into the ground. On one occasion several congressmen visited Iwakuni, and we were to demonstrate the capability of the B-26. One of our most experienced pilots, Major Joe Stein, put on a strafing demonstration over the bay, which was off the end of the runway. Stein was our operations officer, with over four thousand flying hours. After making several low-level, high-speed strafing runs, he must have momentarily lost his concentration and neglected to watch his airspeed and altitude and flew into the bay, killing everyone on board.

"Combat missions and their low-level nature were bad enough and were taking their toll on our crews. Even normal night and weather operations could quickly turn into disaster. On a typical night search-and-destroy mission I took off at four in the morning. The weather was clear and forecast to remain so. I computed my fuel for the length of the mission plus thirty minutes. At Okchon I sighted a train, and I blew away three of its cars with rockets. Then, southeast of Taejon I blasted a locomotive with my 50-calibers, the steam streaming out of numerous holes from the hapless engine. Next, we turned to Sintansin and I destroyed four more boxcars, leaving them burning on the tracks. As I returned to Iwakuni, I was informed that the weather was getting progressively worse. Well, things happen. Once I arrived I elected to make a GCA radar approach. The controller gave me heading and altitude. When I arrived and he said I was over the runway and 'Take over visually,' I was still three hundred feet up and couldn't see the ground. I executed a missed approach. On the second approach I elected to fly the same pattern, but I descended to one hundred feet, and I still couldn't see the runway. As I again aborted my landing attempt, my crew chief told me that we had just enough fuel remaining for one final approach. I really didn't want to bail out. I told the GCA controller of my fuel situation, and he gave me an abbreviated pattern. I was following his instructions when suddenly the usually calm and crisp voice of the controller rose in pitch, and he screamed, 'Climb, climb, climb!'

"I had my hand on the throttles. I pushed them to full power and pulled back on the yoke as far as it would go. We climbed out of there at a maximum rate. We leveled off at four thousand feet, and I contacted the controller. 'This is it,' I told him. 'After this approach, we'll be out of fuel.' The weather had deteriorated to zero-zero—zero visibility, zero cloud height. The shaken controller told me he would take me over the end of the runway. I was to land if I could see anything or not. 'I will tell you when you pass over the numbers (the runway heading painted on the runway's end),' he said. The controller did a perfect job. 'Over the runway,' he announced, his voice steady and professional again. I saw the numbers pass under my left wing, eased back on the yoke, pulled the power, and we settled down to a perfect landing. The engines sputtered as we taxied, then died. A tug towed us into our parking area. The controller did a superb job of bringing me down, but he made a most unusual error when he tried to bring me in on that third attempt. He gave me a reciprocal heading, nearly flying me into a nearby mountain.

"I flew a total of thirty-nine B 26 combat missions. In November 1950 I broke my leg. After it healed, I was assigned to the 9th Bomb Wing at Yokota as a B-29 copilot and flew another eleven combat missions, for a total of fifty. Out of twenty Class 49C flying-school classmates that went to Japan with me in late 1949, only a handful returned home alive. We tried hard to stop the North Koreans to give the army a chance to build up its strength. We succeeded but paid the price. The high attrition of Pilot Training Class 49C earned us the dubious nickname 'Class 49 Crash!' "

Dick retired from the air force in 1975 and went to work as manager in a large construction company doing work in Saudi Arabia and on the Los Angeles Metro project. He now resides in southern California.

Chapter 6

The B-29 Bomber War

On October 28, 1951, the last daylight B-29 attack was conducted. From then on Bomber Command would operate only at night.

Harry G. Summers Jr., *Korean War Almanac*

Our missions were not only long—twelve hours—but often bone-chillingly cold and mind-numbingly boring. Time over the target was brief. The rest of the eleven hours and fifty minutes, we just droned on through an empty sky, trying desperately to stay awake.

Joe Gyulavics, B-29 pilot

Colonel Joseph J. Gyulavics

In 1951, Second Lieutenant Joseph Gyulavics, fresh out of pilot training, found himself in the cockpit of a B-29 flying out of Okinawa, carrying his bomb load up the Yalu River to strike a North Korean airfield. It was soon after an RB-45C had been shot down by Russian MiG-15s in the same area. B-29 bombers, based at Yokota Air Base, Japan, and at Kadena Air Base on Okinawa, were the principal users of the important pictorial intelligence gathered by the high-flying RB-45C reconnaissance jets also based at Yokota. "Suddenly, my aircraft was at the center of several Chinese communist searchlights. We were fired upon by flak from their side of the Yalu, the side we weren't allowed to bomb. I was nearly blinded by the intensity of the lights, unable to see or do anything. A strange thought passed through my mind: 'How did I get to be here?' When I passed beyond the range of the Chinese communist flak, the lights suddenly shifted away, leaving us in near total darkness. That was almost as disconcerting as the initial illumination. We made it back to Kadena without further incident.

"Halfway through my pilot training, the Korean War broke out. The minute I graduated, I was assigned to Randolph Field for B-29 combat-crew training. I crewed up as a copilot with a bunch of misfits, or so I thought. A regular leper colony. An old ex–B-17 pilot (he was in his early thirties), a bombardier who was an alcoholic, and a radar navigator who was an overweight schoolteacher. Before we went to Korea, the former B-17 pilot thought we should take a shot at getting the flight surgeon to ground us or at least have him declare us unfit for combat duty. He claimed he had enough wartime experience flying in the Eighth Air Force out of England in 1944. He could pop his right arm out of its socket with ease and had one of the crew do it for him. He—with his arm dangling—the bombardier, and the navigator walked into the flight surgeon's office asking to be medically excused from flying combat. The flight surgeon took one look at them and kicked them out of his office.

"Our leper colony actually turned into a pretty good combat crew. We flew missions against North Korea out of Kadena as part of the 19th Bombardment Group. It was a long haul to Korea and back—twelve hours. We got to Kadena about the time they lost seven B-29s on one day and nine B-29s the next, shot down or damaged beyond repair. We thought, 'Oh God, here we go. World War II all over again.' Someone at headquarters wised up, and we started flying our missions at night. The Koreans didn't have night fighters worth a damn, but their searchlights were good. They would pinpoint us, and then the flak started working us over. We only got hit once, in the number two engine (the inboard engine on the left side). That time we landed at Fukioka, Japan, on New Year's Eve 1951. We went into the Officers' Club in our sweaty flight suits and joined the ongoing New Year's celebration. No one took notice of us. On one of our early missions, we flew in a bomber stream up the Yalu River. Our target was Sinuiju Airfield, just south of the river, one of their big fighter bases. The searchlights were on the Chinese side of the Yalu River, and we were not allowed to hit them. It was then that I flew my first ECM mission. On that particular flight, we were getting ready to go when a staff officer held us back, saying, 'No, you are not going to be part of the bomber stream. You are going to go in first, by yourselves, and then you are going to orbit south of the target. You will take this black box with you, and the radar operator is going to turn it on when you get into your orbit.' He handed the navigator a black box. Unbeknownst to us, our aircraft had been modified with the necessary antennas and cabling to accommodate the ECM transmitter, which was a simple noise jammer, preset to the frequency of the radar that guided the searchlights. All the radar navigator had to do was turn it on and off.

"The night was very dark. We pulled off into our orbit after we dropped our bombs. Then we watched the bomber stream come along behind us with the searchlights pointing right at the B-29s. On top of each tepee—the top of two, three, or more searchlights—there was a B-29. The flak was zeroing in on them. We turned on the jammer, and then the searchlights fell off. Pretty soon they came back again. We turned the jammer on and off and broke the searchlights' tracking ability. We got to thinking, as we sat in our orbit, if they found out who was doing it to them, we were a sitting duck. We were scheduled to orbit until the last bomber made it through. The jammer worked. We made it home.

"When flying up there, we would nearly always fly over Wonsan Harbor and turn up the peninsula to our IP, the initial point. Well, every time we came near Wonsan Harbor, our own navy would shoot at us. Our navy sat in that area with its carriers. You would think anybody in the U.S. Navy would know that when you had a stream of

The B-29s of the 19th Bomb Group on Okinawa still bore their World War II nose art. *Command Decision* once flew with the Twentieth Air Force in World War II and was back again with the Twentieth, fighting another war, 1951. J. Gyulavics.

bombers coming over from the south, they were ours. But their ships would fire at us every time. Fortunately, nobody got hit. I guess it was an example of a lack of coordination or procedures, or maybe just a lack of common sense. We complained about it, but it didn't do any good. Every single time we went near Wonsan, our navy would fire off at least a few rounds.

"While I was on Okinawa, two of our squadron aircraft were shot down by flak. One we never heard from again. The other crew was captured. The pilot lived in the same Quonset hut I lived in. He was forced to make propaganda announcements over the radio about the imperialist Americans and what they were doing to the Korean and Chinese people. We couldn't believe that he would do that because he was such a gung-ho fellow. He carried a big knife from World War II with a swastika on its handle. He carried the knife and all kinds of other stuff. He told everybody he was going to go down fighting if he

Atomic Tom **carried plain five hundred–pound bombs, 1951. J. Gyulavics.**

ever had to bail out. I don't know what they did to him. Intelligence asked me to identify his voice. Sure enough, it was him.

"The bottoms of our B-29s were painted black. They were World War II aircraft which had been pulled out of the boneyard in Arizona. That's the way they were painted when they went there in 1945. Every aircraft still bore the nose art some World War II air crew had painted on them. We also had one modified B-29 on the base, but it wasn't in our bomb group. It could carry the ten thousand–pound blockbuster bomb. I don't know who flew that plane or what targets they attacked. We flew our mission, came home, took a shower, went to the club, and ate. That was our routine. We didn't discuss our missions a lot with the other crews, so we never learned anything about that strange B-29. Our other targets, besides airfields, were mostly bridges all over North Korea.

"Our missions were not only long—twelve hours—but often bone-chillingly cold and mind-numbingly boring. Time over the target was brief. The rest of the eleven hours and fifty minutes, we just droned on

123

Roland Eskew and Andrew Grybko were gunners on Joe Gyulavics's B-29, 1951. J. Gyulavics.

through an empty sky, trying desperately to stay awake. But the inevitable moment of stark terror every airman dreads came. We were coming home from a Yalu River mission about two or three in the morning. Everybody was sleepy. We were on autopilot, descending from our bombing altitude. When you were descending, you pulled your throttles back, and you lost your heat. We were freezing and half asleep. When I glanced out the window to my right there was another airplane, right off our wing, gliding past us like a ghost. We were nearly touching. No matter how much you try to separate the airplanes, eventually you are all heading back the same way. Had it been a midair collision, nobody would have known why it happened.

"We never flew formation. Our bombing altitude was usually twenty-five to twenty-eight thousand feet. It took a lot of fuel to get to altitude. Over South Korea we'd begin our climb. Right after the target we'd descend again. We carried forty five-hundred–pounders. With a twenty-thousand–pound bomb load, it was routine for us to use up nearly every foot of the runway on takeoff. We didn't do any weight and balance calculations in those days. We'd taxi to the end of the

124

runway, put the power up, and off we went. With a good crosswind at Kadena and a wet runway, we would have to use our brakes and throttles to stay on the runway and not get blown off. In order to add more power on one side, we had to pull power off on the other side. By doing that we increased our takeoff roll. At times it was pretty dicey getting airborne when we ran out of concrete. I flew twenty-five missions out of Kadena, just under three hundred hours flying time. Then we went home."

Chapter 7

B-Flight out of Kimpo
Special Operations

Headquarters, Far East Air Forces, APO 925, General Orders Number 303, 30 June 1953.

By direction of the President, under the provisions of the Act of Congress approved 9 July 1918, . . . the Silver Star for gallantry in action is awarded to MAJOR DAVID M. TAYLOR, 13618A, United States Air Force. MAJOR TAYLOR distinguished himself by gallantry in action against an armed enemy of the United Nations as a pilot, 6167th Air Base Group, Fifth Air Force, on 23 April 1953. On that date, MAJOR TAYLOR flew an unarmed, unescorted C-47 cargo-type aircraft on a search mission behind enemy lines. In the vicinity of Yulli, North Korea, near which an F-84 had been shot down, MAJOR TAYLOR flew his aircraft at tree-top level for approximately one hour to search for the downed airman. In making the search, eight or ten passes were made over the same spot, each pass under fire from enemy troops. With no thought of his own safety, MAJOR TAYLOR disregarded the intense light arms and automatic weapons fire which resulted in hits and damage to the aircraft, and continued the search until directed to leave by the Controller. By his high personal courage in the face of the enemy and outstanding devotion to duty, MAJOR TAYLOR reflected great credit upon himself, the Far East Air Forces, and the United States Air Force.

By order of the Commander: S. R. Brentnall, Major General, USAF, Vice Commander

Colonel David M. Taylor

Silver Star, Distinguished Flying Cross (3), Bronze Star (2), Air Medal (9),
Purple Heart

Dave Taylor was born in 1921 and grew up in the small Mississippi town of Grenada. He occasionally played with his younger cousin, Trent Lott, who would one day become majority leader of the U.S. Senate. Young Dave's horizons were not limited by the surrounding cotton fields. He soon became enamored with flying while helping fuel Ford trimotors at the nearby airfield in exchange for an occasional ride. Flying soon got into his blood, although there appeared to be little chance he would be able to follow his dream. When World War II started, Dave volunteered and in 1942 was assigned to flight training as an aviation cadet. In quick succession he passed through primary, basic, and advanced training, and on May 24, 1943, Dave received his pilot wings and the brown bars of a second lieutenant in the U.S. Army Air Force. His mother pinned the lieutenant bars on her young son's shoulders at Ellington Field, near Houston, Texas.

Intensive B-17 crew training followed at a succession of airfields from Washington state to Florida. Twice, Dave's crew and the units they trained with were certified combat—ready. Twice, his combat-ready squadron was designated a replacement training unit to train others for combat in the skies over Europe. At times Dave wondered if the war he wanted to fight would be over by the time he got his chance. Dave was promoted to first lieutenant and progressed to instructor pilot status. He was very good at flying the B-17. His skills confirmed many times over, Dave Taylor's crew finally received its long-awaited orders to proceed as a replacement crew to England. The meaning of the term *replacement* didn't really sink in until he got there. He had handpicked his crew of nine—copilot, bombardier, navigator, radio operator, and four gunners, all well trained in their respective specialties. On October 9, 1944, the men took a brand new B-17 bomber from Hunter Field in Savannah, Georgia, and flew it along the northern Atlantic route via Goose Bay, Labrador, and Scotland to England.

"After first being part of a replacement pool, we were eventually assigned to the 336th Bomb Squadron, 95th Bombardment Group, Heavy. The 95th was part of the 13th Combat Wing of the 3rd Bombardment Division, commanded by Major General Earl Partridge," Dave recalled. "General Partridge replaced Major General Curtis E. LeMay that spring, who had gone on to organize the B-29s in the Pacific. Our combat wing consisted of the 95th Bombardment Group at Horham, the 100th at Thorpe Abbot, and the 390th at Framlingham. I flew a B-17G out of Horham, one of many air bases located in rural Suffolk and adjacent Norfolk Counties, halfway between Norwich to the north and Ipswich to the south.

"The winter of '44 was bitter cold. Our Nissen huts, heated only by a potbellied stove, provided little comfort. The real problem was getting enough coal to keep the stove going. The Brits controlled the coal. My buddy and I figured out a little scheme. He would approach the English guard at the coal yard, make small talk, and offer the guard a much-prized American cigarette. While they were chatting, I jumped into the coal bin from the opposite side and threw chunks of coal over the wall. The guard never caught on, or maybe he didn't want to. We had lots of coal all winter long and a cozy hut.

"We were not assigned living quarters by crews but rather by rank. Officers and enlisted men were housed in separate huts, which had a dubious advantage: when a crew was lost in combat, an entire hut was not emptied at once. Near each bed was an oxygen container. Early in the mornings, those chosen to go on a mission were awakened. We usually took an oxygen mask and did some prebreathing before washing up, eating, and going to the briefing. Those not selected, at least in our hut, took a swig of wine from a large, twenty-five-liter, straw-wrapped wine flask mounted on the ceiling. We had run surgical tubes from the flask to each bed. After fortifying ourselves this way, we rolled over and went back to sleep. We tried hard to give our barren existence some touches of congeniality. We were just kids, ranging in age from the late teens to midtwenties.

"Not only was the place cold, the food was lousy too. There were two mess halls at Horham—one for the air crews, and another for the permanent party. The permanent party consisted of staff and other nonflyers who remained at the base while air crews moved on—some died, some went home after thirty-five missions, some became "guests" of the Germans. The mess for the permanent party served good food both in quality and method of preparation. The air-crew mess was lousy in both respects. We couldn't do much about that. I became the best chicken procurer in England. I quietly entered nearby henhouses, tucked an obliging chicken under my blouse, and soon we had fried chicken to supplement our diet of Spam and powdered eggs prepared by a disinterested kitchen staff. Another opportunity to improve our food situation offered itself when the group staff wanted to fly on my crew. One day the group commander announced that he was going to fly with me as my copilot. He was a lieutenant colonel. 'You're not flying with us,' I told him in my capacity as pilot in command, 'unless you eat like us.' The group commander was unaware how bad the food was for his air crews, and after entering our chow line and seeing what was offered, he took us over to the other mess. After that the food situation in the air-crew mess improved for a while, but it soon reverted to its former deplorable state. Eating a good meal before a combat mission was important. Our missions were six to eight hours in duration, under extremely difficult conditions. If we were shot down, we knew we probably wouldn't eat again for at least three days. That's what experience had taught us.

"Our first missions after arriving at Horham were training missions to familiarize ourselves with local procedures and the area. We did some practice bombing. I remember during this time we came under V-1 rocket attack. The 95th Bomb Group and our next-door sister group at Thorpe Abbotts, the 100th, received special attention from the Luftwaffe. Our group had flown the first daylight raid against Berlin on March 4, 1944, and had been in the thick of things ever since. It was no surprise that the Germans took a special disliking to us. I was disdainful of the V-1s, and when the alarm was given, everyone else raced for the nearest shelter. I stayed in my bunk. I heard an ominous "putt-

putt-putt-roar" and then smelled the exhaust from the V-1 as it passed the open window of my hut. Silence followed. Then I heard a loud explosion beyond a nearby hill. I catapulted out of bed, dove through an open window, and leaped into the nearest trench, filled with water. More V-1s followed with the same result. They exploded harmlessly on that hillside, doing no damage. The next day, Dirty Gerty, as we called the German woman broadcasting to us over the radio, announced that the 95th Bomb Group had been wiped out. We had a good laugh.

"Before my first combat mission I received several visits from old-timers, pilots who had nearly finished their thirty-five combat missions and were looking forward to going home. (The number of combat missions required of heavy bomber crews before going home varied from twenty-five in early 1943 to thirty-five starting in May 1944.) They just wanted to give me a heads-up. As the newest replacement, I would have to fly in what was referred to as Purple Heart corner. My crew would be the most exposed and vulnerable aircraft in the lowest squadron, flying in the low echelon, on the right wing of the element leader. We would have the least defensive support from any of the other aircraft in the formation. 'Watch out for the new German missiles,' the old-timers said, frowning. 'They leave telltale smoke trails as they streak toward your aircraft. You'll see the smoke, but never the missiles. They're too fast.'

"Flying the Purple Heart corner on our first combat mission was enough stress without also having to worry about German missiles. Our target was the rail yard at Giessen. As we got into the area, I saw the dreaded smoke trails. By that time I was too busy flying a tight formation and holding our assigned altitude to worry much about missiles. Our group lost one aircraft that day, and on the way home I discovered I wasn't really that afraid. I completely forgot about the German antiaircraft rockets. At the intelligence debriefing, when I reported the smoke trails, I learned that there really weren't any new German missiles. It was a story the old-timers carefully nurtured and told to replacement pilots. Rather, the smoke trails I saw were our own marker bombs dropped by the lead aircraft, on which the following

Smoke markers and conventional bombs falling on Steenwijk, Holland, March 24, 1945. D. Taylor.

aircraft immediately behind the lead would release their bombs. The rest of us just dropped our bombs into the cauldron below. The marker bombs emitted trails of smoke on their way down which looked much like missile trails coming up, at least that's what I thought. Never having seen an antiaircraft missile before, how would I know?

"A typical combat mission started with the wake-up call for those designated to fly. From the time they woke us until we landed was a long day. Only part of it was the seven to nine hours of flying time. After washing up, we got dressed and donned our bulky flying gear and headed for the mess. After eating, we assembled in the briefing room, where we learned for the first time where we were going. Our group of three squadrons, twelve B-17s per squadron, was dispersed on hardstands along the perimeter road which ran around the field touching each end of the three crisscrossing runways. Regardless of weather conditions, the engine start and takeoff procedure was followed in complete radio silence. At engine start, we warmed up our engines and ran

131

through the pretakeoff checklist. The control tower then fired a yellow flare to start the taxi sequence. At our assigned time, and watching the aircraft ahead of us move out, we taxied toward our takeoff position. I knew who came ahead of me. When he started to move, I got ready to go next. When the tower fired a green flare, the group started the take-off sequence. It was an intricate process and not without its problems.

"On fourteen of my twenty-seven combat missions, mine was the lead aircraft. On three of those fourteen I lead the entire Eighth Air Force. Being lead meant that as we approached the target, I had to keep the aircraft at our assigned altitude, usually around twenty-five thousand feet, at an airspeed of 170 knots from the IP to the target. From the IP to the target, the bombardier flew the aircraft while I worked the throttles to control our airspeed and watched the altimeter to maintain our assigned altitude. As lead aircraft, our bombs were smoke bombs to mark the target for the others. On April 3, 1945, we flew a mission against submarine pens at Kiel. I was lead. Just before the IP I had to shut down one engine because of flak damage. On only three engines, I was barely able to maintain the formation's airspeed. The aileron was shot up, too, with a large hole, making the entire air-craft shake. On top of that the bombardier was jerking the aircraft around. He had a hard time locating the target. The Germans had constructed a dummy target, and only at the last moment did our bombardier identify the real target. He jerked the aircraft onto the new heading, and we released the smokers. We hit the right target that day, judging from the fireballs we saw on our way out. When I was hit, I should have relinquished my position as formation leader to the deputy lead and headed to Sweden. In Sweden, I knew, we would have been interned for a time and subsequently released when a C-87 (the trans-port version of the B-24 bomber) came over from England to pick us up. The C-87 came to pick up ball bearings to be sent back to the States, where they were in critical supply. Air crews were incidental cargo for this nighttime run.

"I never thought of turning over lead to anyone else as long as my aircraft could fly and I could stay with the formation. At the rally point, our mission complete, I throttled back on the three good engines so as not to lose another and dropped out of formation. I headed for a lower altitude and denser air to stabilize the aircraft. Upon reaching the North Sea, I leveled off at ten thousand feet, continuing to head for England. Soon, an American P-51 fighter came swooping down and flew alongside us. Through hand signals, the fighter pilot gave me to understand that he was going to stay around. That was a great relief. He climbed back to altitude and circled above us as we lumbered slowly toward England. We were joined by a second B-17. I thought the aircraft looked strange, not quite like our own. It had no familiar group markings. Flying abeam us, the stranger kept edging closer and closer. Suddenly the P-51 showed up behind him and shot him down. It turned out to be a reconditioned B-17 used by the Germans to shoot down stragglers and to call out altitudes to their flak. With the help of that P-51 pilot, we made it home on three engines.

"On my fifteenth mission, against Nuremberg on February 21, 1945, I was lead again. Before reaching the IP, my engineer put my flak suit on me. He was to fasten the flies on my left shoulder to leave my right arm free to adjust the autopilot while the bombardier was guiding the airplane to the target with the Norden bombsight. The flack was intense, and things didn't go as planned. The engineer had fastened the flies of my flak jacket on the right instead of the left side, causing the jacket to continually slide off, hitting my right arm when I tried to adjust the autopilot. When the jacket hit my arm, it also caused my helmet to drop over my eyes. This happened over and over again—I adjusted my equipment, the flak jacket slid down as I moved my right arm, my helmet slid over my eyes. When I could see, I saw flak. The Germans were firing salvos in boxes at 25,000 feet, then changing altitude and firing at 24,500 feet, and so on. The effect was a massive blanket of flak. We were taking a lot of hits. The little black puffs of smoke were so numerous that they looked like a blanket, the kind of stuff some people said they could walk on. When I could see the fireball within a puff of smoke, I could expect to be showered with shrapnel. It was no place to bail out and hope to reach the ground alive.

133

"Our group commander was flying as command pilot in the right seat. I was working with the bombardier to keep the aircraft aligned on target. When the bombardier called 'Bombs away!' the cockpit was engulfed in smoke so thick I couldn't see the command pilot to my right. He thought the plane was on fire and hit the bailout button. The tail gunner jettisoned the exit door, and the rest of the crew got ready to jump. The scene below us was flak hell. I got on the mike and yelled to the crew, 'Do not bail out! Do not bail out!' I could see all four engines were still turning. The bailout lights continued flashing. I saw the command pilot rise in his seat to head toward the bomb bay to bail out. I punched his lights out, adjusted the autopilot into a gradual turn, and pushed the button to open the bomb bay doors. As the bomb bay doors opened, the smoke was instantaneously sucked out of the cockpit. The cause of the smoke turned out to be a damaged smoke bomb which had gone off just as we called for the doors to open. The bomb probably got hit by shrapnel. I jumped out of my seat and headed for the bomb bay, leaving my chute behind. There wasn't enough room to take my chute along. I gave the faulty bomb a kick and watched it drop away. I balanced on a narrow ledge over the open bomb bay: below me was twenty-five thousand feet of empty space, a blanket of flak, and the raging fires we had started in Nuremberg. I got back to the cockpit and found to my delight that the airplane was still flying without any major problems. The command pilot had come to again, the Germans had missed our altitude, and we had only scattered flak damage. I turned at the rally point and headed for home. Two of my men told me later they were ready to jump when they heard my command not to bail out. A second later would have been too late for them. We returned to Horham a happy crew. As for my command pilot and group commander? I wrote him up for a decoration."

Dave recalled his worst mission. "We had a radio operator on board who spoke German. We usually referred to them as Mickey operators. His job was to listen to the German fighters and disrupt their attacks by inserting himself into the stream of shouted warnings, sightings, and commentary by giving out false information in German as if he was one of them. The flak was really heavy that day, ripping numerous holes into our aircraft. A large piece of shrapnel hit below the Mickey operator, tearing a large hole into the fuselage under his legs, knocking out the central oxygen supply, and severing electrical cables. More shrapnel forced me to shut down an engine. I had my hands full flying the airplane and analyzing what I had lost and what still worked. The Mickey operator was terrified, looking down at the gaping hole below his legs, ice-cold air rushing up at him. His electric suit had failed, and he wasn't getting any oxygen. He thought he was dying—and he was. He started screaming over and over again on the intercom, 'I'm dead. I'm dead. I'm dead,' totally blocking the intercom so I couldn't talk to the rest of the crew. I had to make a choice. I went first to check on Jones, the ball-turret gunner. He didn't have portable oxygen because of a lack of space in the turret; the Mickey operator did. I donned a portable oxygen mask and rushed to the rear of the plane to see if Jones was all right. It was the job of the waist gunner to get oxygen to the ball turret gunner. The waist gunner had pulled Jones out of the turret and given him oxygen. Except for exposure to the cold and a bad headache, Jones suffered no lasting effects. After I got back to my seat, I dropped the plane down from twenty-five thousand to ten thousand feet so we could breathe. I had to leave the formation and returned to England alone. The Mickey operator survived.

"We could always tell when the assigned target was a bad one. Outside the briefing room would be a large number of military police and ambulances. As we sat in the room, the briefing officer would pull the curtain slowly from left to right past Cologne, Hamburg, Berlin, and sometimes as far as Königsberg. The farther he pulled the curtain to the right, the more distraught many of the air crew became. Even late in the war, German antiaircraft defenses were deadly. A man could take only so much stress, and on difficult missions some would break. The military police and the medical orderlies were there to put them into straitjackets and take them away. I saw firsthand what fear could do to a man on one of my missions. He was my copilot. I asked him to take the controls. Looking over, I saw him raise his hands, and then he froze.

He tried to force his hands down onto the controls, but he couldn't do it. I could see him trying. His face bathed in sweat, muscles rippling, he couldn't get his hands to move. He was frozen stiff with fright.

"I remember one particularly bad mission. I was looking at my best friend flying next to me, off my right wing, and he was looking over at me. I still remember the look on his face. Then he took a direct hit. His aircraft exploded. There was nothing left for me to see. On many of our missions, the killing started before we got going. On bad-weather days—and there were many of those in England; we called them crash-and-burn days—after takeoff we were to assemble over a radio beacon near our base. In theory it was a good procedure. In practice it left a lot to be desired, and we never fixed the problem throughout the war. As we took off, the lead aircraft made a spiraling left turn until breaking out of the overcast and then waited for his squadron mates to join up. Unfortunately, there were numerous bases nearby. As we spiraled up to altitude, our turns got wider and wider, like an inverted cone, and in time our cone would overlap with the cone of another base. The aircraft crashing into each other never knew what happened.

"On takeoff I frequently could see the bodies of my friends strewn across meadows, hanging over fences. Others burned to death in the inferno of a crashing aircraft. Do you know what a human body looks like after it has burned in an air crash? A little black ball which you can hold in your hands. That's all that's left of a man." Dave paused, the recollections of tragedies flitting past his inner eye as if they happened yesterday. He frowned. His eyes shone brightly. The *Mighty Eighth War Diary* notes that between June 1942 and May 1945, more than 6,500 B-17 and B-24 heavy bombers were lost over Europe. One in six, more than 1,000 aircraft, were lost to accidents rather than to enemy action. The Eighth Air Force heavy bomber force in England was maintained at 2,000 aircraft (Freeman 3–8).

Dave continued: "Once our group assembled, or whatever was left of it, we'd join up with other groups. We flew tight formations, the tighter the better, until our wingtips nearly touched. It provided the best defense against German fighters. Our targets varied from industrial to military. On a mission to Fulda I wrote in my log book, 'The target is women and children.' I simply saw things differently then."

Dave Taylor separated from the Army Air Force in late 1945. The Berlin Airlift brought him back into the Air Force to stay, and in 1953 he found himself in Special Operations, flying C-46, C-47, and B-26 aircraft out of Kimpo Air Base, near Seoul, Korea. It was his kind of flying, mostly at night and dangerous. At that point in his air force career, danger was a normal part of Dave's life, and he didn't let it influence him too much. He was not a foolhardy pilot, but he had acquired a taste for pushing the limits of the envelope. He took his chances and counted on the odds being in his favor. On May 24, 1953, two months before the Korean armistice, Dave flew one of his most dangerous missions of a flying career full of danger. As reported by the Associated Press, a South Korean agent operating behind North Korean lines liberated the five survivors of a downed B-29 bomber. The agent probably had previously been inserted by Dave or by another member of his flight, euphemistically called B-Flight, which was short for Base-Flight. In the case of Kimpo Air Base, B-Flight included special missions, meaning those other than the routine flying support usually provided by such an organization.

The South Korean agent was most likely a double agent. Using his radio, the agent informed his American contacts of the opportunity to rescue the downed air crew, commanded by its pilot, a first lieutenant. Dave Taylor received the go-ahead to extricate the crew with his specially modified C-47 transport. The rescue aircraft was a forerunner of more sophisticated but similar rescue systems employed years later in Vietnam. The system used a combination of harness and cabling extended between upright poles to allow an aircraft with a hooking device to come over low and pull a downed airman off the ground to safety. Dave made several flights to locate the downed B-29 crew. Once he found them and thoroughly reconnoitered the area from the air, he dropped the ground portion of the rescue equipment, which included two tall poles to allow the suspension of rescue lines. Dave couldn't shake his suspicion that something wasn't right, that it was a trap. To

Major Taylor's modified C-47, which was used to rescue downed airmen behind enemy lines, at Kimpo, 1953. D. Taylor.

confirm authenticity and to assure himself that this was not a setup, Dave dropped a camera and a homing pigeon. He asked the agent to take pictures of the crew and to return the film via the pigeon. The pigeon returned, but the film showed pictures only of the agent and not of the air crew. On the day before the rescue was to take place, Dave returned to the area and spoke over the radio to the lieutenant, asking him to authenticate himself by revealing private information that only he knew. The lieutenant did so and assured Major Taylor that everything was all right.

In the early morning hours of May 24, 1953, Dave took off in his slow C-47 to effect the rescue. As he approached the pickup site, he made contact on the radio and proceeded to approach the clearing at treetop level. Dave remained suspicious, and his senses were alert. Again, something didn't seem right. He had the lieutenant go through several authentications before committing himself and his crew. He saw the two poles, and his tail hook was extended. As he flew between the poles, the trap was sprung. The rescue poles turned out to house fifty-caliber machine guns. "The bullets were coming straight up between the two engines and the cockpit. They ripped into our belly. I punched the throttles forward, climbed, and by constantly changing heading penetrated a wall of small-arms fire as we escaped the trap. I believe to this day that I was deliberately betrayed for reasons I cannot fathom. I consider him a traitor," Dave said of the B-29 pilot. "He could have warned me off, and he didn't. I wanted to napalm the whole area, that's how mad I was." Instead, Dave returned to the area several days later in a B-26 bomber rigged with a voice recording system. He circled over the mountain hideout and spoke briefly with each of the five B-29 crew members to verify that they were alive. To his surprise, the men spoke as if nothing unusual had transpired. "They gave me no hint whatso-ever of distress. That was the last contact I had with them. After the armistice, the B-29 crew was not returned by the North Koreans, and they were eventually declared dead by the air force. I wonder to this day why an American officer allowed me to be ambushed.

"When I made that rescue attempt, I had a formation of F-84s flying overhead to give me support the instant I got into trouble. They did nothing as they watched the sky erupt around me with tracers flying in all directions. I practically stood my airplane on its wing and made it fly sideways to get out of there. I got my crew out alive, but it was close. I was mad as hell. After landing I got that 84-lead together with our colonel. I wanted the same bunch of guys to go back and bomb and strafe that valley the next day. I wanted to know they had the balls to do it. The colonel agreed, provided I could assure him that the prison-ers were no longer there. I was never able to provide the colonel that assurance. Why didn't the 84s support me? Because they thought there was too much flak down there. That's what their leader said.

"A similar incident happened to me earlier in the year. I was flying a night flare mission for some 84s. There I sat, at low level, punching flares out of my unarmed, slow-moving C-47, an easy target for the North Korean flak. Down below, I could see a long line of trucks. I couldn't get the 84s to come down and hit them. The flak was too heavy, they told me later. Yeah, didn't I know that? I was down there. In anticipation of similar responses, my crew and I removed the chutes from a number of flares and added dynamite and scrap metal. On the next flare mission when the 84s were reluctant to come down low be-cause of the flak, I had my *presentos* ready. We punched them out of the flare tubes, and without chutes the flares dropped quickly. Flares burn very hot, and with the added dynamite they blew the assembled trucks right off the highway. We did that several times until someone blew the whistle on us. In a way I understood the F-84s attitude. They didn't have wet suits, and the waters around Korea were cold. A man would die in only minutes if he had to punch out over water. Of course, that's what you did, because no one wanted to bail out over land if he could help it and become a prisoner of the Chinese. Once the F-84 guys were provided the necessary wet suits—and I helped get the suits for them from navy stocks—they were much more willing to take risks. Their success against ground targets improved greatly."

One of Dave Taylor's more hush-hush missions was to insert Korean agents into the North Korean hinterlands. On one of those missions he took his C-47 way up north. "It was night, and in the distance I could see the lights of Vladivostok twinkling. After I made my drop I had to keep on doing something else in the area, or anyone who saw me would know where to look and quickly pick up our agents. I kept flying up and down snowy ridges until, when topping one ridge, I saw a long line of trucks moving below me. The trucks were difficult to spot in the dark because they had snow on top of their tarps and were driving without lights. What to do? Such a fat target and no guns. No *presentos* either. Then I had an idea. I slid behind the ridge, turned, and as I crested the ridge again, I pushed my aircraft's nose down, facing the trucks, and turned my bright landing lights on. Trucks slid in every direction down the mountainside, exploding in bright flashes as they hit something in the valley below. My crew had a good laugh. We turned and disappeared behind the ridge. I decided to give it one more try. But the next time around, they were waiting for us. I had to do a max-power climb to get out of range of their guns.

"One frequent problem I experienced with our South Korean agents was that they often refused to jump. Usually there were two of them, and if one wouldn't go, the other wouldn't either. When I flew a C-47, it wasn't that much of a problem. When the bell rang and the green light came on and the agent froze in the door, my jump master would cut him loose and push him out. Most of the time we used a modified B-26. We fashioned two seats in the bomb bay for the agents, and when it was time to go I would open the bomb bay doors, the jump master signaled to them, and all they had to do was roll forward—that is, if they wanted to jump. If they didn't want to jump, the jump master couldn't do a thing because he couldn't get to them. His threats and scowls couldn't get those guys to move once one of them froze. The word got around quickly among the Korean agents, and soon more and more of them played this 'I don't want to jump' game with us. I fixed that problem quickly. I had one of my maintenance people insert a pin in the bottom of each seat. The pins had cables attached to them which led to the jump master. Then, when the agents didn't want to jump, he pulled the pins. The seats dropped, and so did the agents. The word soon got out among the agents, and the problem went away.

"Of course we had our fair share of double agents. On a mission deep over North Korea, I was flying a C-47, and one of the agents had two bandoliers of hand grenades slung across his chest. As he was preparing to jump, the two jump masters standing to his left and right, he yanked a grenade off one of the bandoliers, pulled the pin, and threw the grenade into the aircraft. The jump master, who had made three jumps in World War II behind enemy lines, cut the agent's throat with his knife as he was falling away from the aircraft. The assistant jump master grabbed the live grenade and threw it on top of the falling agent, who exploded in a violent flash. I saw the explosion, looking out the window, but had no idea what had transpired.

"In April 1953, just weeks before the armistice was signed on July 27, I attempted one final rescue mission on the spur of the moment—something you should never do. I was walking into base operations when a navy captain I knew spotted me and hollered, 'I have a pilot down. Will you go and get him?' Without hesitation I responded, 'I'm gone.' Off we went, just north of Panmunjom. When I got into the area, I could see the wreckage of the fighter still burning fiercely, emitting black swaths of smoke. No sign of the pilot. I dropped the nose of the C-47 until I got down to treetop level, clipping the tops of the trees with my propellers. The ground fire was intense. I tried several times, but it was no good. I couldn't locate the pilot and had to abandon the mission. When I landed at Kimpo, the navy captain met me on the flight line. He walked around my aircraft and exclaimed, 'I've never seen an aircraft with so many holes.'"

Dave Taylor in front of his aircraft, 1953.
D. Taylor.

It was late in the afternoon, but there was one more story Dave Taylor had to get off his chest. He smiled broadly as he told it. "The Chinese had noise-actuated searchlights," he confided, breaking into loud laughter. "They were almost impossible to get away from once they had a track on you. I figured there had to be a solution to that problem. What I did was to fly really tight turns, flying one engine at max power while powering down the other, slamming in opposite rudder, and while the maximum sound traveled in one direction, I traveled in another. I repeated that trick several times until I had the searchlights going all over the place, unable to track me. Then I let them have several of my *presentos,* and that was the end of the Chinese sound-tracking searchlights." Dave laughed loudly.

Dave Taylor went on to serve in the early days of the Vietnam War, at the time of the Gulf of Tonkin incident in 1964. Serving in the famed Triple Nickel, 555th Fighter Squadron, on Okinawa, he moved its F-102 fighters as well as a squadron of C-130s into position in South Vietnam. He bedded them down without a mobility plan or any kind of preplanned support, quite a feat for one lone air force colonel. "I told my sergeants, if I get there and run out of anything, I'll come back and hunt you down and kill you. I didn't run out of anything." Before Colonel Taylor left Vietnam, he checked out in the F-4C, which replaced the F-102. He had come a long way from flying B-17 bombers

142

at speeds of 170 knots to flying supersonic jet aircraft. Upon his retirement in 1972, after having carried the American flag proudly and valiantly in Europe, Korea, and again in Vietnam, Colonel David M. Taylor retired to his farm on the other side of Charlottesville, Virginia. At the age of eighty, Dave stands tall and straight, and his penetrating blue eyes haven't lost their twinkle. In a rare tribute to this courageous airman, in 1972, the chief of staff of the U.S. Air Force, General John D. Ryan, presented Colonel Taylor with a personal letter of appreciation for his many services to his country and to the U.S. Air Force. The boy from Mississippi never knew what awaited him when he helped gas up those Ford trimotors in 1935.

Part 3

Strategic Reconnaissance

Had the American public known about the ongoing "secret air war" between the two super-powers they would have been even more in despair than many already were about the state of the world.

Ben R. Rich, *Skunk Works*

The second MiG-17 made his firing pass, and I don't care who knows, it was scary watching tracers go over and under our aircraft. This guy had almost come up our tailpipes. Carl Holt had turned around to operate our tail guns after the first MiG shot at us. It was typical for the two remotely controlled 20mm cannons not to fire. I told Holt he'd better kick them or something, because if our guns don't fire the next SOB would come directly up our tailpipes.

Hal Austin, RB-47E pilot

Strategic aerial reconnaissance during the Cold War years, including the overflight of Soviet territory, was a necessary act of desperation and reflected an inability to obtain information by other means. The information gained from such operations was vital to American policy makers and to the defense community at large. Without this information, often obtained at great risk to the air crews, it was impossible to develop the proper force size and mix of weapons to contain the Soviet military juggernaut or, if need be, to confront it and prevail. Reconnaissance flights were largely conducted by long-range aircraft of the Strategic Air Command, a command known for its secrecy and high level of security. Every planner and crew member involved in reconnaissance operations was sworn to secrecy. The battle for information along the periphery and at times over the Soviet Union and the Chinese communist mainland was mostly unknown to the American public. Losses were accepted as a part of doing business.

By 1948 America's senior military leaders no longer had any doubt that the Soviet Union represented a major threat to the United States. The Berlin blockade had clearly demonstrated Soviet intentions in that part of the world. To make matters worse, in September 1949 a U.S. reconnaissance plane flying off the Kamchatka Peninsula picked up signs of radioactivity. The Soviets had exploded an atomic device. The United States and its allies clearly would soon find themselves threatened by atomic-bomb-carrying Soviet aircraft. In Asia, developments were even more ominous. Chinese communist forces were on the verge of completing their conquest of mainland China, and a belligerent North Korea was petitioning Stalin to let it conquer the south. Although the United States viewed these developments with concern and had helped to establish the North Atlantic Treaty Organization in an effort to contain Soviet pressures in Europe, military strength had not grown commensurate with the threat. The air force was organizing the Strategic Air Command under the driving leadership of General Curtis E. LeMay, but even he had to make do with aging B-29 bombers. The air force of the future was evolving.

At a time of military weakness and political uncertainty, the United States particularly needed accurate, verifiable information about the Soviet Union. While a foreigner could easily travel in the United States and purchase any number of publications regarding U.S. military forces and their location, strength, readiness, organization, and equipment, no equivalent access was available in the Soviet Union. The Soviet Union remained a closed society. The only practical option, other than human intelligence with its many shortcomings, was aerial reconnaissance. From the early 1950s to the fall of the Soviet Union in 1991, the United States and the United Kingdom implemented a cooperative effort to reconnoiter the periphery of the Soviet Union with aircraft equipped with various types of sensors. On special occasions, aircraft, with authority from the U.S. president or the British prime minister, overflew the Soviet Union and its satellite nations to gather critical information. Was there a bomber gap between the United States and the Soviet Union? The answer could be found only by the men who risked their lives and flew over the Soviet Union to obtain that information.

As the years passed and Soviet fighter and surface-to-air-missile technology advanced, overflights of Soviet territory required aircraft to fly ever higher. In 1960 a U-2 photo-reconnaissance aircraft operated by the Central Intelligence Agency was shot down near the Russian city of Sverdlovsk. With that shootdown it became obvious that the time for aircraft overflying the Soviet Union had nearly passed. (One exception was the U.S. Air Force's Mach 3 SR-71, which flew at altitudes higher than eighty thousand feet.) With the exception of peripheral reconnaissance flights and a limited number of ground stations, after 1960 the United States relied mostly on satellites to keep watch over the Soviet Union.

Table 1 is a compilation of known overflights of the western and northern Soviet Union by U.S. and British aircraft. Overflights of the eastern USSR and communist China from bases in Japan and Taiwan, although frequent, are not included. Major events affecting U.S.-Soviet relations are highlighted.

Table 2 is a chronology of reconnaissance and observation aircraft, as well as civilian aircraft misidentified by the Soviets as reconnaissance aircraft, known to have been lost to interceptors, AAA, or SAMs. Some

Table 1

Date	Number and Type of Aircraft	Nationality	Launch Site	Altitude Flown	Details
1949—Soviets detonate an atomic device.					
Apr 17, 1952	3 RB-45C	RAF	Sculthorpe	35,000+	Night radar photography of Soviet air bases in Estonia, Latvia, Lithuania, Belorussia and Ukraine.
Sep 17, 1952	1 RB-50	USAF	Thule	10,000–	Daylight overflight of Franz Josef Land, USSR, looking for airbases/radar sites. None found.
Oct 15, 1952	2 B-47B	USAF	Eielson	40,000+	One aircraft overflew Wrangel Island, the other penetrated into western Siberia and flew east across Siberia, exiting over the Bering Strait. Both aircraft recovered at Eielson. No Tu-4 Bull bombers found.
1953—Stalin dies; Eisenhower elected president.					
Aug 1953	1 Canberra	RAF	Giebelstadt	46,000+	The Canberra photographed Kiev, Kharkov, Stalingrad, and Kapustin Yar. Aircraft was damaged by AAA. Landed in Iran.
Apr 28, 1954	3 RB-45C	RAF	Sculthorpe	35,000+	Night mission. Essentially same routes as in 1952. Radar photography.
May 1, 1954—Soviets fly what appeared to be 100 Bison bombers at the May Day parade in Moscow. The "bomber gap" arises.					
May 8, 1954	1 RB-47E	USAF	Fairford	40,000+	Photograph Soviet air bases on Kola Peninsula and near Arkhangel'sk. Looking for Bison bombers. Found no bombers. Aircraft damaged by MiG-17 cannon fire.

Date	Aircraft	Operator	Base	Altitude	Description
Mar 27, 1955	3 RB-45C	USAF	Sculthorpe	35,000+	Night mission. Nearly same routes as flown by the RAF in 1952 and 1954. Radar photography.
Mar 21–May 10, 1956	20 RB-47E/H	USAF	Thule	40,000+	Photographed the polar region from Novaya Zemlya to the Bering Strait, including northern Siberia. Photomapping and electronic reconnaissance. RB-47E photo and RB-47H electronic reconnaissance aircraft.
Jul 4, 1956	1 U-2	US	Wiesbaden	70,000+	Belorussia, Leningrad.
Jul 5, 1956	1 U-2	US	Wiesbaden	70,000+	
Jul 8, 1956	1 U-2	US	Wiesbaden	70,000+	Found only 30 Bison bombers. No bomber gap existed. U-2 operation moved to Incirlik, Turkey; and Peshawar, Pakistan. Twenty-one U-2 overflights follow.

Oct 1957—Soviets launch Sputnik. The "missile gap" arises. Like the bomber gap, however, the missile gap was illusionary.

Date	Aircraft	Operator	Base	Altitude	Description
May 1, 1960	1 U-2	US	Peshawar	70,000+	Francis Gary Powers, pilot, shot down by SA-2 missile salvo near Sverdlovsk. Last U-2 overflight.

Note: Prior to the advent of the U-2 in 1956, RB-57A and RF-100 aircraft, flying from German airbases, made several overflights of Iron Curtain countries.

Table 2

Date	Aircraft	Operator	Location	Dead
Apr 8, 1950	PB4Y2	USN	Baltic Sea/Latvia	10
Dec 4, 1950	RB-45C	USAF	Yalu River	4
Nov 6, 1951	P2V-3W	USN	Sea of Japan	10
Nov 18, 1951	C-47	USAF	Hungary	0
Jun 13, 1952	RB-29	USAF	Sea of Japan	12
Oct 7, 1952	RB-29	USAF	near Kurile Islands	8
Nov 29, 1952	C-47	China Air	China	2
Jan 12, 1953	RB-29	USAF	Manchuria	0
Jan 18, 1953	P2V	USN	Formosa Strait	6
Mar 10, 1953	F-84G	USAF	Czechoslovakia	0
Mar 12, 1953	Lincoln	RAF	East Germany	7
Jun 5, 1953	DC-3	Sweden	Baltic Sea	
Jun 16, 1953	Catalina	Sweden	Baltic Sea	
Jul 29, 1953	RB-50	USAF	Sea of Japan	16
Aug 17, 1953	T-6	USAF	Korean DMZ	1
Jul 1954	DC-4	Cathay P.	Hainan	10
Sep 4, 1954	P2V	USN	Sea of Okhotsk	1
Nov 7, 1954	RB-29	USAF	Sea of Japan	1
Jan 19, 1955	T-6	USAF	Korean DMZ	1
Apr 17, 1955	RB-47E	USAF	off Kamchatka	3
Jun 22, 1955	P2V-5	USN	Bering Strait	0
Jul 27, 1955	Constellation	El Al	Bulgaria	40
Aug 17, 1955	T-6	USAF	Korean DMZ	1
Aug 22, 1956	P4M	USN	off China coast	16
Sep 10, 1956	RB-50	USAF	Sea of Japan	16
Dec 23, 1957	T-33	USAF	Albania	0
Dec 24, 1957	RB-57D	USAF	Black Sea	1
Feb 18, 1958	RB-57A	Taiwan	China	1
Mar 6, 1958	F-86	USAF	North Korea	0
Jun 27, 1958	C-118A	USAF	Armenia	0
Sep 2, 1958	RC-130A	USAF	Armenia	17
1958	RB-50	USAF	Armenia	
Oct 7, 1959	RB-57D	Taiwan	China	1
May 1, 1960	U-2	US	Sverdlovsk	0
May 25, 1960	C-47	USAF	East Germany	0
Jul 1, 1960	RB-47H	USAF	Barents Sea	4
Sep 9, 1962	U-2C	Taiwan	China	1
Oct 27, 1962	U-2	USAF	Cuba	1
May 17, 1963	helicopter	USA	Korean DMZ	0
Aug 6, 1963		USA	North Korea	6
Nov 1, 1963	U-2C	Taiwan	China	1
Jan 28, 1964	T-39	USAF	East Germany	3
Mar 10, 1964	RB-66	USAF	East Germany	3

July 7, 1964	U-2C	Taiwan	China	1
Jan 10, 1965	U-2C	Taiwan	China	1
Dec 14, 1965	RB-57F	USAF	Black Sea	2
Jan 1, 1966	KA-3B	USN	China	
Sep 9, 1967	U-2C	Taiwan	China	1
Mar 1969	U-2C	Taiwan	China	1
Apr 15, 1969	EC-121	USN	Sea of Japan	30
Aug 17, 1969	OH-23	USA	Korean DMZ	0
Oct 21, 1970	U-8	USA	Armenia	0
Jul 14, 1977	CH-47	USA	North Korea	3
Apr 20, 1978	707	KAL	USSR/near Murmansk	2
Sep 1, 1983	747	KAL	Sea of Japan	269

of the downed aircraft were airliners straying over Soviet territory. The 1978 and 1983 attacks on South Korean airliners revealed the continuing disarray of the Soviet air defense system. Although the loss of life was tragic, such incidents provided invaluable information to American military planners.

RB-47E photo-reconnaissance aircraft refueling from a KC-97 tanker above Lockbourne AFB, Ohio, 1954. Colonel Austin flew the same type of aircraft over the Soviet Union in 1954. H. Austin.

Chapter 8

Taming the RB-45C Tornado

We were flying supersonic [on October 14, 1947]! And it was as smooth as a baby's bottom: Grandma could be sitting up there sipping lemonade. I kept the speed off the scale for about twenty seconds, then raised the nose to slow down.

General Chuck Yeager

We also pushed it through Mach 1 more than once. Our group lost eight airplanes in that first year [1950]. One of the first we lost, we think the guy went through the Mach trying to get down. . . . I went through the Mach with it—rough as hell going through, rougher coming back out.

Hal Austin, RB-45C Tornado pilot

The B-45 was a 1943-vintage design, America's first all-jet bomber, with a rigid, straight wing and a B-17–style gunner's station in the tail. The XB-45 flew for the first time on March 17, 1947, piloted by North American test pilot George Krebs, who died flying the XB-45 on September 20, 1948. With his untimely death, no further significant flight testing was conducted, and the B-45 went into production. Many of its flaws were later discovered by some unlucky air crews. Ninety-six bomber versions of the North American B-45A were built. The aircraft were assigned to the Tactical Air Command with their final duty station the 47th Bombardment Wing at RAF Station Sculthorpe in County Norfolk, England. The last forty-three aircraft built, incorporating advances in design and lessons learned from the A models, were delivered in 1950 and 1951. Ten of the forty-three C models were built as bombers; the other thirty-three were reconnaissance versions. The production line for the B-45 was then discontinued. All of the forty-three C models were assigned to SAC.

In contrast to the A-model bombers, the C model had a solid rather than a glassed-in nose, carried 1,200 gallon wingtip fuel tanks, and, best of all, was capable of in-flight refueling. Air refueling enabled the aircraft to reach nearly anyplace on the globe without having to land as long as a tanker was available to support it. Furthermore, the RB-45Cs were equipped with a remarkable suite of high- and low-altitude cameras designed by the renowned Harvard astronomer James G. Baker. On August 26, 1950, the first of the thirty-three RB-45C production models was delivered to the 91st Strategic Reconnaissance Wing at Barksdale AFB near Shreveport, Louisiana. By the end of 1950, SAC reported that twenty-seven RB-45s equipped the 91st Wing. Its unit equipment (UE) authorization had been set at thirty-six aircraft. The wing began its incremental move from Barksdale to Lockbourne AFB near Columbus, Ohio, in June 1951. By that time, the wing had expanded to thirty-eight B/RB-45Cs, and SAC headquarters had increased the wing's UE aircraft authorization to forty-five. That would be the high-water mark for the RB-45C wing in terms of the number of aircraft it was authorized to have.

In 1952 the C-model bombers were turned over to TAC. SAC finished the year with twenty-two RB-45Cs on its roster. In only sixteen months of operation, eleven of the thirty-three RB-45Cs had perished. One had been shot down by Russian MiGs in a secrecy-shrouded mission near the Yalu River. In January 1953 SAC began the transfer of the RB-45C to TAC, as SAC's inventory of newer RB-47 aircraft increased. The last four RB-45s, assigned to the 91st Strategic Reconnaissance

Squadron at Yokota Air Base in Japan, were transferred to the Far East Air Force on December 1, 1953.

Colonel Harold R. Austin

In late 1949, after flying the Berlin Airlift, Colonel Harold R. "Hal" Austin, then a captain, was assigned to the 324th SRS of the 91st SRW at Barksdale. The wing had two other squadrons, the 322d and the 323d. In the summer of 1950 Hal was selected to transition into the RB-45C. He picked up a brand-new aircraft from the factory in Long Beach and, along with other air crews, began the task of learning to fly a jet airplane. Hal Austin had no checklist, no technical data, and no company technical representative with pilot qualifications who could answer his many questions.

Hal Austin, like his friends Sam Myers and Harold Hendler, now lives in Riverside, California, and he recalled his assignment to the then state-of-the-art RB-45C jet. "Every one of us, of course, had to try to see how high we could get in the new airplane. We got to nearly 50,000 feet—49,500 feet is the highest I took it. It took forever. We were light, having burned off most of our fuel at the end of our mission, when we got to that altitude over our home base of Barksdale. In the early days, no one else was up there except for a few F-86 fighters. We flew cruise-climb for our departures. North American told us to do that. We would normally end up over Barksdale at 43,000 feet. The day I took it up to 49,500 feet, when I pulled the power back, the airplane hardly slowed down. It had no speed brakes, nothing to slow it down. I started pushing the airplane down, which put me in a high-speed buffet, and of course when I pulled back, I was in a stall, or right between buffet and stall. It took me thirty minutes to get back to 40,000 feet. To land, we flew a teardrop approach from over Barksdale. In a steady descent toward the Gulf of Mexico, I would eat up a third of the altitude. Then the second third was in the turn, and the final third would be coming into Barksdale. When I made my turn at the widest point, I was two

154

hundred miles south of Barksdale over the Gulf of Mexico. There was no way to slow that aircraft down. We finally talked the FAA into letting us use a letdown coming straight in. Initially the FAA said, 'What do you mean, you want to let down en route? We've never heard of such a thing.' They finally let us do it. We fussed about the lack of braking from day one with the RB-45. You couldn't get it out of the sky.

"We also pushed it through Mach 1 more than once. Our group lost eight airplanes in that first year. One of the first we lost, we think the guy went through the Mach trying to get down, trying to see what the airplane would do. I went through the Mach with it—rough as hell going through, rougher coming back out. The one that crashed had the tail come off. He was southeast of Barksdale at forty-three thousand feet when it happened. That's the altitude where I pushed mine through, the only time I ever pushed it through. We lost other aircraft going through the Mach before anyone survived to tell us what happened. An aeronautical engineer finally explained to us that the rigid wing passed the vibrations encountered going through the Mach to the tail section. Unfortunately, the airplane wasn't designed to handle such stress. It was basically a World War II airplane powered by jet engines."

All this experimentation by the RB-45C pilots occurred in 1950 and 1951. The first flight exceeding the speed of sound had been made only three years earlier, on October 14, 1947, by Captain Chuck Yeager in the Bell X-1 experimental aircraft. In his autobiography, Yeager wrote of his historic flight, "We were flying supersonic [at forty-two thousand feet]! And it was as smooth as a baby's bottom. . . . After all the anxiety, breaking the sound barrier turned out to be a perfectly paved speedway" (Yeager 130). It wasn't that way for the RB-45, an airplane that lacked the smooth lines of the X-1. After many catastrophic incidents, the RB-45C was limited to speeds of less than Mach .85 (85 percent of the speed of sound).

"Another problem that took a couple of crashes to resolve," Hal Austin continued, "was the bomb bay fuel tanks. We had two one thousand–gallon bomb bay tanks—that was before we went from gallons to pounds—hung on old B-17 bomb shackles. The shackles were not designed for such a continuous load and the stress of day-in, day-out flying pulling a lot of Gs. One instructor pilot, flying in the copilot's seat in the third or fourth plane that crashed, survived. He told us that all of a sudden the aircraft started twisting. He couldn't remember how he got out of the airplane, couldn't recall ejecting. When he became conscious of his situation, he found himself still sitting in his ejection seat, heading for the ground. When the wreckage was examined, the inspectors found the back-bay shackle had given way and hit the bomb bay doors. The doors flipped out and hit part of the empennage, the tail assembly of the airplane. Once that happened, the tail section twisted off, and the aircraft was out of control. North American redesigned the shackles, and that solved the problem. Every major problem we discovered cost one or two air crews their lives. We were, in fact, test pilots.

"The RB-45C was powered by the early model of the J-47 engine, which in later years proved to be quite reliable on the B-47. But that engine wasn't reliable when we were flying it in early 1951. The engine had to be pulled every twenty-five hours of flying time for a complete overhaul. The number one and number three engines had the generators—today they're called alternators. The generators had a solid shaft. When the bearings wore, the shaft began to wobble, finally fail, and tear up the engine, sometimes resulting in an engine fire. When the second engine became disabled, the crew had to bail out. We lost two aircraft from this particular problem.

"Number two and number four engines powered the hydraulics. Number two operated the left aileron, and number four the right. There was no aileron crossover. If I lost number two, and it wasn't windmilling, then I lost my hydraulics on the left side and my aileron control. I was in deep trouble when that happened. If I had an engine problem and I needed to shut it down, I had to do it slowly. If I shut the engine down too quickly, the shroud ring in the hot section in back of the engine could warp, and if that happened, the engine seized. If it was the number two or number four engine, I lost my ailerons. At high speed and with the aileron not working, I had a hell of a control problem. The only alternative, and it was a difficult one, was to steer the aircraft with the rudder. We finally got the aileron crossover problem resolved. The hydraulics were redesigned so number two or number four engine could power both left and right ailerons. It was the only safety modification made to the airplane. It was a great aircraft to fly, except for the aileron crossover problem.

"I recall a landing in early 1951 at Goose Bay. I was on a flight to Sculthorpe, near Kings Lynn on the east coast of England. Our usual route was from Barksdale to Goose Bay, Labrador, then on to Iceland, and finally Sculthorpe. With full tip tanks and bomb bay tanks, we could fly without refueling for five and a half hours, about 2,500 miles. It was routine for us to cross the Atlantic without the use of a tanker. On this trip I landed first at Wright-Patterson AFB in Ohio, where I topped off my tanks. Coming into Goose Bay, I still had too much fuel and had to spend time burning it off. I flew around a bit since I had no way of dumping fuel. When I was light enough, I eased back on the power to make my letdown into Goose. I was right over the spot where a friend of mine had crashed only two weeks earlier and my number three engine seized. It flipped us over. I know we were past ninety degrees. It scared the hell out of me. I rammed the power back up and managed to roll it level. My navigator sitting in the nose of the aircraft and not knowing what was happening, called over the intercom, 'You son of a bitch, what are you doing up there?' I got her down safely, but it was difficult. For a moment, when the aircraft went out of control, I thought we were going to join my friend. They never did find out what happened to his aircraft.

"We also had some comfort problems with the airplane. The canopy was welded shut. I guess they didn't know at that time how to hinge the canopy. In an emergency, the pilots punched through the canopy with their ejection seats. The navigator didn't have an ejection seat, though. He had to bail out of the access door on the left side of the aircraft, forward of the cockpit. In the summer it got pretty hot at Barksdale, and the crew-compartment temperature was unbearable. Every time the maintenance men put a meat thermometer in there to measure the temperature, the thermometer would blow up. Our maintenance people installed brackets alongside the canopy so we could carry a shade. Even with a shade, it was still hot as hell when we first got in. So it was our procedure to taxi out, push all four engines to 80 percent to cool down the cockpit, and finally the crew chief would take the shade off the cockpit."

Although the RB-45s tail guns did not contribute to any flight safety problems, they were not installed in the SAC aircraft, for unknown reasons. There was one exception, however. Aircraft 8-042, which operated out of Yokota as part of the RB-45C SAC detachment in 1952 and 1953, for some strange reason had a set of tail guns mounted in a fixed position. One gun pointed straight back, while the other was mounted in a thirty-degree downward slant. The guns could be remotely fired by the pilot. In April 1952 the RAF used the same aircraft in an overflight of the western Soviet Union; Major Lou Carrington subsequently flew the plane when he won the Mackay Trophy on a flight from Alaska to Japan; and Captain Sam Myers and Lieutenant Francis Martin flew this craft over the eastern Soviet Union and communist China. When the RB-45 reconnaissance aircraft were turned over to TAC in January 1953, tail guns were installed in all aircraft.

"The cockpit of the RB-45 was laid out like that of a fighter," Hal Austin observed. "The visibility was excellent. The air-refueling receptacle was behind the canopy, so the airplane ended up right under the KB-29 tanker and didn't feel the prop wash as much as one did in the newer B-47, with its receptacle in front of the canopy. By 1952 we had resolved our engine problems. We didn't fix them, mind you, except for the crossover problem. We learned how to manage the engines." Austin added wistfully, "A great pilot's airplane."

Air force pilots fly whatever airplanes they are given. In a period of one year, the 91st SRW lost eight of thirty-three aircraft, 24 percent of the force. Each aircraft carried a crew of three. In most cases all aboard the doomed aircraft perished. This was the sort of attrition flying units experienced in combat in Korea and later in Vietnam. But this was peacetime flying in the early 1950s. For Austin to say it was "a great

RB-45C 8-042, piloted by Captain Sam Myers, taking off from Yokota Air Base, Japan, December 1952. H. Myers.

pilot's airplane" when every flight was more or less a test flight was an understatement worthy of an Englishman, not a matter-of-fact American flyer. Austin coped with day-to-day stress by focusing on those aspects of the airplane that gave him pleasure. And the RB-45C was a pleasure to fly when compared to most piston-engine aircraft. The year 1950, when the RB-45C was put in service, was early in the jet age, and the B-45 was one of the jet age's earliest products. If there had been time, the airplane would have been flight-tested sufficiently to discover more of its problems, problems that Hal Austin and his fellow flyers had to discover the hard way. But there was no time for testing. When the RB-45C entered the air force inventory, the Korean War had started. SAC needed a fast, high-altitude-reconnaissance aircraft to complement the slow RB-29s, a fair number of which had already been shot down by Soviet interceptors. The RB-45C was that airplane.

Chapter 9

Recon to the Yalu and Beyond

Citation to Accompany the Award of the Distinguished Flying Cross
Captain Howard S. Myers, Jr, FR34694A, distinguished himself by exceptional meritorious service in the performance of duty as Commander, Detachment 1, 91st Strategic Reconnaissance Wing, and RB-45C Aircraft Commander during the Korean Conflict from November 1952 to March 1953. While piloting a RB-45C jet reconnaissance aircraft, staging from Yokota and Misawa Air Bases in Japan, and forward air bases in Korea, the exceptional ability, diligence, and devotion to duty of Capt. Myers was instrumental in successful collection of highly classified photographic and radar intelligence information over enemy territory, during reconnaissance penetration missions into North Korea, Central and Northern communist Asian countries, and Soviet territory. Accuracy of the intelligence information collected on these missions provided vital targeting data for follow on bomber and fighter strike missions over the North Korean Peninsula. In addition, deep penetration missions into other highly fortified Soviet block countries provided long range strategic planners in the Pentagon and Strategic Air Command Headquarters with vital intelligence and combat capability information. These singular distinctive accomplishments of Captain Myers reflect great credit upon himself and the United States Air Force.

160

Colonel Howard S. "Sam" Myers Jr.

Distinguished Flying Cross, Air Medal (4)

The Korean War was in its third year in November 1952 when Sam Myers's crew and another air crew relieved two RB-45C crews at Yokota Air Base in Japan. The RB-45 arrived at Yokota in September 1950 and flew its first combat mission in November. Sam's navigator on the deployment was Lieutenant Frank Martin, who, like Sam, was assigned to the 322d Reconnaissance Squadron of the 91st Strategic Reconnaissance Wing at their home base of Lockbourne. Sam had been appointed commander of the two-plane Yokota RB-45C detachment, which was part of the Yokota-based 91st Strategic Reconnaissance Squadron. His primary mission was to fly reconnaissance for the FEAF Bomber Command, colocated with the RB-45Cs at Yokota. FEAF's B-29 bombers were based at Yokota and on the island of Okinawa.

At one time in late 1950, the Yokota RB-45C detachment possessed three aircraft, but one was shot down on a mission near the Yalu River. At noon on December 4, 1950, an RB-45C piloted by Captain Charles E. McDonough, the detachment commander, rose into the sky above Yokota Air Base, never to return. The aircraft called in when it penetrated North Korean airspace. Silence followed. It wasn't a routine combat mission. Besides the pilot, copilot, and the radar navigator, onboard the plane was an air force colonel from the Pentagon. Colonel John Lovell worked in air force Intelligence and was assumed to have been involved in planning reconnaissance missions for the RB-45C. Why Colonel Lovell accompanied the mission is unknown. It was unusual for someone with Colonel Lovell's knowledge of reconnaissance operations to expose himself to possible capture. Robert Burns of the *Norfolk Virginian-Pilot and Ledger Star* wrote in 1994,

The RB-45 was no ordinary plane. It was the most advanced photo-reconnaissance plane in the world, and this was its first wartime use. The Air Force knew the RB-45C was a target of Soviet intelligence. Moscow was aware that U.S. Air Force planes were flying over its territory throughout the 1950s, but it didn't become an international issue until the Soviets shot down Francis Gary Powers in a CIA-operated U-2 spy plane on May 1, 1960. Although never officially acknowledged by Washington, men who flew the plane in Korea say their top-secret missions sometimes took them deep into Chinese and Soviet airspace. More routinely, it flew photo reconnaissance over North Korea. Louis Carrington of Tyler, Texas, one of the two other pilots in McDonough's unit, recalls that *Mac* and his crew, attired in blue flight suits, took off into clear skies from Yokota at about lunchtime on December 4. The last word from the RB-45 crew was a routine radio contact 100 minutes after takeoff, signaling their entry into North Korean airspace. The crash site was never pinpointed. No bodies were recovered. (A6)

Major Carrington was himself no ordinary pilot. In July 1952, three months before Sam Myers and Frank Martin arrived at Yokota to re-place his crew, he won the Mackay Trophy, given by the National Aero-nautic Association for the outstanding flight of the year. It was only the second time the trophy had been awarded to a SAC crew. The first Mackay Trophy had gone to the crew of the *Lucky Lady II*, a B-50A of the 43rd Bomb Group, which completed the first nonstop around-the-world flight in 1949. On July 29, 1952, Lou Carrington flew RB-45C 48-042 nonstop from Elmendorf AFB in Alaska to Yokota Air Base, supported by two KB-29 refueling tankers. It was the first transpacific flight of that nature.

Burns pointed out in his story that "the clinching evidence [about the shootdown] came not from U.S. government files, but from Russia, whose MiG fighters shot down McDonough's plane near the Yalu River separating North Korea from China. McDonough ejected from the plane. The one page document that said McDonough had died was found in Russian archives. It was dated December 18, 1950—exactly two weeks after the shootdown—but did not indicate the exact date or cause of death. 'I am informing you that the pilot from the shot-down B-45 aircraft died en route and the interrogation was not finished,' the note said in Russian." McDonough apparently was the only crew mem-ber to eject from his stricken aircraft, and he subsequently perished.

"Our standard missions," Sam Myers recalled, "were day missions over North Korea. We were tasked by FEAF Bomber Command, and as soon as we returned from a mission, their intelligence specialists would retrieve our film, process it, look at the target areas, and then task the B-29s at Yokota and Kadena, Okinawa, against the targets we had located. Some of our missions were deep penetrations into communist China and the Soviet Union. We flew other missions against the coastal regions of the Soviet Union abutting the Sea of Japan and along Sakhalin and the Kurile Islands, often escorted for part of our flight by F-84 fighters. We had a one-hundred-inch-lens camera mounted at a thirty-degree angle in the bomb bay. We could fly at twenty-five thousand feet over water and shoot into the Soviet Union and get great pictures of their airfields. It worked real well for photographing Sakhalin Island. We used our powerful bomb bay camera for high-altitude photography and the nose camera for low-altitude work. Nearly 90 percent of our missions were day photography, the remainder were night radar photography.

"If our missions were flown at night, we used our black RB-45C, tail number 48-027. There was a U.S. Army searchlight detachment at Yokota. My predecessor, Major Carrington, had run a test to determine how visible our aircraft was at night if we were picked up by a searchlight. The Koreans and Chinese used searchlights prodigiously. In the test Carrington ran, the RB-45C flew at thirty-five thousand feet when it was picked up by the Yokota searchlights. The aircraft shone like a bright star. They then painted one aircraft black and flew the test again. The searchlights couldn't track the black RB-45C, so at night we flew aircraft number 48-027. On December 17, 1952, I flew a deep-penetration mission over the Soviet Union and China. We took off from Yokota, crossed the Sea of Japan, and coasted inland at thirty-five thousand feet, just south of Vladivostok. Then I turned northwest toward Harbin, then back south toward Mukden [Shenyang]. After passing an airfield near Mukden, I made a programmed ninety-degree banking turn, and I could see MiGs taking off below me. They didn't catch us. We crossed North Korea, heading toward Japan. When we flew over the battle lines, there were searchlights operating on both sides. The battle lines were lit up all the way across the peninsula, a spectacular view from thirty-five thousand feet. On other missions we staged first to K-13, Suwon Air Base in South Korea. There we refueled, and then we'd go out over the Yellow Sea, up the west coast of North Korea. We penetrated into China and took photographs of activity along the coastal areas, especially ships being loaded. Much of what was being loaded was going to North Korea. The B-29s would then try to catch the ships as they were unloading in North Korean ports.

"The closest I came to getting shot down was over Wonsan on the North Korean east coast, returning from a night mission over China. We had two fifty caliber machine guns mounted in the tail. Although it looked like we carried a gunner back there, we didn't. The two guns in this particular aircraft were fixed. One gun pointed straight aft, the other pointed downward at a thirty-degree angle. I could fire the guns from the cockpit. We were cruising along at thirty-five thousand feet, heading for the Sea of Japan, when by chance I overheard a flight of two navy F9F Panthers calling their carrier, which was sitting right in front of us. The lead navy pilot was saying they had spotted an IL-28 bomber heading for the carrier and they were going in for the attack, thinking my RB-45C was an IL-28. Luckily, I happened to be on their frequency when I heard the radio call. My adrenaline level rose instantaneously, and for a moment I felt like the bull's-eye at a rifle range. I immediately called back to let them know I was friendly. The shipboard radar had seen us coming from the north, assumed we were hostile, and launched the Panthers. The F9Fs finally got the word and broke off their attack, but not before making a pass at us close enough to rock the aircraft with their jet wash."

Lieutenant Frank Martin, Sam's radar navigator, sat in the nose of the aircraft and spent most of his time with his eyes glued to his radarscope. "I had none of the panoramic views of Korea or Vladivostok Sam had from the cockpit of the aircraft. On several occasions we flew up the Yalu River from Antung until we could see Vladivostok. Those were daylight missions for which we had navy fighter escort. I recall one mission over Tsingtao (Chingtao), on the Yellow Sea. There were three MiG airfields in that area. I bet you there were a hundred MiGs sitting on the aprons. I could see them on my radar. They didn't have

Rear view of RB-45C 8-042 on the Yokota flight line with two fixed-position tail guns, 1952. All other SAC RB-45s had their tail guns removed. H. Myers.

a clue we were there. They didn't have the radar to see us, nor, I presume, did they think we would do that in broad daylight. My crew flew a total of thirty-one missions over North Korea and the maritime provinces of China and the Soviet Union while we were there."

Master Sergeant Arthur E. Lidard
Air Medal (3)

In addition to the small SAC RB-45C photo-reconnaissance detachment at Yokota, there was a much more sizable presence of aging RB-29 reconnaissance aircraft to conduct both photographic and electronic intelligence. The ELINT aircraft were addressed by their crews using a World War II moniker, Mickey ships. The RB-29s also were assigned to the 91st SRS at Yokota, a SAC squadron under the operational control of FEAF. Technical Sergeant Arthur E. Lidard, better known as "Lucky," was assigned to the 91st SRS at Yokota in 1951. He got there in the usual roundabout way.

Captain Myers in the cockpit of his RB-45C at Yokota, 1952. H. Myers.

"I was born in Baltimore, Maryland, on February 24, 1926. My first flight in an airplane was with Colonel Roscoe Turner, flying a Fokker monoplane. I was six years old. Roscoe Turner was a well-known barnstormer, three-time winner of the Thompson trophy, and experienced fighter pilot. My father told me, 'Don't you ever tell your mother about this,' because he spent five dollars to take me on that flight. It was 1931, and times were bad. After that breathtaking flight, my dream was to be a pilot and fly airplanes when I grew up. When the war started, I was two years behind in school because my dad was crippled and I had to go to work to help my family. I attended Loyola High School in Baltimore. They sent me to take the aviation cadet examination, and I did quite well on it. I finished in the top 10 percent. I enlisted in the Army Air Force, waiting for a flying slot to open up, but as the war was winding down in 1944, they didn't need any more pilots. Instead, they sent me to B-17 armaments and electronics school at Lowry Field. Then I went to B-29s at Maxwell Field in Alabama. I flew as a scanner.

"When the war ended, I extended for a year because I had no job to go home to. I was transferred into air rescue. I flew on a B-17E as a crew chief. We carried a twenty-two-foot wooden boat with twin inboard Packard engines slung underneath its belly. I never had to actually drop the boat to rescue anyone. In October 1946 I was discharged and went to work for the post office. Two days before Christmas, I called a recruiting sergeant and told him that I would like to come back into the air service. The day after Christmas, they swore me back in. I missed airplanes, and they sure didn't have any in the post office. I came back in as a buck sergeant, a three-striper. Promotions were frozen, and I stayed in that rank for five years—seventy-eight bucks a month for five long years. I was stationed at Bolling Field in Washington, D.C. When I showed up at Bolling, the line chief said, 'Oh, goody, we need you—a crew chief. I'm going to give you a T-6.' I said, 'No, Sarge, that's single engine. I've been crewing B-17s, multiengine aircraft.' He said, 'We give you more than one.'

"I ended up with two T-6s. The most important tool in my toolbox turned out to be a can of metal polish. Man, we shined those things until you could see your face in them. All the brass from the Pentagon flew out of Bolling. The chief came out one day and said to me, 'You've done a hell of a job, Lucky. I wish I could promote you, but I can't. I can put you in a multiengine aircraft, though. You get some flying pay then.'

"He gave me a C-45. It was my baby. I did everything including the twenty-five-hour inspections. The pilots came over from the Pentagon to fly. One old colonel I will never forget. He had four sets of different prescription glasses. The colonel fascinated me. He'd come out and say, 'Hello, Sergeant. Nice day today. Good day for flying. We'll take it up for a while.'

"I knew that 'for a while' meant four hours, to get his flying pay for the month. I got the crew chief next door to hold the fire bottle, because I had to sit in the right seat. The colonel never brought a copilot along. Then the colonel would say, 'Start 'em up, Lucky,' and I'd crank 'em up.

"Read the checklist,' he'd say. I'd read the checklist. Ran the engines. He'd turn it onto the runway, take the power up, and we'd start to roll. That's when he switched glasses. Scary. We'd roll, break ground, and he'd say, 'You've got such and such on the bird dog?'

" 'Yes, sir,' I'd reply.

"He'd say, 'Clean her up, and you got it. Take us up to eight thousand feet.' We'd get to our assigned quadrant in the local flying area and he'd say, 'Fly it around for a while, Sarge. When it's time to go in, you wake me up. It's been a busy day in the Pentagon.' I flew around for a while. Then I woke him up. Going home was a rerun of what had come before, only in reverse. This happened once or twice every month. I got to thinking, this isn't for me. I'm getting twenty days a month flying pay—not even a full month's pay. I had to fly with anybody, and some of the landings were real awful. I went to headquarters every day. They had a bulletin board near the sergeant major's office where they'd post the requests for people that came in. I found what I was looking for. Alaska. I took it in to the sergeant major. 'I'm ready to go,' I said. 'I can be packed and on the way in an hour.' 'Sure you want to go to Alaska?' he said.

" 'At least,' I said, 'you get overseas pay.' Alaska was still a territory. 'It's a C-54 squadron, and I want to work as a flight maintenance technician,' I told him. Two weeks later, I was in Anchorage with the 54th Troop Carrier Squadron. I went through the usual training—made a few trips up the chain [Aleutian Islands] as a student. I played on the squadron baseball team. All the games ran until past midnight. The last game we played the 1st Cavalry Division. They beat us twenty-eight to nothing. When we got to the shower, someone said, 'Don't get comfortable. Ops wants you in the briefing room.' Colonel Sammons, General Nathan F. Twining's son-in-law, was our commander. He had a southern drawl you could cut with a knife. 'We are going on a thirty-to sixty-day TDY to Germany,' Colonel Sammons said. 'We need to get the airplanes ready to go. We want them off the ground heading for Germany as soon as they're ready.' I worked on an engine change that night.

"We got off the following day. We had three crews aboard and a bunch of maintenance men as well as their toolboxes, carbines, and helmets. We left the snowshoes behind. We flew to Great Falls, then on to Scott Field, and to Westover. At Westover the crew rested us for eight hours. The following day we flew to Harmon, then to Lajes Field in the Azores. At Lajes we stayed on the ground long enough to eat. Took off in the evening and landed at Rhein-Main the following morning. We got in on July 1. The airplane went into Berlin that evening. During the Berlin Airlift, I flew almost entirely with my own airplane, and I kept it running. I stayed until February 7, 1949, and completed 185 trips to Berlin. When I got back to Anchorage, seven months later, someone had cleaned out my locker, and all my stuff was gone.

"In 1951 a friend of mine got an assignment to B-29s. His wife had just gotten pregnant. They had tried to have a kid for a long time, and he didn't want to leave her. So I said, 'I'll see if I can take your shipment. I've flown in B-29s before at Maxwell, and I liked them.' A lot of people didn't like the B-29. I made the request, and they said I could take his shipment. I reported to Randolph, near San Antonio, where I was assigned to a crew. We went through training together at Fairchild AFB, in Spokane, Washington, and then reported to the 91st Strategic Reconnaissance Squadron at Yokota. I was really happy about that. The 91st had RB-29s and RB-45s. Our tail marking was a circle X for the 91st SRS. The 98th, also at Yokota, were circle Hs. They were bombers.

"From 1951 until I left in 1952, I flew thirty-five photo missions, three of which were over Beijing, and eighteen yoke missions, for a total of fifty-three. *Yoke missions* were sea-lane surveillance flights off the coast of Russia. We'd fly out over the Sea of Japan at three hundred feet off the water and twelve miles off the coast. We'd take pictures of Russian ships. The Russian sailors waved to us as we passed. We'd wave back at them. The 91st SRS also had two airplanes without numbers on them and no tail markings. Those two B-29s, painted black, had special equipment. When we briefed for those airplanes, they sent some of our gunners home. We still took our CFC gunner, but the two waist gunners and the tail gunner we left behind. We also sent the photo men home because the ship was a Mickey ship, full of all kinds of electronic junk. On the missions we turned in our identification except for our dog tags. They'd give each of us a little box, which we carried in the leg pocket of our flying coveralls. The box held several Mickey Mouse watches—the good ones. There also were several gold ingots in there. And a blood chit that said I was worth twenty-five thousand dollars in gold, alive, half that if dead.

"The Mickey airplane had Curtiss electric props. The electrical motors changed the propeller pitch automatically. With them we could get up to altitude without a lot of prop problems. At high altitude, the conventional props would constantly change their pitch and hunt. Sometimes they would go so fast I thought they'd spin off the airplane. Then I'd shut down the engine and feather the props. The Curtiss props didn't hunt. They were steady even at forty-three thousand feet. We could get up to that altitude if we burned off enough fuel. We would go as high as the plane would go before we entered China. When we got what we had come for, the Mickey operators would tell us it was all right to turn around. Heading east, we'd pick up the jet stream, and all of a sudden that plane almost turned into a fighter. The trip over took forever, but the trip back didn't take much time at all.

"My regular photo-recce plane was the *Honey Bucket Honshos*. The name was painted across the nose of the airplane. My pilot was Captain Zimmer. I was the flight engineer. We would take off from Yokota and head out over the Sea of Japan, climbing all the time. We'd climb maybe two and a half hours, all the way across Korea if we were heading into China. We'd be at forty thousand feet when we penetrated. The Korean missions we flew around twenty thousand to twenty-five thousand feet. The DMZ was always lit up with searchlights. Pyongyang also had a lot of searchlights. When they shot at us, I could see the rounds coming up, looking like corkscrews. The old stuff glowed yellow and didn't get to our altitude, but the new stuff glowing silver did. Sometimes single MiGs came up and paced us. They seemed to call the altitude down to the AAA. The AAA never shot a barrage at us, only single rounds.

"On June 13, 1952, we were supposed to fly a yoke mission, but it was canceled. I don't know why. We had already preflighted our airplane and were ready to go. They said that Captain English's crew could fly part of the yoke and also do photo-recce near Sakhalin. There was no need for two of us to go. Captain English's flight engineer came over and asked me if he could borrow my watch, since I wasn't flying—his had quit running. I said OK. He promised to return it as soon as they were down. It was a good automatic watch. It's probably still running on a skeleton in the Sea of Japan. They got shot down by a Russian fighter near Sakhalin."

It was grim news but was not totally unexpected by the men of the 91st SRS, who knew that the Russians were touchy around Sakhalin. The navy had lost a P2V six months earlier near Sakhalin. The 91st would lose another RB-29 in October in the Sea of Okhotsk. The unit started with twelve airplanes in late 1950 and with the loss of the two RB-29s, the bean counters at SAC headquarters reduced the squadron's authorized UE strength to ten aircraft. By 1954, when the remaining RB-29s were replaced with newer RB-50s, only eight of the original twelve remained. Lucky Lidard thought it couldn't happen to him: "I was young and felt immortal." But there came a mission in 1952 over North Korea when Lucky nearly lost his belief in his immortality.

"That night we briefed for Pyongyang on *Honey Bucket Honshos*, aircraft number 929. It was supposed to be a paper route, a leaflet drop. I helped load the paper bombs. When we got to the mess hall, we had a message waiting for us: 'Take your time.' When we got back to the airplane, they had yanked the paper bombs and reloaded with M-15 flash bombs. We would follow the 98th Bomb Wing for a big hit on the railroad yards near Pyongyang and take poststrike pictures. Fifteen B-29s would be bombing in a stream. By the time the fifteenth bomber was rolling down the runway, we had completed our taxi checklist and did our run-up. Everything looked good on takeoff and climb out. As we turned west, I watched the sun set. Soon it was pitch black.

"We coasted out of Japan twenty-five minutes behind the bomber stream. Engine temperatures and pressures were in the green. We pulled the pins from the fuses of the M-15s and pressurized to eight thousand feet. The gunners test fired the turrets and ran their in-flight ready checks over the Sea of Japan. We leveled off at twenty-five thousand feet and took up a heading into our target. As we approached, we could see the flashes from the 98th bomb drop. We could also see the searchlights and the flashes from the North Korean flak. Over the initial point, we opened the bomb bay doors and started our photo run. We had some flak, dispensed chaff to mislead their radar, and the flak remained erratic. As we finished our run, the radio operator reported that one M-15 bomb was still in the forward bomb bay. The navigator checked the forward bay and called the pilot over the intercom, 'The left rack in the forward bay still holds one M-15, hanging nose down from the rear latch.'

" 'Roger, Nav,' was Captain Zimmer's response. 'Lucky,' he said, 'set up descent. Depressurize the cabin. Send Sergeant Bjork (the radio operator) into the bay, and get rid of the bomb.'

" 'Yes, Sir,' I replied. As the flight engineer, my responsibility was the supervision of the enlisted crew. 'Sir,' I called to Captain Zimmer, 'go and head for home. We are in a descent, and I will slowly depressurize the cabin.' I told the radio operator to go into the bomb bay with the doors open. He started to shake and told me that he couldn't go out there with the doors open. I looked at him, and I knew the man was so afraid he would kill himself if I forced him out there. I called Captain Zimmer and told him that I would go into the bomb bay to get rid of the bomb. When I looked through the port into the bomb bay, I realized that things were worse than I expected. I walked up behind the pilot and told him what I had seen. Every once in a while the vane on the flash bomb rotated. I had no idea how long that had been going on. If it went off inside our airplane, we would turn into a Fourth of July rocket. It was a magnesium, fifteen million–candlepower bomb. Captain Zimmer accelerated our descent and informed the crew to get ready for a possible over-water bailout. I asked the CFC gunner to come forward through the tunnel and ride in the flight engineer's seat and attend to the panel while I went into the bomb bay to get rid of the bomb. I then told the rest of the crew what our situation was and what I intended to do. Just then, the number three engine started to take oil. I suggested to the pilot that we shut down number three and feather the prop. One emergency at a time was enough for me. He agreed.

"I had never been in the bomb bay at night with the doors open. I knew it would be a religious experience. I clipped an oxygen bottle to my flying jacket, adjusted my mask, put a big crescent wrench in one inside pocket, my Stanley screwdriver in the other, pulled on my nylon glove liners, and dropped my flashlight into a leg pocket. When I got to the bulkhead at the hatch into the bomb bay, I pulled a crash ax out of its straps, and I was as ready as I was ever going to be. I looked into the bay and decided to walk along a narrow ledge between the bomb rack and the fuselage. I wasn't going to go down the middle of the bomb bay, over that black nothingness. I removed my backpack parachute. It was decision time. My heart was pounding in my throat.

"We were at fifteen thousand feet when I opened the hatch and stared into the black, endless chasm. There was some light from the bomb bay lights, and we were drawing ground fire, which helped to light up the blackness of the night. I went through the hatch slowly, onto the narrow sill, hanging onto handholds. I told myself, 'Don't look down.' Then I said it aloud, over and over. About that time, I noticed the vane on the hung bomb flipping over almost a full turn. It was windy as a hurricane in the bomb bay. I squeezed my way between the left front rack and the fuselage, hanging onto anything I could grab. I made it to the rear rack.

"I looked at the shackle holding the bomb and tried my screwdriver in the release slot. I couldn't turn it. I tried to turn the release with my crescent wrench. It wouldn't move. Then the wrench slipped from my grasp and dropped away into the dark. I hacked at the shackle three or four times with the crash ax before it, too, spun off into the night. I wedged my twelve-inch Stanley into the latch of the shackle, and, holding the shaft with my left hand, I planted my left foot on the handle. I hung on for dear life with my right hand and pushed with my foot. Suddenly, the shackle released, and the M-15 disappeared into the night. I started to count as the bomb left the shackle—one thousand, two thousand, three thousand. At the count of fifteen thousand, a brilliant flash of white filled the darkness below and behind us and stayed bright as the bomb fell away. I gave a hand signal to the navigator to close the bomb bay doors. When they *whoosh-whumped* closed, I struggled my way back through the hatch and into the ship. Once on the interphone, I informed Captain Zimmer that I was repressurizing to get some heat in the aircraft and to let us remove our oxygen masks. I suggested to the pilot that we restart number three so we'd have four engines for landing, but it wouldn't turn. We were at eleven thousand feet over the Sea of Japan. I set up three-engine cruise and realized I was shaking and soaked in sweat.

"By the time we arrived over Yokota I had recovered my sense of immortality and joked over the intercom about having to pay for the crescent wrench and the crash ax. Captain Zimmer laughed and called for the before-landing checklist, and then he added, 'We'll go to town tomorrow for dinner, Lucky, and I'm buying.'" Lidard indeed counts himself lucky to have survived his experience in the bomb bay of a B-29. After retiring from the air force, he settled in northern California.

Chapter 10

More Secret Than the Manhattan Project

My first encounter with airplanes and flying was in 1929, I was eleven. I got a ride in a Ford trimotor. That was like going to heaven.

Hack Mixson, air force pilot

Even though the story leaked out of the woodwork two or three years ago, I still find it strange to talk and write about it. While it was happening it rivalled the Manhattan Project for secrecy. In fact, I think it outranked the Manhattan Project.

Squadron Leader John Crampton, DFC, AFC and Bar, Royal Air Force, Retired

Colonel Marion C. Mixson

Distinguished Flying Cross (2), Air Medal (5)

"I was born in Charleston, South Carolina, March 20, 1918. My first encounter with airplanes and flying was in 1929. I was eleven. I got a ride in a Ford trimotor. That was like going to heaven. If an airplane flew over Charleston, I'd run outside to take a look. There weren't that many airplanes then. Once a German Dornier seaplane landed in Charleston Harbor. It was a monstrous thing, exciting. Aviation was spread pretty thin in those days, but I always knew I wanted to fly. I believe it was my nanny who first called me Hack, and the name stuck with me ever since. I was raised in Charleston, went to the public schools there, and after high school attended Presbyterian College in Clinton, South Carolina. College was a pretty uneventful four years. When I graduated from Presbyterian in 1939, I ended up with a commission as a second lieutenant in the infantry. My brother, Lawrence, was four years older than I. In World War II he served in the navy in the Pacific, where both of his destroyers, the *Osborne* and the *Renshaw,* were heavily damaged in combat with Japanese naval forces. I went to work in the family business in Charleston, the Mixson Seed Company, selling seed and fertilizer throughout the southeastern states.

"In the fall of 1939, I soloed a little 45-horsepower Aeronca. What a thrill it was to soar above Charleston on my very own. I'll never forget that first solo flight. Fortunately, I had a friend, Robert Carroll, who owned several airplanes. The best one was a Rearwin Cloudster made at Fairfax Airport in Kansas City, Kansas. It had a 120-horsepower five-cylinder radial Ken-Royce engine—pretty powerful stuff for that day. Between 1939 and 1941, I flew several hundred hours with Robert and his brother, Edwin. I flew every time I got a chance. In July 1941 Edwin and I took off from Charleston to fly to Los Angeles. We stopped in Atlanta and got gas. Spent the night in Monroe, Louisiana. Went on to Fort Worth, Texas, and had lunch there. It was about ninety-five degrees. Then we headed to Wichita Falls, flying at three thousand feet. I was flying. All of a sudden the old RPM just went down and kept on going down. I said to Edwin, 'I can't maintain altitude. I'm going to have to land.' In those days, the sectional charts showed farm- and ranch houses. Edwin located the nearest farmhouse on the map, I headed for it, and we landed in a field by a rock cairn next to the house. We got out and checked everything and found nothing wrong. We cranked the engine up again, and it ran like a breeze. So we took off and flew to Wichita Falls. The mechanic there couldn't find anything wrong with the airplane either. Being cautious, we decided not to go on to Los Angeles and instead flew to the Ken-Royce plant at Fairfax Field in Kansas City. They modified the engine so we didn't have to manually grease the rocker boxes with a squirt gun. We met Mr. Rearwin, the owner of the plant, and his two sons, Ken and Royce, after whom he named the engine. They checked the engine themselves and declared everything was fine. We still had our doubts, though, and flew back to Charleston.

"Two weeks later Robert Carroll, who owned the plane, and I set off on the same trip. Same itinerary—gas in Atlanta, overnight in Monroe, lunch in Fort Worth, even sitting at the same table. It was ninety-five degrees again. As we flew along, heading for Wichita Falls, I said to Robert, 'See that farmhouse down there? I landed right in that field.' By that time, the old engine slowed down. Robert landed within a hundred feet of the same rock cairn. We went all through the engine, and everything checked out again. Then we flew to Wichita Falls. The same mechanic who checked the engine two weeks earlier checked it again and declared there was nothing wrong with it. This time we decided to continue our flight to Los Angeles, spending the night in Albuquerque, New Mexico.

"We left early the next morning. As we crossed the New Mexico–Arizona line, all of a sudden the cockpit filled with smoke. Smoke in the cockpit is scary. We decided to put it down and landed about seven thousand feet up on a mesa. We did a bad landing and stripped the landing gear. There we were—in the middle of the Zuni Indian Reservation—with a busted airplane. I saw some Zuni Indians and walked toward them to ask them for help, but when they saw me coming, they ran away. Luckily, a guy came along in a Buick convertible on his honeymoon, taking the back trails. He gave me a ride to St. Johns in Arizona. There I found a fellow with a flatbed truck who agreed to take the plane, Robert, and me to the factory in Kansas City for twenty-five dollars. He didn't know how far Kansas City was—about a thousand miles. Once we got to Kansas City, we gave him an extra fifty dollars.

The problem with the plane? One of the new oil lines which automatically lubricated the rocker boxes had malfunctioned, causing the smoke in the cockpit. In Kansas City, at the Rearwin factory, they fixed our plane. Mr. Rearwin built a good engine, but his modification was bad.

"In December 1941 I was called to active duty at Fort McClellan. I put a letter in through channels to transfer to the air corps. I had three hundred hours of flying time, I wrote, and I should be in the air corps, not in the infantry. I think my first letter got thrown in the trash. Then I sent a letter directly to the Army Air Corps. Four days later I was at Maxwell Field in Alabama, getting a physical. Two weeks after that I was at a small airfield near Fort Worth, Texas, to begin training in the PT-17. I went on to the BT-13 and after that to little twin-engine plywood planes, AT-10s. After I graduated from pilot training, I was sent to the 13th Bomb Group at Westover, Massachusetts, a B-25 outfit. Out of Westover I flew antisubmarine patrols along the Atlantic coast.

"In July 1943 I was assigned to the 461st Bomb Group, which was forming in Boise, Idaho. Before I knew it, I was a B-24 flight commander, since I had more experience in that airplane than most others, which wasn't much. I was still a second lieutenant and less than a year out of flying school. My crew—there were ten of us—were all experts in their fields and great guys. Sam Gilio was the engineer and waist gunner. He had been a prizefighter as well as a mechanic for American Airlines for ten years. Sol Adler, the radio operator, spent ten years at sea, copying Morse code. Sol would sit, looking like he was asleep but copying everything that came in over the radio. My bombardier, Howard Kadow, was a jeweler from Brooklyn, New York. Howie was brilliant. The copilot, Tom Lightbody, was an Irish cop from Pelham, New York. Hank Wilson, a lawyer, was the best navigator there ever was. And Gino Piccione, Ed Miller, Herb Newman, and Chester Kline were our gunners. The four gunners were all pretty young, eighteen or so. Ed Miller, the largest man on the crew, was the ball turret gunner. Usually the smallest man took this position. We ten trained at Fresno, California, and at Wendover range in Utah. We finished up about Christmas of 1943.

In February 1944 our group deployed from Florida to Dakar, North Africa, and then to Marrakesh. We flew a couple of missions out of Tunis and then moved to our permanent field south of Foggia, Italy, Toretta 1. On April 13 I was formation leader for the 461st Bomb Group in an attack against an aircraft plant near Budapest, Hungary. Our escort fighters, P-38s, didn't show. I didn't think we would make it back from that mission. We were viciously attacked by waves of enemy fighters, firing rockets, cannon, and machine guns. They came at us head on and from all sides, flying abreast, firing their rockets into our formation. Rockets tore off the wing of one aircraft; out of control, it collided with another. Both exploded. A third aircraft went down. Of the remaining thirty-five B-24s, thirty were damaged. I was awarded the Distinguished Flying Cross for that mission. In June 1944—I was a captain by then—we finished our twenty-five missions. I was told by my group commander, Colonel Lee, 'If you take your crew home and come back, I'll make you a squadron commander.' I took them home about the time everybody else landed in France. When we returned in September, Colonel Lee, who had by then been promoted to general, gave me the 764th Bomb Squadron.

"On December 17, 1944, we were going to destroy the last little bit of oil the Germans had—the Odertal refinery in Upper Silesia. It was the longest mission ever flown by the 461st Bomb Group. I led the group, and two other B-24 groups joined us, flying at lower altitudes, the 484th and the 451st. Ninety-three heavy bombers. Intelligence briefed us, 'Don't worry. You are the high group. You will be flying at twenty-six thousand feet. No one will bother you up there. Keep your ball turrets up. You got plenty of fighter cover.' Twenty-six thousand feet was the maximum formation altitude for the B-24. Keeping our ball turrets up in the belly of the aircraft rather than extending them downward meant increased range on this long mission and better formation flying, though once the decision was made, it was not easy to reverse if it proved to have been the wrong choice. The ball turret gunner had to remove his chute to crawl into the turret. After entering, the gunner would then lower the ball electrically. The procedure took a fair amount of time.

"Well, we got up into Germany and didn't see our fighter escort. At that altitude it was difficult to keep the formation together. We were heavy, flying through the brilliantly blue December sky, working hard to keep the formation together. The plane was unpressurized, and the crew was on oxygen all the time, wearing bulky, heated flying gear. Finally, we saw a large group of fighters approaching. Our escort, we thought. Wrong. They were German Me-109s, seventy-five of them. And we had our ball turrets up. The 109s jumped on my group first.

"Planes were exploding and going down everywhere. Seventy more German FW-190s pounced on my group. In fifteen minutes eight of my bombers were shot down, five more damaged. Only fifteen of an original thirty-one in my group made it to the target. Losses were lighter in the lower groups. On the return leg, as I was passing Vienna, a German calls me on the radio. He used our correct call sign, and in perfect, German-accented English he said, 'Where is the rest of your formation?' Then he laughed and signed off. It had been a beautiful day when we took off that morning in Italy. The Luftwaffe hadn't been bothering us for weeks. We got complacent. Put our ball turrets up. That was a mistake. That ball turret was a killer, and we didn't have those guns to defend ourselves. We paid dearly for that mistake. Our escort never showed up, and I still don't know why to this day.

"I flew about thirty-five combat missions. Some missions counted double, giving me a total of fifty. Every week or so we would go up to Ploesti. Ploesti was always bad—they had a lot of flak there. Munich was bad, as was anything around Vienna. The Germans often put up a spotter plane to give their antiaircraft guns our altitude. The flak was always heavy in our target areas. That was World War II for me.

"After the war ended, I stayed in Italy for another year. It was one of the best years of my life. I was sitting in the replacement depot ready to go home when I got a call to work for General W. L. Lee, my former boss and group commander who headed the Air Force Subcommission in Rome, which was part of the Allied Commission for Italy, headed by

Ellery Stone, a two-star admiral. After the telephone call—I'm pretty elated about this time—I chatted with a major, who was heading for home, and in the course of our conversation told him that I had only minutes ago received an assignment to Rome. I had a case of bourbon whiskey with me. He said to me, 'You're going to need all that whiskey?' I said, 'Yeah, I think I am.'

" 'I tell you what,' the major said, 'I got a deal for you. I have a C-47 over at Marcianise, near Naples. I commanded a service squadron. During the year I picked the wing off of one plane, a wing off another, and I made me an airplane—my airplane. If you give me six of those bourbon bottles, I'll check you out in that plane and you can have it.' That sounded good to me, so we went over to Marcianise. It was raining lightly when we got there. We made two little runs around the field, and the major declared me checked out in his C-47, took my six bottles of bourbon, and disappeared. I then flew the airplane up to Rome. Days later I learned that at the Pomigliano depot near Naples sat thirty-nine brand new C-47s which the Russians were going to get. They were sold to them for twenty thousand dollars apiece, three for fifty thousand dollars. The third C-47 was intended for spare parts. The planes had only ferry time on them. At the first opportunity, I jumped into my piece of flying junk and flew it over to Pomigliano, where the brand-spanking-new C-47s sat. The American captain in charge of the planes was friendly and easygoing. Giving him the biggest smile I could muster, I said to him, 'Favano, I want to take this piece of junk I flew in with and put it at the end of that line and get me one of those new ones.' He laughed and agreed. We changed the serial numbers around, parked the old C-47 next to the others bound for Russia, and I flew off in my own brand-new C-47. I flew that airplane for a year. When the time came for me to go home, there was no one to turn the C-47 in to, because the airplane didn't exist. By that time Admiral Stone had gotten word about my plane and quickly solved my problem by giving it to the Italian air force.

"Incidentally, all those B-25 and B-17 bombers in Italy at the end of the war were destroyed. None were sent home. For a while I flew a brand-new B-25. German prisoners took the armor out of it, stripped the paint, and polished the airplane to a high gloss. Although I had orders to turn the plane in to be destroyed like all the other bombers, I kept stalling for about two months. Finally I got a message that if I didn't turn in the plane I was going to be court-martialed. So I flew it down to the Pomigliano depot; my buddy came down in a C-47 to take me back. By the time we finished filing our clearance for our return trip, they had drained the gas out of that beautiful B-25, cut the engines off, cut holes in the crankcase and into the propeller blades. That airplane was completely smashed in about an hour.

"Late in 1946 I returned home to Charleston and was discharged from the Army Air Force with the rank of lieutenant colonel. At twenty-eight I tried to reenter the Mixson family wholesale seed business. I was used to staying at the Plaza Athenai in Athens, the best hotels in Paris, Rome, and Cairo. I found myself traveling through South Carolina and Georgia, staying in hotel rooms with one lightbulb hanging from the ceiling. In 1948 I got a message from the air force offering me a regular commission, giving me twenty-four hours to accept or decline. Naturally, I accepted. I was assigned to the 343d Squadron of the 55th Group at MacDill Air Force Base in Tampa. They were flying B-17s, C-45s, and C-47s equipped for aerial photography—a mapping outfit. Within weeks, we transferred to Topeka, Kansas, and then, in October 1949, the 55th Group was disbanded. I was transferred to the 91st Reconnaissance Group at Barksdale AFB in Louisiana. I stayed there from October 1949 until June 1950, when I went to the Air Command and Staff College in Alabama. That month the Korean War started and I was promoted to lieutenant colonel. When I reported back to Barksdale in December, the group had transitioned to the RB-45C four-engine jet. I was given command of the 323d Squadron."

With the impetus of the Korean War, British Prime Minister Clement Attlee and U.S. President Harry S. Truman agreed to a combined aerial reconnaissance program for flights over the western Soviet Union. At the time, the only aircraft able to implement such a program was the RB-45C Tornado. RAF Sculthorpe, hidden away among the hedgerows of rural and remote East Anglia, was home to B-45A Tornado bombers of the 47th Bombardment Wing. The reconnaissance version of the B-45 was assigned to SAC. Although there were organizational differences between the bomber and reconnaissance units, having the same aircraft type at one air base simplified maintenance and support functions. In all other respects, the three squadrons of B-45A bombers and the one rotational squadron of RB-45C reconnaissance aircraft remained separate.

"Soon after I checked out in the RB-45 at Barksdale, I was sent in May 1951 to RAF Sculthorpe. Our presence at Sculthorpe consisted of the twelve aircraft of the 323d SRS, which I commanded. By the time I arrived at Sculthorpe, RAF air crews had already joined the squadron and flown one or two joint missions. By the end of July, I returned to the United States, accompanied by three RAF air crews to continue their training at Barksdale AFB. We landed at Barksdale in a KB-29 about nine o'clock in the evening. The Brits wore their heavy RAF winter uniforms. When we left England early that morning it was chilly. When we landed at Barksdale at nine o'clock in the evening it was ninety degrees, the humidity was 99 percent, and a thunderstorm and a tornado had just come across the end of the field. The RAF flyers soon got used to their new Louisiana environment and quickly made friends and acquaintances among the American air crews.

"The three RAF crews and a couple of extras were led by Squadron Leader John Crampton. Crampton was a tall, lean man with extensive World War II experience. The lead radar navigator, Flight Lieutenant Rex Sanders, had similar combat experience over Germany. Only those two were privy to the real purpose of their training at Barksdale. For the others, and anyone else asking questions, the story was that the Royal Air Force was considering acquiring a number of RB-45Cs on loan and wanted to conduct air-refueling trials. B-29s had been provided to the RAF under a previous agreement, so this seemed a reasonable explanation. Each RAF crew consisted of a pilot, a radar navigator, and a flight engineer. The flight engineer sat in the seat normally occupied by an American copilot. None of our aircraft carried defensive armament, so there were no gunners on the crews.

"As for my role in this extremely sensitive and highly classified operation, I was in charge of the planned overflights of the Soviet Union as far as SAC was concerned. To a limited degree I was involved in the mission planning and accompanied Crampton and Sanders to bomber command at High Wycombe near London to sit in on their briefings. There the routes were drawn up, and we met with Air Chief Marshal Sir Ralph Cochrane, Vice-Chief of Air Staff, to discuss issues regarding the loan of the aircraft. I don't think SAC or anybody else on the American side had any real input into where the Brits were going. The RAF did the planning and provided the air crews; the U.S. Air Force provided the aircraft."

Captain Howard "Sam" Myers, the Berlin Airlift veteran, was assigned to the 322d squadron at Barksdale. Sam had his first flight in the RB-45C in May 1951. By July, Sam recalled meeting RAF air crews both in the officers club and on the flight line. He thought they were there to learn how to fly the RB-45 in case they acquired some for the RAF. He quickly struck up a casual friendship with a couple of the RAF pilots and navigators, but by August, the RAF flyers vanished. "I moved them up to Lockbourne AFB in Ohio, the new location for the 91st SRW," recalled Hack Mixson, "when my squadron, the 323d, moved there. A major part of their training took place at Lockbourne and was conducted among the three squadrons—the 322d, the 323d, and the 324th. The Brits cracked up one aircraft—didn't hurt anybody but ruined the airplane. That crew washed out of the program and was replaced by another."

In September 1951 Sam Myers transferred with the rest of his squadron from Barksdale to Lockbourne and again ran into his RAF friends. In November, Sam was on his way to England as the 322d squadron replaced the 323d. He flew his RB-45C via the usual northern route to RAF Sculthorpe for a three-month TDY assignment. Soon after his arrival at Sculthorpe in December, Sam again encountered his RAF colleagues, who had returned after completing their RB-45 training at

American and British RB-45C air crew and technicians, RAF Sculthorpe, 1952. Sam Myers is front right. H. Myers.

Lockbourne. "During my stay at Sculthorpe," Sam recalled, "I had an RAF copilot and RAF radar navigator on several occasions. They stayed current in the aircraft by flying with us. We flew mostly along the periphery of the Soviet Union, but occasionally we flew over Soviet satellite countries. Cooperation between us and the RAF was excellent. They were great flyers."

Hack Mixson explained that "we rotated the three 91st Wing squadrons into Sculthorpe. Because of my experience with the RAF crews and as the only one knowledgeable of the real purpose of their being there, I remained behind in England when my squadron rotated home. All in all, I got to do about four three-month TDYs over there."

Meanwhile, plans were made for the first deep penetration of the Soviet Union. Four RB-45s at Sculthorpe were stripped of their U.S. Air Force markings and repainted with Royal Air Force roundels on the fuselage and RAF colors on the tail fin. Aircraft numbers were omitted. On March 21, 1952, a night mission was flown into East Germany, east of Berlin, to find out how the Soviets would react to such an incursion. Their reaction wasn't sufficient to dissuade the planners from going ahead with the overflight they had planned for the night of April 17, 1952. In a 1998 letter to the Air Force Museum at Wright-Patterson Air Force Base, Squadron Leader John Crampton recalled, "Even though the story leaked out of the woodwork two or three years ago, I still find it strange to talk and write about it. While it was happening it rivalled the Manhattan Project for secrecy. In fact, I think it outranked the Manhattan Project. While off base we weren't allowed to THINK about it. It was all well above top secret. It was at Sculthorpe that Hal Connor, the tough little Texan who commanded the squadron, selected four of his airplanes (one was a spare) for our operational use." Hal Connor was the commander of the 322d squadron, to which Sam Myers was assigned and which pulled a rotational tour of duty at Sculthorpe. Connor, however, was not aware of what the RAF was up to; Hack Mixson and a handful of highly placed military and political officials were the only Americans who knew that.

On the night of April 17, 1952, three RB-45Cs in RAF colors rose into the East Anglia sky and proceeded to their individual air-refueling areas—one over the North Sea; another over Copenhagen, Denmark; and a third south of Frankfurt, Germany. The three aircraft topped off their fuel tanks from U.S. Air Force KB-29 refueling tankers and proceeded on their individual routes, flying at thirty-five thousand feet in total radio silence into the heart of the Soviet Union. One plane photographed targets in the Baltic states of Estonia, Latvia, and Lithuania; in Poland; and in the former German province of East Prussia. The second aircraft flew across Belorussia as far as Orel. The third plane was piloted by Squadron Leader Crampton, with Sanders as his radar navigator. This craft flew the longest and most southern route, crossing the Ukraine and penetrating as far as Rostov on the Black Sea. Each route had frequent turning points to include a maximum number of potential targets.

A month after the RAF flew its deep-penetration mission into the Soviet Union, Sam Myers prepared to return to the United States. "I went out to the flight line to preflight my aircraft for the return trip. I distinctly remembered a logo painted on the nose of the aircraft—it was gone. And there was the slightest hint of an RAF roundel on the fuselage. It was clearly one of the aircraft used by the RAF for its over-flights, but at the time, I could only guess."

In October Hack Mixson was alerted for another possible RAF mission planned for late December. "Four aircraft were repainted at RAF Sculthorpe in RAF colors," Hack recalled, "but at the last minute the mission was canceled. It was December 18, 1952, just before Christmas, and everyone wanted to get home. I called Headquarters Strategic Air Command in Omaha, and they decided to have us fly the airplanes home without first repainting them. While there were four airplanes, the RAF only had three full air crews to fly them. They were short a pilot for the fourth crew. So I flew one of them back with a British engineer in the copilot's seat and Rex Sanders as my radar navigator. It was a long and tiring ten-hour flight, since the engineer couldn't help me fly the plane. Snow was blowing at Lockbourne when we arrived. There were some surprised looks by the ground crew when we taxied in, resplendent in the colors of the Royal Air Force. In January 1953 SAC began transferring our RB-45s to the Tactical Air Command, and I left Lockbourne temporarily to get checked out in the new six-jet B-47.

"Between January and March 1953 I checked out in the B-47 at McCoy AFB near Orlando, Florida, along with Hal Austin and many others who once flew the RB-45C. Late in the year, once we got operational in the RB-47, the 91st Wing deployed to Nouasseur Air Base in Morocco, North Africa. While at Nouasseur I got a message to see General LeMay at Offutt—immediately. I caught a ride on a plane and headed back to Nebraska. Once I got to Offutt, LeMay told me to get down to Shaw AFB in South Carolina; pick up four RB-45s; take them to Wright-Patterson AFB in Dayton, Ohio, for modifications to their radars; and then fly them over to Sculthorpe. TAC crews flew the airplanes to Wright-Patterson. The modifications to the radar took about a month. The radar fix was implemented under the supervision of English radar experts, who significantly improved the picture to very crisp and clear. When the aircraft arrived at Sculthorpe in early April 1954, Crampton and his bunch were waiting for the airplanes. They were

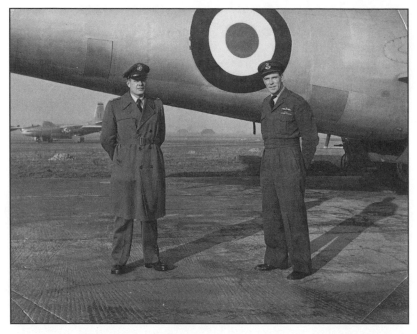

Lieutenant Colonel Mixson and Squadron Leader Crampton, RAF Sculthorpe, December 1952. M. Mixson.

repainted in RAF colors, and we waited for the launch date on routes nearly identical to those flown in 1952. The date of the mission was April 28, 1954, ten days past the two-year anniversary of the 1952 flight."

Again Squadron Leader Crampton took the longest, most southern route, extended as far as Volgograd, the former Stalingrad. In his letter Crampton wrote of this mission: "The RB-45C squadrons who were our kind and courteous hosts during that very dicey period from which I have always thought we were very lucky indeed to survive, especially now that we know that the Russkies knew we were to fly the second mission in 1954, and shot at us all 'round our route—and frightened the life out of me over Kiev when they finally got our height right and sent up a highway of predicted flak, a real highway, fantastic it was, but by the grace of God they got our speed wrong and chucked the stuff just ahead of us. Even the hot shards of shrapnel missed us." Although

Air crew and maintenance personnel assembled in front of four RB-45Cs bearing RAF colors, December 1952. M. Mixson.

all three RB-45Cs returned safely, it was a close thing. It was the last flight in the RB-45C for the RAF. Crampton found the operation "a good example of real USAF/RAF get-togetherness. There was never anything quite like it!"

Lieutenant Colonel Francis T. Martin Jr.

Distinguished Flying Cross, Air Medal

But it was not the last overflight of the Soviet Union by the RB-45C. In early May 1954, the 19th Tactical Reconnaissance Squadron (Night Photo Jet) from Shaw AFB, South Carolina, flying the former SAC RB-45Cs and led by its commander, Major John B. Anderson, flew its aircraft en masse via Goose Bay, Labrador, and Iceland to RAF Sculthorpe. The planes arrived at Sculthorpe on May 8. Major Anderson

RB-45C refueling from a 91st SRW SAC KB-29P tanker over the Baltic Sea near Copenhagen, Denmark, April 17, 1952. M. Mixson.

and the 19th TRS air crews were met and greeted by the Sculthorpe base commander, Colonel David M. Jones, and Brigadier General Joseph R. Holzapple, the 47th Bomb Wing commander. The 19th TRS became part of the 47th Bombardment Wing, with its three squadrons of B-45A bombers and one squadron of KB-29 refueling tankers. It was probably the most powerful wing the United States had stationed in Europe at that time. Soon the 19th TRS air crews were involved in extensive photomapping of much of Europe. One of its members was Captain Francis T. Martin Jr. a radar navigator with extensive combat experience in the RB-45C over North Korea and communist China.

Frank Martin was a farm boy, born in 1928 in Roslindale, Massachusetts. "While I was still in high school my family moved to the country, to Medway, where my father and I raised chickens for eggs and meat. We had a rabbi kill the chickens, and I had a delivery route in Boston where we sold kosher food. I continued to commute to Boston to finish my schooling. The war got everybody interested in aviation, particularly us youngsters. My father had been a torpedoman in submarines in the First World War, and several of my uncles served in either the army or navy during the war with Spain, in the Philippine Insurrection, and the First World War. I wanted to become a navy flyer, so I joined the navy. Then the war ended, and they just discharged our whole class. At age eighteen I decided I wanted to start a career in photography. I heard that the Army Air Force would give you your base of choice if you enlisted, so I did. In 1946 I was sent to the photo school at Lowry Field in Denver, Colorado. When I graduated, I stayed there as an instructor. I really enjoyed air force life, so I decided to try again and applied for pilot training through the aviation cadet program. It turned out I had insufficient depth perception, disqualifying me, but I was offered a slot in the navigator aviation cadet program, which had just opened at Ellington Field in Texas. I graduated in 1951. I continued with my training, qualifying as bombardier and radar navigator. Since I had expressed an interest in photography, I was assigned to the 322d Reconnaissance Squadron at Barksdale AFB in Louisiana. The squadron flew the new RB-45C photo-reconnaissance jet. Within weeks of my arrival at Barksdale, the squadron transferred to Lockbourne AFB in Ohio.

"At Lockbourne I was quickly checked out in the RB-45. The Korean War was in full swing, and by December 1951 I was flying photo reconnaissance out of Yokota Air Base, Japan, over North Korea. That time I flew twenty-one combat missions. Upon my return to Lockbourne I ended up on Sam Myers's crew, and I went back to Yokota with him for a second combat tour. Our missions were pretty straightforward, mostly day photo missions over North Korea. There was a small percentage of special missions. On several of those we flew up the Yalu River from Antung [Dandong] until we could see Vladivostok. The pilots could actually see the MiGs taking off at Vladivostok, but the MiGs could never catch us. On the daylight missions up the Yalu we always had navy fighter escorts, F9F Panthers. Then we flew night radar deep-penetration missions into China as far as Mukden [Shenyang].

Other missions, day and night, we flew along the Kurile Island chain and along Sakhalin Island. For the night missions we flew 8-027: the aircraft was painted black. Some of us got jumped by MiGs near the Kurile Islands and Sakhalin. The B-45s made out all right, but some of the others in our squadron—the slower RB-29s—didn't.

"In January 1953 I transferred to TAC, along with our airplanes. Most of the RB-45 crews of the 19th TRS at Shaw AFB came from Lockbourne. When all of the RB-45s finally arrived from SAC and had their tail guns reinstalled, the squadron went into an accelerated training program. In May 1945 we transferred to RAF Sculthorpe, and I stayed there until 1958. We had less than twenty airplanes in the squadron and had some supply problems with spare parts. Everybody was saying we couldn't do our mission. So two or three times we got the entire squadron off the ground—every airplane—to show that we could do our mission. In June, only a month after our arrival at Sculthorpe, one of our aircraft set a record for the most flying time in the B-45 for a thirty-day period, 108 hours.

"We did a lot of mapping in Europe—Norway, for example. That was very difficult because of the steep mountains rising sharply from sea level to thousands of feet. If we had a camera focused for sea level, it wouldn't be in focus for higher up. When you do mapping work they get very, very stringent. It was a difficult mission for us, but we did it. We did some work in North Africa too, and we even did some archaeology work for some of the colleges in England to help them with their digs. From the air they could see outlines which were not readily discernible on the ground.

"On March 27, 1955, my squadron flew three deep-penetration missions over the Soviet Union. The pilots were Major Anderson, our squadron commander, and Captains Grigsby and Schamber. I was the radar navigator on Anderson's aircraft. Our copilot was First Lieutenant Flynn, and the gunner was Master Sergeant Bryant. The aircraft with the longest route, which was ours, had to recover in Germany for refueling. We didn't have enough fuel to make it back to Sculthorpe. Our routes were essentially the same as those flown by the Royal Air

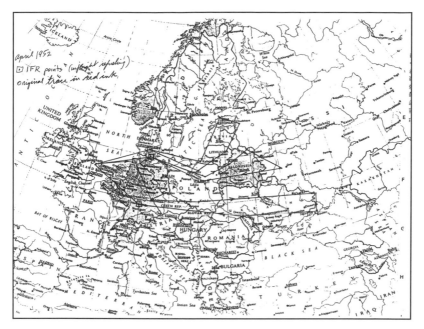

Routes flown by RAF and U.S. Air Force crews in RB-45C photo-reconnaissance aircraft based at RAF Sculthorpe, England, in 1952, 1954, and 1955. H. Myers.

Force in 1952 and 1954. Our mission planning was highly classified, very secret. We didn't know the routes of the other crews. It was all kept very quiet. Somebody else did all the map preparation and planning for us. We just took what Intelligence gave us. We didn't know until the last minute where we were going.

"The three of us took off reasonably close together. I remember a strange incident just as we were crossing the border into East Germany. We were not yet at our cruising altitude, still climbing to thirty-five thousand feet. The night was pitch-black. We had no lights on anywhere. Major Anderson said to the copilot, 'Did you see that? The plane going to the west.' There was a plane heading west as we were going east, pretty close to our altitude. His lights were out just like ours. I flew with my radar on for the entire mission. That was my primary means of navigation. I believe one of the things the Intelligence people were trying to do at the time, other than taking radarscope photography of assigned targets, was to find out what the Russians would do in the way of identifying and stopping us. I think it was important to find out if they would launch night fighters and what radars they would turn on to locate us. It was a coordinated effort to find out everything they had and could do. It was a dark night, and we didn't see any reaction other than the one airplane that passed us early in the flight. The same was true for the other crews: they encountered no hostile reaction from the Russians. Upon landing we were met at the airplane by Intelligence personnel, who took the radar film and every scrap of paper or map we had in our bags."

Like the RAF missions in 1952 and 1954, the three RB-45Cs from the 19th TRS did have an aerial refueling just prior to entry into Soviet-controlled airspace. Anderson's aircraft, flying the longer southern route, had to recover at Fürstenfeldbruck Air Base in Germany and return to Sculthorpe the following day. Anderson's flight was the last time such mass reconnaissance flights were flown over the western Soviet Union. All twelve crew members of the three RB-45Cs were awarded the Distinguished Flying Cross for extraordinary achievement while participating in aerial flight during 1955. Frank Martin's last flight in the RB-45 was on June 28, 1957. "It was a cool airplane. I liked the B-45," Frank said. Before returning to the United States in May 1958, Frank transitioned into the newer RB-66, which replaced the RB-45 in the TAC inventory. He returned to the Strategic Air Command and flew B-52s early in the Vietnam War before retiring to Maryland's Delmarva Peninsula, near Salisbury, to raise chickens.

Colonel Hack Mixson continued to serve for many years in the secret world of strategic reconnaissance. In 1955 he transferred to a supersecret reconnaissance program run by the CIA, piloting Kelly Johnson's high-flying U-2. Hack was involved in nearly every aspect of that program, from getting the aircraft operational, to hiring air crews, to flying them out of various locations in Germany, Japan, Thailand, and Pakistan. After five years of constantly being on the move with the U-2 program, Mixson assumed command of the 55th SRW, in which he had served as a young major in 1948 soon after being recalled to active duty. The wing had been reactivated and still operated out of Forbes AFB in Kansas, flying RB-47H electronic-reconnaissance aircraft. Hack retired from the air force in 1970 as commanding officer of the 100th SRW, a U-2 wing, at Davis-Monthan AFB, near Tucson, Arizona. He settled in Tampa, Florida, not too far from MacDill AFB and the occasional smell of jet fuel. As with so many of his generation's flyers, it was quite a ride. Hack Mixson went from a little forty-five-horsepower Aeronca via the B-24, RB-45, and RB-47 to the U-2 spy plane. "I loved every minute of it," Mixson said, "and every airplane I ever flew."

Chapter 11

Challenging the Russian Bear

President Eisenhower turned his attention to what he would
subsequently describe as "the most effective proposal of the [1955
Geneva Summit Conference] . . . mutual overflight by the U.S. and
USSR of each other's country as a technique of inspection, what became
known as the "open skies" plan. . . . He observed that in his opinion,
since the Russians already knew "the location of most of our
installations, mutual agreements for such overflights would undoubtedly
benefit us more than the Russians, because we know very little about
their installations."

Peter Lyon, *Eisenhower*

The fourth MiG . . . finally made a lucky hit as I was in a turn, through
the top of our left wing, about eight feet from the fuselage, through the
retracted wing flap. The shell exploded into the fuselage in the area of
the forward main fuel tank, right behind our crew compartment.

Hal Austin, RB-47E reconnaissance pilot

The Strategic Air Command was the creation of World War II
bomber General Curtis E. LeMay. Men such as Harold Austin popu-
lated the cockpits of SAC bombers and tankers during the 1950s and

'60s. It was a tightly knit, war-seasoned group of flyers who believed that no other flying command, sister service, or foreign air force could hold a candle to them. They were mostly survivors of epic World War II air battles over Europe, of B-29 raids against Japan, of the assembly-line flying of the Berlin Airlift, and, of course, of Korea. These combat-hardened survivors of adversity constituted the core of SAC air crews.

LeMay's heritage was German, like that of many other great American soldiers. In late 1942 LeMay, then a thirty-four-year-old colonel, took the 305th Bomb Group to England. Quickly determining that the current formations were suicidal, LeMay recalled how he climbed into the top turret of one of his airplanes, plugged into the radio extension, and personally placed each pilot in that formation (LeMay 234). This was the evolution of the wedge-shaped combat box finally adopted by everyone in the Eighth Air Force. LeMay's tactics allowed the obsolescent B-17 bombers to strike deep into the heart of Nazi Germany in broad daylight and survive. Although the Eighth Air Force took fearsome losses, the Americans prevailed. By the time the 29th Infantry Division landed on Omaha Beach, there was no Luftwaffe there to greet them, thanks to the Mighty Eighth. In 1944 LeMay transferred to the Pacific and took over B-29 operations against Japan. With single-minded resolve, he developed the tactics for B-29 raids against Japan. It seemed only natural for a man with such tactical genius and strategic vision to be selected to command the newly created Strategic Air Command, a combat command reporting directly to the Joint Chiefs of Staff in the Pentagon.

LeMay took over a mixed bag of aircraft and crews in 1948. By the time he relinquished command in 1957, SAC was as deadly as a cat at a mousehole. SAC was an air force within an air force and the envy of those who were not part of it. He built SAC in the image of his Eighth Air Force but many times more lethal. He focused on his people, who had been the key to his success in World War II and who would be the key to building SAC. When LeMay first took over SAC, he ran a maximum simulated bombing effort against Wright-Patterson AFB, near Dayton, Ohio, with the small force then at his disposal. He wanted to see how bad it really was. LeMay wrote later, "Our crews were not accustomed to flying at altitude. Neither were the airplanes, [as] far as that goes. Most of the pressurization wouldn't work, and the oxygen wouldn't work. Nobody seemed to know what life was like upstairs [above fifteen thousand feet]. . . . Not one airplane finished that mission as briefed. *Not one.*" Not only that, but during an inspection of a SAC mess LeMay found low quality even there. "Let any reader think of the many bad messes he must have encountered during World War II, and apply that to SAC in 1948–49, and he'll know what is meant. The s-on-s was there all right, and it wasn't even good s-on-s. Steaks obviously came from the nearest shoe repair shop; potatoes had been cooked in the laundry; the spaghetti and macaroni might have interested an entomologist or a herpetologist, but not any hungry customers" (LeMay 433, 437).

If LeMay's people were not properly trained, he knew it wasn't their fault. If their equipment was World War II leftovers, that wasn't their fault either, nor was the fact that they were poorly motivated and fed. He changed that. At its peak in the late 1950s and early 1960s, SAC was a force of nearly two thousand B-47, B-52, and B-58 all-jet bombers, supported by a large fleet of KC-97 and KC-135 tankers. The tankers allowed the bombers to strike anywhere in the world with predictable accuracy. The planes flew ever higher in the '50s to evade enemy defensive antiaircraft fire, and when the SA-2 SAM made its appearance, the flyers transitioned with equal ease to low-level attack profiles down to two hundred feet above the terrain.

If SAC's aircraft were the best the United States could build, the crews surely were among the best the United States could train. LeMay established a "lead crew" concept taken right from his Eighth Air Force playbook. A lead crew was designated an S-crew, a select crew. All other crews were designated E-crews, meaning that they were combat ready but were not lead crews. Select crews had to be the best in competition with all other crews in their wing, with a wing usually consisting of three flying squadrons each with fifteen aircraft. The bomb wings were rated on navigation and flying skills, including aerial refueling, time on target, how close their simulated bombs came to the target, and the employment of electronic countermeasures against simulated threat radars. Radar bomb scoring units, known as RBS sites, many located on railroad cars throughout the United States, served as the targets and impartial evaluators. Reconnaissance crews were rated in the same manner as bomber crews. Since these crews did not carry bombs, their crew ratings were determined by the quality of their photography and how accurately they acquired, analyzed, and located radars.

The select crews of each wing were assigned to the standardization and evaluation division (STANDBOARD), which at least once a year flight-checked each air crew and certified it combat ready. In no-notice exercises (cocoa alerts) personally ordered by the commander in chief of the Strategic Air Command, a wing's readiness was put to the test. Failure invariably lead to the wing commander's dismissal.

Readiness to fight on a moment's notice and performance by the book was SAC's credo. It seemed an almost Prussian application of discipline to American flyers in its demand for absolute obedience and following rules. It wasn't everyone's cup of tea. "SAC took the fun out of flying," said Colonel Ed Gorski. Many would agree with him. But SAC became incredibly powerful and effective as a peacekeeper in a nuclear world.

Colonel Harold R. Austin

Distinguished Flying Cross (2), Air Medal

Men such as Colonel Hal Austin were trained to fly anywhere, anytime, and prevail, without asking questions. Hal's turn came on May 8, 1954. By 1949 Hal Austin had become a charter member of the newly formed and rapidly expanding Strategic Air Command flying RB-45C reconnaissance aircraft, first out of Barksdale and later out of Lockbourne AFB. In those early years, he frequently deployed on TDYs to England. "Flying was a thrill in the nearly empty skies of postwar Europe. I never made more than two or three radio calls on an entire mission. In between those two or three calls, I flew at whatever altitude I chose. One of my jobs was to photomap the Rhine River basin and Spain. This was an important prerequisite for the future stationing of ballistic missiles in Europe. What a way to see Europe."

In 1953, still a member of the 91st Strategic Reconnaissance Wing at Lockbourne AFB, Hal Austin transitioned from the RB-45C to the more advanced RB-47E. "The B-47 was a sleek aircraft with swept wings, a raised cockpit which provided fighterlike visibility, and lots of speed. I loved flying the B-47. It was an aircraft of advanced design which eliminated many of the troublesome shortcomings of the RB-45C." The B-47 soon became the SAC mainstay. In April 1954 Crew S-51 of the 91st SRW, consisting of Captain Harold Austin, his copilot Captain Carl Holt, and Major Vance Heavilin, the radar navigator, deployed with seven other RB-47E photo-reconnaissance aircraft from Lockbourne to RAF Fairford. Fairford, near the campus of Oxford University, was a Battle of Britain base, many of which were used by SAC aircraft during the Cold War. Hal and his crew spent a couple of weeks familiarizing themselves with the area by flying short training flights and had enough time off to enjoy the nearby historic sights and the many offerings of London. The Columbia Officers' Club, a large mansion donated during the war by a patriotic and grateful Englishman, fronted Bayswater Road and sat across from Hyde Park. The club was conveniently located near Marble Arch and Speaker's Corner. There was no better and certainly no cheaper place to stay, and the three men took full advantage of the opportunity.

Fairford's March weather was exceptionally bad, and their group of eight RB-47s was recalled to Lockbourne after only two weeks. During the two weeks, however, they flew two long-range reconnaissance training missions against the island group of Spitsbergen, high above the Arctic Circle. Once Hal and his crew returned to Fairford in April, they again were directed to plan a flight to Spitsbergen. On May 6, 1954, Austin and five other RB-47E photo-reconnaissance aircraft took off in the early morning hours for their distant target. The countryside reverberated from the throaty roar of powerful jet engines until all six

RB-47E photo-reconnaissance aircraft at Lockbourne AFB, Ohio, getting ready for a morning launch, 1954. H. Austin.

B-47s faded into the morning mist. Slower KC-97 tankers had departed earlier that night to meet them at the prearranged rendezvous point off the coast of Norway. That evening at the local pub, some older Englishmen confessed over a glass of warm beer that they thought World War III had started when they heard those Yank airplanes taking off.

The six RB-47E reconnaissance bombers, outfitted with the same camera suite as in the RB-45C, flew in a loose trail formation called *station keeping* on a great circle route, north out of England. Past the Faroes, over open ocean, the bombers refueled from their waiting KC-97 tankers and continued northward between Jan Mayen and Bear Islands until reaching their target. When they turned their cameras on, the navigators noted in their logs that they were at eighty degrees north latitude, where the ice never melted. They were only miles from Soviet Franz Josef Land, just a few minutes' flying time east of Spitsbergen. The small crew of the lone Soviet Kniferest early warning radar on Franz Josef Land must have come to life when the American B-47s showed on their radar screen. But after the momentary excitement, even alarm, and after reporting the Americans to Murmansk control, with the blips again faded off their radar screens, the Soviets reverted to their monotonous existence on the Arctic ice.

The 3,500-mile flight took nearly nine hours of flying in an ejection seat, a seat not built for personal comfort. On returning to Fairford, the crews slid down the aluminum access ladders from their cramped cockpits, feeling every bone in their bodies. Time for a good stretch, a hot shower, and a yard of ale at the bar. But maintenance logs and numerous chores had to be completed before the flyers could leave the smell of JP4 jet fuel behind them. Austin and his crew didn't know that the feint they had just flown over Spitsbergen and the one earlier in March were major rehearsals for a mission Austin's crew was slated to fly two days later, on May 8. They also did not know that three RB-45Cs, manned by British crews, had flown a night reconnaissance mission deep into the western Soviet Union only ten days earlier.

"In the early morning hours of May 8, Carl, Vance, and I had an ample breakfast at the club. We stopped by the in-flight kitchen on our way to the secure briefing area to pick up three box lunches and two thermos bottles filled with hot coffee. It was going to be just one more mission. We intended to pick up our charts and then go out to the aircraft for preflight, have a short cigarette break, and get ready to launch. As we entered the secure briefing facility, we were met by our wing commander, Colonel Joe Preston. 'What does he want?' I thought. The colonel turned to me and said, 'Please follow me.' 'Yes, Sir,' I replied. We followed Colonel Preston into a classified briefing room built for target study for bomber crews, providing security from sophisticated listening devices. Colonel Preston held the door for us as we entered the room, which was definitely out of the ordinary. He closed the door behind us and left. In the briefing room were two colonels from SAC headquarters. The colonels had no smiles on their faces and immediately got down to business. One of them, a navigator, handed Heavilin a strip map. We looked it over and saw where our flight was to take us—over the Kola Peninsula past Murmansk, southeast to Arkhangel'sk, then southwest before turning west across Finland and Sweden back to Fairford. We were stunned.

" 'Please sit down, gentlemen,' said the second colonel. He wore pilot wings. Neither colonel wore a name tag on his blue Class-A uniform. 'I will give you your mission brief, weather, and intelligence. You will photograph nine airfields as annotated on your maps.' Later I learned that the purpose of the mission was to determine if the Soviets had deployed their new Bison bombers to any of these fields. 'You will launch in a stream of six aircraft, just as you did on the 6th. Three aircraft will fly the Spitsbergen route. You and two others will proceed to your turning point one hundred miles north of Murmansk. You, Captain Austin, are number three. The other two will turn back at that point. You will proceed on your preplanned mission. The entire mission from taxi to exit from the hostile area will be flown in complete radio silence—no tower calls, no reporting back when reaching altitude, no radio contact with the tankers, no radio calls if anyone has to abort. Radio silence is essential to the success of this mission.'

"Then the pilot colonel reviewed the weather at the altitudes we were supposed to fly, the camera turn-on points noted on the strip maps, and he briefed us on expected opposition. 'Only MiG-15s,' he said. 'They can't reach you at forty thousand feet. No contrails are expected to form in the areas you will be passing over.' That information was important to us if we didn't want to streak across the sky looking like a Times Square ad. 'You'll be flying through a clear air mass. The weather couldn't be better for this mission.' The briefing over, Heavilin started to annotate his chart. 'Don't do that,' directed the navigator colonel. 'Everything you need to know is on those charts.' The two SAC colonels measured their words carefully, only saying what needed saying. They answered no questions and offered no additional comments to us. On the way out, one of the colonels reemphasized the need for absolute security before and after we returned from our mission. We would not discuss any aspect of the mission outside a cleared area, we were given to understand, nor with anyone not having a need to know. No talk about the mission, period.

"Colonel Preston met us as we exited the building and drove us to our aircraft. An air crew was already there, just finishing preflight. From the looks of it, they were none too happy to have been asked to do our job. As they slid down the ladder from the crew compartment, the pilot said to me, 'The aircraft is cocked'—a bomber term—and he, his copilot, and his navigator walked to their crew car without saying another word and drove off. We climbed into the aircraft and strapped into our seats. Every one of us was quiet, I recall, tending to our own thoughts."

Major Heavilin noted that his map had been annotated with radar offset points, such as lakes and other natural and man-made features, that would show well on his radarscope. Austin was number six in line, last for takeoff. "I taxied after number five moved out. Number one lined up at the end of the runway, set his brakes, and ran up his engines. The other five aircraft sat in line on the taxiway, waiting to take their turn on the active. When number one received the green light from the tower, he released his brakes, and the aircraft slowly moved down the runway. The other RB-47s launched at two-minute intervals, buffeted by the violent jet wash from the preceding aircraft. When I took the active, a trail of black smoke from the exhaust of the other five pointed the way for me."

Takeoff data computations were in front of Austin and Holt, strapped to their thighs. They were a team, no longer individuals. Prompts and responses were automatic. As the copilot, Holt called the checklist:

"Throttles."

"Open. All instruments checked," Austin responded. Austin slowly moved the six throttles to 100 percent. Oil pressure was within operating limits, he noted, glancing down the row of gauges on his instrument panel. Fuel flow was stabilized. He checked the EGT for all six engines at 100 percent. The EGTs were within limits.

"Steering ratio selector lever."

"Takeoff and land."

"Start, six lights out." Austin released the brakes of the shuddering aircraft, which began its slow roll down the twelve thousand–foot concrete runway. Carl Holt quickly turned left and right and checked the engines. He saw black smoke coming from all six and reported to Austin, "Engines and wings checked."

They continued their takeoff roll. When the aircraft reached seventy knots, Holt called out, "Seventy knots now." Heavilin responded, "Hack." Fourteen seconds later, their acceleration good, Heavilin called out "S-one, now." Decision speed—their last chance to ground abort. Austin's eyes were on his EGT gauges, compass, and airspeed indicator. Temperatures looked good. Speed looked good. They continued their takeoff roll. He held the aircraft down: it wanted to climb because of ground effect before it had sufficient airspeed to sustain flight—a novice trap that had cost lives. Austin could feel the plane grasping for its element. At the 7,500-foot marker, the 180,000-pound craft strained to rise, and Austin let it go. "Unstick," he called. The nose rose slightly, and the aircraft began its long climb heavenward. Climb speed was looking good, Austin noted mentally.

"Landing gear," Austin called, and Holt placed the gear lever in the up position. They were at 185 knots indicated and gaining speed.

"Flaps." Holt put the flap lever in the up position and kept his hand on it, simultaneously watching the airspeed. They were at 210 knots at 20 percent flaps, and he continued flap retraction. The aircraft's nose started to pitch down, but Hal had already cranked in nose-up trim and smoothed out the predictable perturbation.

"Climb speed," Holt called.

"Climb power set." Hal set it to 375 knots indicated. They continued with their checklist as they climbed straight ahead to thirty-four thousand feet. Their mission didn't officially exist. They had filed no flight plan, which was nothing new to understanding British air traffic controllers. Holt continued to check that the HF radio was on, the APS-54 radar warning receiver was set to the nose/tail position, the chaff dispensers were on, and the IFF was on standby. He called, "Altimeters."

"Set, Pilot."

"Set, Nav."

They reset their altimeters to 29.92 inches of mercury. When they passed over open water, Holt tested his guns. They fired. "I guess it's a go," Holt said over the intercom. Hal clicked his mike button twice on the control column in response. A little more than one hour into their flight, the navigator picked up the tankers on his radar at the briefed air-refueling orbit and gave Hal a heading and altitude. The tanker pilot saw Hal approaching from above and departed the orbit for his refueling track. At the two-mile point, Hal pulled back on the throttles to decrease his rate of closure. They were five hundred feet below the tanker and slowly eased in behind the KC-97 Stratocruiser, its four engines churning at maximum power in a slight descent. Hal looked up at the tanker looming ahead and above and moved into the observation position. He watched for light direction from the boom operator—two amber, one green, two red lights on the belly of the large KC-97. He saw the forward amber light come on, urging him to move in closer. He moved in slowly. The green light illuminated, and he held in the contact position. He could see the boom operator in the tanker flying his boom toward the open refueling receptacle on the nose of the RB-47, right in front of his face. The aircraft pitched in the wake of the turbulence generated by the KC-97.

"Contact," Hal muttered into his oxygen mask. Normally, he would have said it out in the open. Not that day. The green light illuminated on the air refueling panel, and Austin and Holt knew they had a good contact. The tanker transferred fuel into the empty tanks of the receiver at the rate of four thousand pounds per minute until all of the RB-47's internal fuel tanks were full, causing an automatic pressure disconnect. Hal dropped away from the tanker, saluted the boom operator, and initiated a climb to thirty-four thousand feet to rejoin his two companion aircraft. Three lone RB-47s, high above the cold Atlantic waters. Soon someone would pick them up on radar. Time passed slowly. The aircraft was on autopilot. Not much for any of them to do but listen to the static on the HF radio for a possible recall. No recall came. The three aircraft turned east toward the Barents Sea. Hal, Carl, and Vance got out their box lunches and ate their ham and turkey sandwiches and hard-boiled eggs, drank their cold milk, and put their apples aside to be eaten later, if there was time. They had coffee. They were at forty thousand feet.

"How much further to the turn?" Hall asked his navigator.

"Oh, four minutes and thirty seconds, I'd say," Vance replied.

They put on their oxygen masks, tight. The cabin pressure was at fourteen thousand feet. Should they get hit and lose pressurization, anything loose would be flying into their faces, so they made sure everything was tied down, buttoned, zipped, or out of the way.

"On my command, turn to a heading of one-eight-zero." Hal clicked his mike button in response to the navigator's direction. "Turn now," the navigator called out to Hal. The big aircraft turned surprisingly easily toward the Kola Peninsula, the Soviet Union. The other two RB-47s preceding them made their 180-degree turns to the left, away from the land, and headed home. "We coasted in over the Kola Peninsula at forty thousand feet at twelve noon Greenwich mean time," said Hal Austin, looking at the floor. His voice was terse, his facial muscles tight. "We were about four thousand feet above our optimum altitude for our weight. Our first targets were two large airfields near Murmansk. The navigator turned on his radar cameras at the coast-in point and started the three K-17 large-area visual cameras in the bomb bay. The weather was clear as a bell. You could see forever. Perfect picture-taking weather."

Carl Holt also remembered that moment well. He looked back from his position behind the pilot, and what he saw did not make his heart jump for joy. "It was a clear day as we coasted into the Soviet Union. Suddenly, we started to generate contrails like six white arrows pointing to our airplane. As we passed over our first target, I could see the fighters circling up to meet us, and I knew it would only be a matter of time before they reached our altitude."

"About the time we finished photographing the second airfield near Murmansk," Hal continued, "we were joined by a flight of three Soviet MiG-15s. I don't know whether or not they were armed. I don't believe they were. They kept their distance and stayed about half a mile off our wing. About twenty-five minutes later, another flight of six MiGs showed up. These too were MiG-15s, appeared to be unarmed, and kept their distance. I guess they confirmed we were the bad guys. A few minutes after their arrival, another two flights of three each arrived behind us with obvious intent to try to shoot us down. By this time we had photographed five of our assigned target airfields and were turning southwest near Arkhangel'sk toward our last four targets. We had been over Soviet territory for an hour. We had been briefed that the MiG-15 would not be able to do any damage to us at forty thousand feet with our airspeed at 440 knots. Well, you can imagine what we called those Intelligence weenies as the first Soviet MiG-17, not a MiG-15, made a firing pass at us from the left rear and we saw cannon tracer shells going above and below our aircraft. And the MiG was still moving out rather smartly as he passed under us in front. 'Enough of this forty thousand feet stuff,' I thought. I pushed the RB-47 over, descending a couple thousand feet and picking up about twenty knots indicated airspeed in the process."

Carl Holt remembered, "When I saw the flashes of fire from the nose of the fighters, I knew it would not be a milk run. I had trouble getting the tail guns to fire, and since I was in a reverse seat position, I could not eject in case of a direct hit. Also, the radar firing screen would not work [because the MiGs stayed outside the RB-47's radar envelope], so I felt a little like Wyatt Earp, looking out the back end of the canopy and firing at will. I did not hit any of the fighters, but it kept them out of a direct rear firing pass. They could only make passes from either side at a greater than forty-five-degree angle to stay outside the area covered by our guns."

"The second MiG-17," Hal Austin said, "made his firing pass, and I don't care who knows, it was scary watching tracers go over and under our aircraft. This guy had almost come up our tailpipes. Carl Holt turned around to operate our tail guns after the first MiG shot at us. It was typical for the two remotely controlled 20mm cannons not to fire. I told Holt he'd better kick them or something, because if our guns didn't fire the next SOB would come directly up our tailpipes. Fortunately, when the third MiG started its pass, our guns burped for a couple of seconds. General LeMay did not believe in tracers for our guns, but the Soviet pilots must have seen something, because the third guy broke off his pass and the flight of six, and the next flight of six MiG-17s which joined us later stayed about thirty to forty degrees to the side, outside the effective envelope of our guns. Of course, the MiGs didn't know that our guns wouldn't fire again.

"The fourth MiG of the second group of MiG-17s finally made a lucky hit as I was in a turn, through the top of our left wing, about eight feet from the fuselage, through the retracted wing flap. The shell exploded into the fuselage in the area of the forward main fuel tank, right behind our crew compartment, knocking out our intercom. We felt a good *whap* as the shell exploded, and all three of us were a little bit anxious—scared is a better word—but we continued to do our mission as briefed, basically because of habit. I firmly believe that's what good, tough, LeMay-type SAC training did for his combat crews. Later we also discovered the shell had hit our UHF radio. It would no longer channelize, meaning it was stuck on channel 13, our command-post frequency, which we had on the set at the time."

"After we were hit in the left wing and fuselage," recalled Carl Holt, "one MiG tried to ram us by sideslipping his fighter into our aircraft. On one ramming pass, he stalled out right under our aircraft, and our vertical camera took one of the first close-up pictures of the new MiG-17."

"By then we had covered our last photo target," Austin continued, "and turned due west toward Finland to get the hell out of there. The six MiGs which dogged us since Arkhangel'sk must have run short of fuel. They left. Six others appeared to take their place, two of whom initiated firing passes but didn't hit anything. After those two made their unsuccessful passes, the third came up on our right side, close enough to shake hands, and sat there for two or three minutes. As we departed the area south of Helsinki, Finland, he gave us a salute and then turned back toward the Soviet Union."

"We proceeded to cross neutral Sweden, then Norway. Over the North Sea, we headed south-southwest, looking for our tanker," Hal Austin recalled, but "our excitement for this mission was not over by any means. An airborne standby KC-97 tanker was holding for us about fifty miles from Stavanger, Norway. We really weren't sure how the damage to our left wing and fuselage would affect fuel consump-

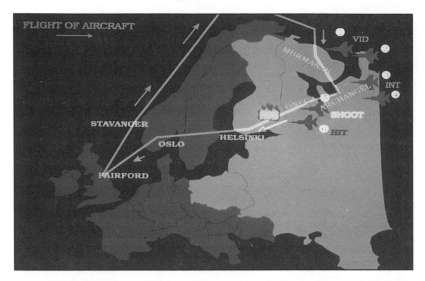

Route of Austin's May 8, 1954, overflight of the Soviet Union. The various points at which MiGs attempted to shoot him down are shown. The last attempt was over Finland. H. Austin.

tion. Initially, it didn't look bad. As we came into UHF radio range of the tanker, I heard him calling in the blind on command-post common, the only frequency we had available on our radio. He came in garbled. His transmission was breaking up. We were running about thirty minutes behind schedule, and I heard the tanker pilot say that he was leaving his orbit at the scheduled time. I tried frantically to acknowledge his call, but when I later spoke to the tanker pilot he said he never heard me. Of course they had not been briefed about our mission, but they were aware that six RB-47s went through refueling areas that morning and that only five had returned. Usually they were smart enough to figure out the situation.

"As we coasted out of Norway, it was obvious we had fallen behind the fuel curve. I climbed to forty-three thousand feet and throttled back to maximum-range cruise. I thought we could get back to a base in England, not necessarily Fairford. We knew there was a tanker on strip alert at RAF Mildenhall awaiting our call. Carl Holt had spent much of the time since the last MiGs departed sitting in the aisle below me, acting as the intercom between me and the navigator. You don't realize how handy the intercom is until you don't have one. Holt was monitoring our fuel consumption and beginning to panic as we reached a point about 150 miles from the Wash. Carl wasn't afraid for himself. He was worried about losing our film. He said to me, 'All this effort was for nothing if we have to bail out of the airplane and have no film for Intelligence to process.' He was right. At one hundred miles off the Wash, I started calling for the strip tanker from Mildenhall to launch. Jim Rigley, the tanker pilot, later said to me, 'I heard a word or two of your transmission, enough to recognize your voice.' He was one of our tanker guys from Lockbourne. We all knew each other. He attempted to get permission to launch. The tower wouldn't give permission because the RAF had an emergency of some sort working at nearby RAF Brize Norton. Rigley announced that he was launching, and he did. When he returned to base, the local American commander, a colonel, threatened him with a courts-martial and British air-traffic control gave him a violation. Both situations were later fixed by General LeMay.

"In all my nine years of flying up to that time, I was never more thrilled to see another airplane in the air than I was to see that beautiful KC-97 tanker. As soon as I saw Rigley's airplane, I headed straight for him. We as a crew already decided to try to land at Brize Norton and were in the process of letting down when I spotted Rigley. At the same time, Holt looked at our gas gauges from the aisle below me and yelled, 'We're going to run out of gas.' The gauges were analog gauges and usually moved a little if there was still fuel remaining in a tank. None of the gauges moved, and Holt was sure we were about to flame out. In the meantime, Rigley had his crew looking upward, searching for a glimpse of us. They caught a glint of what they thought was our airplane rapidly descending toward them. Rigley leveled off at three thousand feet, heading south, toward land. He was positioned perfectly to allow me to use an old RB-45 refueling maneuver. Since we had no way to slow that aircraft down other than pulling back on the throttles, we came up from behind the tanker, flew below him, and then got on his tail in a climbing turn. This bled off the airspeed in the RB-45. The

211

old maneuver worked perfectly. When I pulled up behind the lumbering KC-97, its engines were giving all they could to keep us from stalling. The boomer skillfully flew his boom into our refueling receptacle.

" 'Contact,' Holt called out to me. 'We are taking on fuel. All gauges show empty.'

"Tell me when we have twelve thousand pounds, Carl."

" 'Now,' Holt called out at the top of his lungs, still sitting below me in the aisle.

"I punched the boom loose, gave the boom operator a salute, and headed for Fairford. I got down to five hundred feet and buzzed the control tower. They gave us a green light to land. When we reached the ramp and brought the aircraft to a stop, the crew chief was the first up the ladder. He saw the damage we sustained. 'What kind of seagull did you hit, Sir?' he shouted at me. I smiled back at him. I couldn't give him a straight answer. Colonel Preston met us at the aircraft. We jumped into his staff car, and he took us to our quarters, where we took a quick shower and changed into Class-A blues. Then he drove us to London and we met with the U.S. ambassador to Great Britain at his home. The ambassador greeted us cordially and offered us a drink. Then he whispered, 'Let's go outside. I think my house is bugged.' The next morning my crew flew back to Lockbourne. I took another guy's RB-47E to get back since mine obviously needed repairs. We arrived at Lockbourne in the afternoon, and the following morning we took a B-25 base flight aircraft and flew to Offutt—headquarters SAC at Omaha, Nebraska. The commander in chief himself, General LeMay, wanted to attend our mission debriefing. We met in a room in the old Douglas aircraft plant because the new SAC headquarters was still under construction. It was a three-hour meeting. The first question the general asked was, 'How come they didn't shoot you down?'

" 'I guess they didn't have the guts,' was my answer to him. There was no doubt in my mind that the MiG-17 pilots could have shot us down if they had been willing to come right up our tailpipes. General LeMay responded, 'There are probably several openings today in command positions there, since you were not shot down.' "

Carl Holt also reflected on that occasion. "Having flown combat in World War II and later been recalled during the Korean War, I thought we were in a Cold War with Russia, not a hot one, since all the reconnaissance plane shootdowns had been kept secret. During our debriefing with General LeMay, I said to him innocently, 'Sir, they were trying to shoot us down!' Smoking his usual long cigar, the general paused, leaned back in his chair, and said, 'What did you think they would do? Give you an ice cream cone?' His aides smiled. I was serious. I didn't smile."

Three months after the debriefing of crew S-51 at Offutt, General LeMay visited Lockbourne, where he was met by the wing commander. After the usual saluting back and forth, the general came right to the point of his visit. He wanted to meet with Captain Austin, Captain Holt, and Major Heavilin. When they arrived, he asked the wing commander to leave. General LeMay decorated each member of crew S-51 with two Distinguished Flying Crosses, in lieu of the Silver Star, for their reconnaissance flight over the Soviet Union. According to Austin, the general apologized, saying, "The award of the Silver Star had to be approved in Washington, which could cause two problems: first, they'd get the thing screwed up, and, second, I'd have to explain this mission to too damn many people who don't need to know." Hal asked if they could see their photography. The answer was "no." But to the question, "How did we do?" the general answered, "You got all targets."

Colonel Austin's epic May 8, 1954, overflight of the Kola Peninsula accomplished at least two things. First and foremost, it assured the American military and political leadership that the Soviet Union had not massed its new jet bombers at potential staging bases on the Kola Peninsula. The second, although unintended, result was to again point out reconnaissance aircraft's vulnerability to shootdown. The RB-47 could not fly high enough to escape the MiG-17's cannon fire, and even more capable Soviet aircraft would soon follow. Alternative solutions had to be found. The higher-flying U-2 reconnaissance plane was an interim solution itself, and by 1960, technology caught up with it, too, when SAMs demonstrated that they could reach its sixty thousand–foot

operating altitude. Earth-orbiting satellites, as well as the remarkable high-altitude Mach 3 SR-71, eventually provided the necessary solutions. But in 1954 it took the courage of men such as Hal Austin, Carl Holt, and Vance Heavilin to fly over the Soviet Union to provide the United States the critical information needed to defend itself.

Hal Austin at his home in Riverside, California, holding the framed cutout from his RB-47E where the MiG-17 cannon shell impacted, December 1998. W. Samuel.

Chapter 12

Flying the Top of the World

To this day, the SAC Thule missions remain one of the most incredible demonstrations of professional aviation skill ever seen in any military organization at any time.

R. Cargill Hall, "The Truth about Overflights"

We launched up to five tankers an hour before we took off, to be able to take the fuel off of at least three of them. One tanker usually developed engine problems and had to turn around before he got to the refueling area. . . . At the final refueling point, high over the polar ice cap, they could only give us ten thousand pounds each if they wanted to make it back to Thule themselves. . . . We loved our tanker buddies, who were always there when we needed them. They could only surmise what we were doing or where we were going, but they knew after flying ten hours or more we had covered five thousand nautical miles.

Joe Gyulavics, RB-47H reconnaissance pilot

The Cold War had some truly cold aspects to it, speaking from a climatological perspective. Waged from air bases near or above the Arctic Circle, the U.S. long-range reconnaissance war against the Soviet

215

Union was essential to ensure national security. The two principal air bases from which the polar-region reconnaissance missions were flown were Eielson AFB near Fairbanks, Alaska, just below the Arctic Circle, and Thule Air Base, on Danish Greenland, at approximately seventy-eight degrees north latitude, on Baffin Bay. Both man and machine were put to severe tests in winter. Flyers and maintenance men who served in these inhospitable climes never forgot the conditions under which they had to get aircraft ready to fly, especially at Thule. Cold froze the inside of the nose when anyone stepped out of a vehicle or a building. Vehicle tires shattered like glass. Static electricity dogged nearly every move made in the dry Arctic air.

In temperatures below minus forty degrees Fahrenheit, the simplest function became difficult to execute. Closing a valve or opening a hatch, operations that under normal conditions required little thought, became difficult to perform and were carefully planned. Aircraft landing at Thule could close the airfield with ice fog for hours or even days at a time. To maintain aircraft in such a hostile environment and to fly them routinely were challenges that required skill, perseverance, and a little bit of luck. Cabin fever, combined with deep boredom, became another enemy. Given enough time and the right circumstances, such conditions could drive a man to the edge of his sanity.

At Thule the 55th Strategic Reconnaissance Wing maintained Operating Location 5 (OL-5) in support of its RB-47H electronic-reconnaissance flights. On occasion, RB-47E photo-reconnaissance aircraft from Lockbourne also operated from Thule. A comparable setup existed at Eielson AFB in Alaska, where the 55th SRW maintained OL-3. From these two locations, the 55th SRW launched year-round electronic-reconnaissance flights. Life in the remote and hostile Arctic world was controlled by the environment. Each building at Thule was built like a cold-storage vault, with large icehouse-type doors and triple foot-thick walls perched on three-foot-high pillars. Many buildings had their own water supply, delivered by truck and pumped into fresh-water tanks. Water used for washing was drained into an intermediate tank and then reused to flush toilets. The final waste was eventually pumped into a truck and shipped out. In the spring, snow and ice melted, including mounds of frozen human waste from truck spills and water that had accumulated as a result of the constant drip, drip, drip from access pipes. The ensuing putrid smell often pervaded the entire air base. Colonel Joe Gyulavics, an RB-47H pilot who flew out of Thule on several occasions, put it this way: "It was pretty gruesome living."

Water was a precious commodity and was used sparingly when the winds were blowing. It wasn't that water was scarce; to the contrary, there was plenty available from a nearby freshwater lake. The problem was delivery. Water was delivered by truck. When the winds were blowing or when the base was closed by ice fog, the trucks could not operate, and each building had to make do with what water was available in its tanks. Showers were short. None of the luxuries of the lower forty-eight states applied at Thule. Going to the toilet was frequently a dreaded undertaking. Manual flap-valve pumps were used to pump waste water into the toilet. The user then had to manually pump the waste into a tank. This required frequent opening and closing of valves, and the pumps frequently backfired and splattered waste onto the individual. The only flush urinal on Thule was in the Officers' Club, which didn't open until three o'clock in the afternoon. Lieutenant Colonel Bruce Bailey, a 55th Wing Raven who flew out of Thule, recalled, "We sat around with our legs crossed, miserable, in pain, and unable to stand straight when the time came, waiting for the club to open."

Another Thule phenomenon was the suddenly arising winds, referred to as "phases." The intensity of the Arctic winds was defined in terms of their velocity—phase I, II, III, and IV. Phase IV winds were the most dangerous, threatening human life and requiring outdoor activity to come to an immediate halt. Phase II and III winds closed down flying operations, and Phase I winds resulted in a warning to air crews attempting to land at Thule. In actuality, any phase usually resulted in the closing of the base and outdoor activity coming to a halt. It wasn't just the winds that closed the base but also the accompanying loss of visibility due to blowing snow and the danger of freezing to death. The transition from lower to higher, more dangerous wind velocities could occur quickly. An effective warning system was devised by using the base radio station, KOLD, which operated twenty-four hours a day. Everyone working outdoors carried a small portable radio to receive warnings. Phase wind warnings and freeze notices were announced on KOLD. Warnings such as "Flesh will begin to freeze in forty-five seconds," were common. Warnings considered not only the outside air temperature but also the windchill factor. In anticipation of the sudden occurrence of a phase, every building was stocked with water and emergency food. Once a phase hit, it was nearly impossible to go anywhere.

The final hazard at northern locations was psychological. The dark season played with a man's mind. At seventy-seven degrees north latitude, darkness was a significant factor. "Some people," noted Colonel Charles Phillips, "suffered severe psychological problems during the November-February period. On the shortest day of the year, December 21–22, if the weather was clear, I could see a glimmer of light to the south for a few minutes at noon. Otherwise it was dark around the clock." Colonel Gyulavics recalled, "We had slot machines in the Officers' Club which could keep people busy for hours. And there were free movies every night. But it got to where we didn't even bother to go to see a movie anymore. We adapted as best we could. A few came close to the edge, but I am not aware of anyone actually breaking under the stress of living at Thule."

Thule-based reconnaissance flights over the Soviet Union were long and required tanker support. "At times, we took off from Thule and recovered at Eielson. A few days later we would fly a mission in reverse and recover at Thule," Joe Gyulavics recalled. "Long means that the flights were over nine hours in duration. Over nine hours meant that the air crew had to sit in their ejection seats for that entire period of time. Into the early '60s tanker support was provided to the RB-47s by KC-97 aircraft. For a reconnaissance mission flying over the polar ice cap to reach its targets in the Laptev and Kara Seas usually required the support of several KC-97s. Refueling was critical. We launched up to five tankers an hour before we took off, to be able to take the fuel off of at least three of them. One tanker usually developed engine problems and had to turn around before he got to the refueling area. Sometimes two wouldn't make it. I worked out light signals with the tanker crews, since we never used our radios on these flights, so if I met one or two of them heading back prematurely, I would get behind them and take whatever fuel they could off-load. At the final refueling point, high over the polar ice cap, they could only give us ten thousand pounds each if they wanted to make it back to Thule themselves. On the return leg, we didn't refuel, so we had to have enough fuel to make it back on our own. To rely on a refueling was too risky because of possible high winds or unexpected ice fogs. We loved our tanker buddies, who were always there when we needed them. They could only surmise what we were doing or where we were going, but they knew that after flying ten hours or more we had covered five thousand nautical miles."

In 1956 Project Homerun was flown out of Thule between March 21 and May 10. The operation was top secret, and not even the participating air crews were fully aware of its scope. During that period, sixteen RB-47E photo-reconnaissance aircraft from the 10th SRW at Lockbourne teamed with four RB-47H electronic-reconnaissance aircraft from the 55th SRW at Forbes to photograph and electronically record the entire north polar region well into the Siberian interior. The region from the Kola Peninsula across the Kara and Laptev Seas to the Bering Strait was the target area. Two squadrons of KC-97 tankers provided the necessary air-refueling support. The air crews lived under Arctic conditions aggravated by the number of men stationed there. They flew from a snow- and ice-covered ten thousand–foot runway barely discernible from the surrounding fields of ice and snow. All missions were flown in absolute radio silence.

"The unique thing about Thule," Joe Gyulavics continued, "was landing on a snow-packed runway. At low temperatures, it really was no problem. You could practically brake on the cold snowpack like it was concrete. Of course, you had to be judicious about it. If you steered too fast, you kept on going, as if you were in a car on ice. Our antiskid brakes helped. In spring, when there was melting, it could get touchy at times. Getting ready to take off one time, I taxied up to a little apron near the lip of the runway. There was a slight uphill grade, and two KC-97s sat on the apron before me, running their engines, melting some of the snow. When I came up the incline, it had turned to slick ice. I couldn't see the ice from the cockpit. All of a sudden, the airplane started sliding backward and sideways. I had no control. On a tandem gear, this was not a pleasant experience. The nose was rotating, and there were snowbanks all around. I hit the number one and two engines and swung around, hoping I wouldn't damage the wingtips or run the tail into a snowbank. I finally managed to swing her around. When we returned from that mission, the crew chief found a sizable dent in the left wingtip. Things like that only happened at Thule."

"Thule Air Base itself was adjacent to a Danish headquarters and weather station," Charlie Phillips recounted, "and seventy-five miles from the nearest Eskimo village, Qanaq. When the once-remote Danish weather station at Thule was expanded to become an American air base, the Eskimos living there were relocated to the newly built village of Qanaq, located on a beach next to the ocean north of Thule to accommodate both summer and winter hunting and fishing. We had virtually no contact with the Eskimos."

Only once during two deployments to Thule did Joe Gyulavics meet an Eskimo. "It was in 1956 during Project Homerun. We test fired our guns as soon as we leveled off, about thirty to forty minutes out. You think you are out there with nothing but snow and ice beneath you from frozen horizon to horizon. Because of the total darkness, we couldn't see anything. You can imagine my surprise when after landing one day I was asked if I test fired my guns. Yeah, I answered, we do on every mission at the same place. A couple of Eskimos had come in to the Danish Council carrying several 20mm shell casings. 'They fell from the sky,' the Eskimos said. Even near the North Pole, you couldn't be sure there wasn't someone out there."

During project Homerun, crews fought outside temperatures of forty degrees below zero Fahrenheit or lower with fur-lined parkas, bulky mittens, heavily padded flight suits, and clumsy mukluk boots. Maintenance people had a particularly difficult time with tasks that required them to remove their bulky Arctic mittens. One man held a stopwatch with a second hand, while the other man worked. They completed tasks in stages, switching off to keep their fingers from getting frostbitten. Photo- and electronic-reconnaissance aircraft frequently operated in pairs, with an RB-47E photo aircraft teamed with an RB-47H electronic-reconnaissance aircraft. However, the planes did not fly in formation or even in sight of one another. All air crews were briefed individually, and because of a strictly applied need-to-know security rule, no air crew knew exactly where the others were going. The Thule missions of 1956 photomapped the islands of Novaya Zemlya and their atomic test site. These aircraft flew behind the Ural Mountains and across Siberia and confirmed that the Soviet Union's northern regions were poorly defended against air attack. Subsequently, many of the SAC bomber routes against the Soviet Union were planned to cross the top of the world. Throughout this difficult operation, not one RB-47 was lost as a result of accident or Soviet fighters. Not that the Soviets didn't try on occasion. Joe Gyulavics remembered "a bunch of fighters coming up out of Novaya Zemlya. We heard them launch. The Ravens picked up the fighter radars on their receivers. I saw the contrails of the Russian fighters, but they couldn't overtake us. An interesting time. We thought we were invincible and immortal. We never thought of any downside."

Colonel Charles L. Phillips Jr.

Distinguished Flying Cross (3), Air Medal

Lieutenant Colonel Charles L. Phillips was assistant director of operations for the 4083rd Strategic Wing at Thule in 1958. Charlie was a World War II veteran, like so many of the air crew who served in SAC. In 1945 he flew twenty-nine combat missions against Japan in B-29s out of Saipan, dropping firebombs from altitudes too low for high-

221

altitude antiaircraft guns to be effective and too high for Japanese automatic weapons fire to reach. That tactic was one of General LeMay's innovations. In the process, pilots discovered the jet stream, which could almost bring to a standstill a B-29 bomber flying into the wind. Charlie's missions had been grueling fifteen-hour flights, and he sympathized with the RB-47 reconnaissance crews, which flew similarly lengthy missions out of Thule. Charlie had been able to get out of his seat to stretch aching muscles, but the RB-47 crew had no such luxury.

Charlie Phillips was born to Presbyterian missionaries on July 6, 1918, in Pyongyang, Korea. He attended the local American school, whose students came from Korea, Japan, and Japanese-occupied provinces in China. The school sat on the downwind leg of a Japanese flying school, and Charlie used to visit the base and watch the Japanese planes taxi and take off. He developed an early interest in flying. On one occasion, he saw from his classroom window the propeller coming off a plane that had just taken off. Next, the engine fell off the plane. The pilot parachuted. Charlie and a friend ran out of their class to help the pilot, who landed in an adjacent field. The schoolmaster did not take kindly to such wild enthusiasm and moved Charlie's desk away from the window. In 1931, on a visit to the United States, Charlie's father took him and his brother for a twenty-minute airplane ride in a Waco cabin plane. For Charlie it was an unforgettable experience—he loved the feeling of flying and the view of the world it gave him. He wondered how he could become a pilot. In 1935, after graduating from high school, Charlie returned to the United States and entered UCLA. In 1940 he joined the Army Air Corps, earning his pilot wings and a commission as second lieutenant just five weeks before the Japanese attack on Pearl Harbor.

While at Thule, Phillips recalled, "I lay on my cot in BOQ 713, listening to the howling winds outside. I thought of my next-to-last combat mission, my twenty-eighth, which I flew on August 6, 1945, the day the first atomic bomb was dropped on Hiroshima. I ran out of fuel after an unexpected encounter with the jet stream and had to ditch my aircraft. I was apprehensive about putting the big bomber in the calm waters of the Pacific. My crew tumbled about considerably when I did, but fortunately only one of us was severely injured. On August 9 the second atomic bomb was dropped by a B-29 from Tinian. Still, peace negotiations with the Japanese dragged on. On August 14, I launched along with three hundred other B-29s against the Japanese army arsenal at Osaka. I expected to be recalled any moment because I thought a peace agreement was imminent, but it didn't happen. We dropped our lethal load of high-explosive bombs and watched as the Japanese arsenal below us was reduced to rubble. Shortly after we landed at Saipan, the Japanese surrendered. I know it was August 14, 1945, in the United States, the fifteenth on Saipan."

When Thule closed and an aircraft had to divert to an alternate or emergency airfield, few options were available. The most practical choice open to a pilot was emergency airfields on Greenland itself, fields that offered a minimum of support and required a maximum of pilot skill. Recovering aircraft from emergency airfields such as Weather Station Nord became a major operation fraught with risk to the aircraft as well as the maintenance crews who tried to get the marooned jet airborne again. One such emergency landing occurred in April 1958 at Station Nord, on the northeast tip of Greenland. An RB-47H, tail number 3-0281, of the 55th Wing and piloted by Captain Kenney Addison, was returning from a routine reconnaissance mission along the Siberian frontier when Thule closed for phase III winds. The winds blew across the runway at a right angle and resulted in zero-zero conditions—zero visibility, zero ceiling. Either the severe crosswinds or the limited visibility was enough to keep the RB-47 from landing. Only two practical alternatives offered themselves to the tired air crew. One was Sondrestrom, on the west coast of the southern third of Greenland, with an approach up a fjord and a runway facing a towering ice shelf. The other option was Nord. The crew chose Nord, a barren airstrip adjacent to a Danish weather station that offered only a snow- and ice-covered eight-thousand-foot runway. However, Nord had runway lights, the only sure way for a pilot to positively locate the runway in wintry conditions.

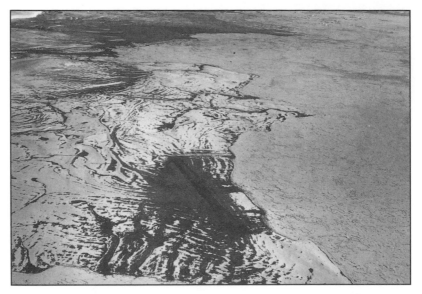

View of the airstrip at the Danish weather station Nord, 1958. C. Phillips.

"I was startled when my phone rang," Charlie Phillips related. "The senior command-post officer asked me to try, if I possibly could, to come over. I dressed quickly and as warmly as possible. I pulled the hood of my fur-lined parka around my face and stepped into the Arctic whiteout. It was unusual for anyone to be asked to go outside after a phase had struck. When I reached my destination, my parka was encrusted in a thick layer of ice and frost. I was told that the RB-47 aircraft which had launched the night before had landed at Station Nord and that as soon as the winds died down, I was to lead a rescue party to get the aircraft back to Thule. I sat down and began planning the recovery of the stranded RB-47H with the tail number 3-0281."

Aircraft 3-0281 had made an uneventful landing at Nord. Captain Addison had taxied the aircraft to the center of a small parking area near a building that he presumed was the weather station. Before shutting down the engines, he blew the approach and landing chutes off to the side. Then, as the engines spooled down with a high-pitched whine, an eerie silence settled over the aircraft. In spite of their helmets, the air crew's ears had endured hours of incessant wind noise as they had cut at five hundred miles per hour through the cold skies of the Arctic world at thirty-eight thousand feet. One of the three Ravens sitting in the aisle below the pilots opened the entry hatch and let down the aluminum ladder. The six crew members emerged slowly, dressed in their bulky winter flying suits, stiff from sitting for hours strapped in ejection seats. The crew secured their classified logs and tapes and locked the aircraft. Then they turned to their Danish host, who greeted them in good English. It was an occasion to celebrate. Rarely did anyone drop by in the winter months for a visit, emergency or otherwise. The arrival of the Americans was a welcome interruption. The air crew quickly learned that Danish aquavit kept ice-cold and drunk in one bold gesture was lethal. They enjoyed the cheese that was served along with the sleep-inducing drink and soon excused themselves. Their host provided blankets, and they slept on the heated concrete floor of the laundry room. To fly back to Thule, they knew they would need outside assistance. They had no way to start their engines.

Three days after 3-0281 landed at Nord, the winds died down at Thule, and Charlie Phillips and his rescue party got under way. "I took two KC-97 aerial-refueling tankers with full fuel loads from the 100th Air Refueling Squadron and sent them off to Nord. The 100th came from Pease AFB in New Hampshire. They were pulling a six-week rotational tour at Thule. Then I had an MD-3 power cart loaded on a Berlin Airlift–vintage C-54 transport to power up the RB-47, I put my maintenance crew on the same plane, and I followed in one of the KC-97s. First and foremost on my mind was the safety of my men and the aircraft we were to rescue. I knew that everything we had to do needed to be done carefully and deliberately. I wouldn't have anything bad happen to that airplane. As the team leader, I decided to personally handle the potentially most dangerous operation myself—operating the forklift in close proximity to the RB-47. I was told that a forklift was permanently positioned at Nord to unload aircraft delivering fuel to Nord in fifty-five-gallon drums. After our arrival, I had the Danish lift operator explain its operation to me, and then I practiced driving, tilting, and lifting for half an hour before I certified myself as being ready

Colonel Phillips operating the forklift, 1958. Maintenance men standing on the lift pallet are connecting a flexible fuel hose to the tanker's extended boom.
C. Phillips.

to operate the lift. The outside temperatures as usual were in the forty below zero Fahrenheit range. With the forklift, I lifted the maintenance officer, a major from the 55th Wing, up onto the nose of the RB-47 to enable him to connect a flexible refueling hose to the aircraft's refueling receptacle. I carefully drove the lift within inches of the RB-47, lifting the major on a pallet to his icy perch.

"Once the hose connection was made from the refueling boom of the tanker to the receiving receptacle of the RB-47, the KC-97 started three of its four engines—one to power its brakes, the other two to run its fuel pumps. Since there was no tug to tow the KC-97 into position, the huge tanker aircraft had to be backed in by reversing the propeller pitch. It was a slow and tedious process. Once the first tanker discharged its fuel, it had to be disconnected from the RB-47 and taxied away, and the second tanker had to be backed into position, again very

Final connections being made to the KC-97 boom nozzle, 1958. Toggles are in place and fuel is ready to flow to the RB-47. Note the tail number on the left forward gear door of the RB-47H. C. Phillips.

carefully. During the refueling with the KC-97s, the icy wind blast from their running engines frosted up the RB-47. The frost had to come off the jet before it could fly. I had two ropes tied around the waist of one of my men and lifted him with the forklift up on a wing of the RB-47. Two men on each side of the wing held the ropes tied around the wing walker's waist to keep him from slipping off while he brushed off the ice and snow, using a push broom. A hazard to the man cleaning the ice off the wings was a double row of vortex generators sticking up on top of each wing near the tips. Each blade was two inches high. A fall onto these knifelike blades could cause serious injury. The operation took over six hours from start to finish. No one was injured, and nothing was damaged. We also installed new approach and landing chutes in the RB-47. Then I wired the command post at Thule for instructions, which came by teletype over the Danish weathernet. Judging from the telegram, the Thule weather forecast wasn't all that good. Conditions varied, with blowing snow; winds at twenty-five knots, gusting to thirty-five; and moderate to severe turbulence. We were advised to depart after 0200 Zulu, Greenwich mean time, on the twenty-eighth, during the best anticipated weather conditions. KC-97 tankers would be standing by at Thule to launch in case additional fuel was required. The RB-47 was to use Goose Bay, Labrador and Sondrestrom in Greenland as alternates.

"When the time came for the RB-47 to leave, everyone at Nord came out to watch. I remember the RB-47 taxiing to the end of the snow-packed runway and then, as it so often happened, the heat from its six engines generated a huge ice cloud. The cloud settled between the RB-47 and us watchers. We didn't know if the cloud also enveloped the RB-47. Then we heard the throaty roar from six jet engines, and suddenly the aircraft emerged from the other side of the ice cloud as it rose into the milky white sky above Station Nord, heading for Thule. We all cheered. At that moment it was *our* plane. We had put our full energy into getting that bird airborne, and we felt good about our accomplishment. There were smiles all around. I shook hands with everyone and thanked them for their hard work and a job well done. After the two KC-97 tankers departed, our Danish hosts invited the rest of us to share some food and drink with them. We did for an hour or two, then exhaustion and the aquavit overcame us. We slept on the same heated concrete floor in the weather station's laundry room where the B-47 crew had slept before us. We left the next day in the C-54."

On July 1, 1960, only two months after the shootdown of Francis Gary Powers's U-2 photo-reconnaissance aircraft near Sverdlovsk, an RB-47H reconnaissance aircraft with tail number 3-0281 took off in the early morning darkness from RAF Brize Norton. The RB-47, the same aircraft that two years earlier had recovered at Station Nord, was on a peripheral reconnaissance mission. Its route was similar to that flown in 1954 by Captain Harold Austin, except that the plane did not intend to penetrate Soviet airspace, as Austin had. Captain Willard Palm was the aircraft's commander, Captain Bruce Olmstead the copilot, and Captain John McCone the navigator. The three Ravens flying in the reconnaissance capsule in the bomb bay were Captain Eugene Posa and Lieutenants Oscar Goforth and Dean Phillips. Over the icy waters of the Barents Sea, aircraft 3-0281 was shot down by a Soviet MiG-19. Captains McCone and Olmstead survived, spending seven months in the infamous Lubyanka Prison, a place of torture and sorrow since the days of the czar. Premier Nikita Khrushchev released the two men as a goodwill gesture toward newly elected U.S. President John F. Kennedy in January 1961. The other four crew members perished. It was Lieutenant Oscar Goforth's first Cold War reconnaissance mission.

Chapter 13

The Last Flight of 3-4290

Copilot Hank Dubuy watched the MiGs as they positioned themselves behind his aircraft and took a couple of pictures. The lead MiG suddenly initiated the attack by firing its cannons. It was war. Hank dropped his camera. As the shells slammed into the aircraft, he requested permission from his pilot to fire. "Shoot the bastard down," exclaimed Mattison. . . . As he proceeded to drop the aircraft toward the lower cloud layer, Mattison called for the navigator to give him a heading, "to get the hell out of here."

George Back, RB-47H electronic warfare officer

Citation to Accompany the Award of the Distinguished Flying Cross
    First Lieutenant Joel J. Lutkenhouse distinguished himself by extraordinary achievement during aerial flight as an Electronic Warfare Officer, from 30 March 1965 to 20 May 1965. During this period, he participated in a program of vital international significance and demonstrated outstanding effectiveness and courage in the accomplishment of missions conducted under exceptional flight conditions. The professional competence, aerial skill, and devotion to duty displayed by Lieutenant Lutkenhouse reflect great credit upon himself and the United States Air Force.

Major George V. Back
Distinguished Flying Cross (4), Air Medal (6)

Captain Henry E. Dubuy
Distinguished Flying Cross, Air Medal

Lieutenant Colonel Joel J. Lutkenhouse
Distinguished Flying Cross (4), Air Medal (6)

Lieutenant Colonel Robert J. Rogers
Distinguished Flying Cross (3), Air Medal

On a warm and softly pleasant January afternoon in 1961, at the age of twenty, Joel Lutkenhouse passed through the main gate of Harlingen Air Force Base and became an aviation cadet. Harlingen, a small, dusty agricultural community in the lower Rio Grande Valley of Texas, was home to a navigator training base, one of many flying training bases scattered along the Texas-Mexico border. There, in a land of ever blue and empty skies, potential air force navigators spent the better part of a year learning the intricacies of aerial navigation in twin-engined Convair T-29 aircraft, the military version of the widely used Convair 240 airliner.

The oldest of five children in a hardworking New York family, Joel entered Staten Island Community College in 1958. In the school cafeteria one day, a classmate mentioned that he would soon be leaving to enter the air force's aviation cadet program, on his way to becoming a pilot. "You don't have a college degree," Joel countered, "How did you get in?"

"You only need two years of college, Joel," his friend replied, "not a degree. You can pick up a degree sometime in the future if you want to do that. Right now, I want to learn to fly. I am really excited. I can't wait to leave. Why don't you come too? If I can get in, you can, for sure. You are a lot smarter than I am." His friend smiled. For days Joel pondered the challenge. It represented an opportunity to become an officer, to give his life direction. Joel decided to take a closer look. He visited the local air force recruiter and took the required tests. Although he passed, his score was not high enough to qualify him for pilot training, so he entered the program as a navigator candidate. In January 1961 he found himself at a dusty, palm-tree-studded air base in what he thought was the remotest corner of the United States. As he looked around, he knew Harlingen wasn't anything like New York. "But down the road, on an oil-stained tarmac, I saw row upon row of twin-engined T-29 navigation trainers. I suddenly felt excitement rising within me. They were my future. I really wanted to fly. I knew it was the biggest thing I'd ever done in my life, and I promised myself I wasn't going to fail at it." Over the next ten months Joel Lutkenhouse forgot about New York. With studying, flying, and classroom work, there was precious little time left for sleep, much less dreaming about his past.

In November 1961 Joel Lutkenhouse exchanged the shoulder boards of an aviation cadet for the brown bars of a second lieutenant and was awarded the aeronautical rating of navigator. But instead of being assigned to a flying unit to practice what he had learned, he was selected to continue training for another year to become an electronic warfare officer (EWO). He had no real concept of what that involved, but he knew he would master it too. After a short vacation at home, he reported to Mather AFB near Sacramento, California. Mather was the exact opposite of Harlingen, nestled in the lush wine country of northern California. Instead of taking celestial shots with a sextant, flying pressure patterns, and taking loran (long-range navigation system) readings, at Mather Joel learned about radar and how to defend against it should he ever have to employ his newly acquired skills in war.

Upon graduation in November 1962, Joel was assigned to the 376th Bomb Wing at Lockbourne AFB, Ohio, the same air base from which Sam Myers and Hal Austin once flew the RB-45C and RB-47E. Joel's squadron flew B-47E bombers carrying a manned capsule in the bomb bay. The phase-V capsule accommodated two EWOs, who controlled a large number of electronic jammers and chaff dispensers used to provide electronic-countermeasure support for SAC bombers slated to attack the Soviet Union in the event of nuclear war. Four times during his two years at Lockbourne, Joel *reflexed* to RAF Brize Norton in the

United Kingdom. There Joel sat alert with other B-47 bomber crews for two out of three weeks. Being on alert meant living in his flight suit in a concrete bunker near his aircraft, ready to launch at a moment's notice should the claxon sound. The claxon never sounded in earnest for Joel. In May 1964 the 376th Bomb Wing disbanded, and Joel received orders to report to the 55th Strategic Reconnaissance Wing at Forbes AFB in Topeka, Kansas. The 55th was composed of two squadrons of RB-47H electronic-reconnaissance aircraft, the 38th and 343d, and one squadron of RB-47K photo-reconnaissance jets, the 338th. Joel was assigned to the 343d squadron. Once certified combat ready, he was assigned to crew E-96 as a Raven 3. In this unit, the EWOs were referred to as Ravens, and "Raven 3" meant that he would occupy position three in a capsule in the bomb bay of the RB-47.

Another young air force officer was on a career track that for many years nearly paralleled Joel's: Second Lieutenant George V. Back. George was a little older than most lieutenants. Born in 1936 in Syracuse, New York, he had joined the Army National Guard at a young age. By the time he entered aviation cadet training at Harlingen in 1961, he already held a reserve commission as second lieutenant in the infantry. But he had always wanted to fly, and when the opportunity offered itself, George, like Joel, entered the aviation cadet program. He and Joel were in the same cadet class at Harlingen and received their air force commissions on the same day. Together they completed electronic warfare training in California, and upon graduation they reported to the same wing at Lockbourne. Upon deactivation of that wing in 1964, both Joel and George were reassigned to the 55th Wing, and they ended up on the same crew, E-96.

In George Back's words, "The 55th was considered a closed union, and we were the first brown bars to come into the unit in a couple of years. Most of the crew members were lieutenant colonels, majors, or senior captains—intimidating for us young guys, and we thought we better do things right. Matt—Lieutenant Colonel Hobart Mattison, my aircraft commander—was a no-nonsense officer when it came to flying. Every mission we lined up under the left wing of the aircraft for inspec-

View of RB-47H 4-304, piloted by Lieutenant Colonel Rust of the 55th SRW, on its way to the Barents Sea, 1963. Photo taken from an accompanying KC-135 tanker. Author was on the aircraft as a Raven 2. W. Samuel.

tion—our parachutes on the ground in front of us, our helmets on top of the chutes, and Matt conducted a short premission briefing. After the briefing, we did a left face, marched forward till clear of the parachutes, and began our individual preflights. In flight we addressed crew positions when talking on the interphone—'Raven to Pilot,' and so on. We said what needed saying and then shut up. No frivolous banter. First names were left to the Officers' Club."

On March 30, 1965, Joel Lutkenhouse and George Back deployed with crew E-96 to Yokota Air Base, near Tokyo, Japan. Yokota had hosted various air force reconnaissance elements over the years and at that time served as a base of operation for a detachment of the 55th Wing. Detachment aircraft flew missions along the periphery of the Asian mainland from the Gulf of Tonkin to the Sea of Okhotsk. Their principal objective was to update the electronic order of battle. These missions' bread-and-butter targets were early warning radars and SAM and AAA acquisition and tracking radars, their technical parameters, and locations. Many of the routes flown were canned, meaning that they were flown repeatedly, without significant variation, thereby providing the Soviet military with tacit assurance that these missions were routine and without hostile intent.

At times routes and tactics were modified to cause the Soviets to turn on their radars to reveal wartime techniques normally not used in peacetime operations. Radar emissions were recorded for subsequent analysis, and the emitters' locations were incorporated into the master EOB. These flights also kept tabs on the deployment of new or improved radar-guided weapons systems and detected the introduction of new techniques that might render U.S. tactics and countermeasures marginal or ineffective. It was a never-ending game of one-upmanship to ensure that American technology and tactics were on top most of the time. Reaction to reconnaissance flights over the years had varied, depending on the sensitivity of the information gathered or on the whim of a Soviet politician or military commander. Since the early 1950s, a number of reconnaissance aircraft, air force and navy, had been lost to hostile action, mostly to Soviet fighters. These losses usually received little publicity from either side unless it proved politically advantageous, such as the downing of Francis Gary Powers's U-2 by Soviet SA-2 SAMs in May 1960, an event that Premier Nikita Khrushchev used to embarrass President Dwight D. Eisenhower at that year's Paris summit. The last 55th Wing aircraft lost to hostile action had been an RB-47H shot down by a Soviet MiG-19 fighter over the Barents Sea in July 1960, five years earlier.

Although most reconnaissance missions were flown along the periphery of nations hostile to the United States and outside their territorial waters, reconnaissance aircraft were frequently intercepted by single-seat MiG-17, MiG-19, and MiG-21 fighters or by two-seat Yak-25 interceptors. Such intercepts did not automatically cause a reconnaissance flight to abort. Aborts occurred only when the fighters showed clear hostile intent, which usually did not become apparent until the MiGs were alongside or behind the reconnaissance aircraft and in firing position. Evasive maneuvers to escape the attackers were often extreme and violent and at times resulted in the overflight of neutral airspace as the RB-47 attempted to flee its pursuers. On April 28, 1965, crew E-96 of the 55th Strategic Reconnaissance Wing was going to become part of a very hot Cold War mission.

The front end of crew E-96 was composed of Lieutenant Colonel Hobart D. "Matt" Mattison, an experienced and skilled aircraft commander; First Lieutenant Henry E. Dubuy, who flew as copilot and gunner; and Captain Robert J. Rogers, the radar navigator. The back-end crew, the Ravens, were Captain Robert C. "Red" Winters, who flew as Raven 1; First Lieutenant George V. Back, flying as Raven 2 on his first operational deployment; and First Lieutenant Joel J. Lutkenhouse, Raven 3, also on his first operational deployment. Each Raven controlled a set of similar receivers, analyzers, recorders, and direction-finding equipment. The essential difference between their positions was the discreet radio frequencies they monitored. Prior to each mission, the Ravens received tasking orders and priorities of what to look for in specific geographic areas and within their frequency spectrum.

On takeoff, the three Ravens sat strapped into web slings in the aisle below the pilots. Once the aircraft was airborne and temporarily leveled off at two thousand feet above the terrain, the Ravens crawled aft on their hands and knees through a tunnel to their capsule in the bomb bay. There, the Raven 2, the last to enter the compartment, locked the capsule door and the Raven 3 pressurized the compartment. Then they strapped into their ejection seats. As the aircraft climbed to its assigned altitude, anywhere between thirty and forty thousand feet, the pressurization in both the front and rear crew compartments was kept at fourteen thousand–feet pressure altitude, which implied that the crew was supposed to be on oxygen for the entire length of the mission. Crew members went off oxygen to smoke a cigarette or to relieve the numbing pressure of the oxygen mask on the face. The reason for maintaining a thinner atmosphere within the crew compartments was to diminish the explosive effects of rapid decompression should that occur. Fuel tanks were housed in the aircraft fuselage. Directly behind the pilots, in order, were the main forward fuel tank, the center main fuel tank, the bomb bay fuel tank, the aft auxiliary fuel tank, and the aft main fuel tank. The aft main fuel tank was located in the tail section, forward of the vertical stabilizer, in the area where the American star was painted on the fuselage. The Raven capsule fitted in the bomb bay was surrounded by fuel tanks, and the smell of JP4 in the compartment was a common aspect of life in the capsule. The copilot, who sat directly behind the pilot, also served as aircraft gunner. His seat swiveled around to allow him to operate the twin 20mm guns and the associated radar system. The guns were not known for their reliability. It was standing operating procedure (SOP) to abort a reconnaissance mission if the guns failed upon test firing—not an order, but an SOP. Crews frequently ignored the SOP, pressed on, and got the job done. Getting wind of such independent crew initiatives, SAC headquarters directed maintenance personnel to tape the ends of gun barrels before takeoff. If the guns failed to fire when tested over open ocean, the tape supposedly would not be perforated. If the crew returned from a mission with taped guns, some punitive action would be taken against the pilots. The guns usually fired a few rounds before jamming, so little changed.

The two pilots sat in conventional upward-firing ejection seats, while the navigator's seat ejected downward without having first to cut through a hatch, as was the case with the Raven seats. For both the Ravens and the navigator, ejection below five hundred feet above ground level was problematic, even with their zero-second lanyards connected to assure immediate chute opening. Over the years of B-47 bomber operations, the reliability of the ejection seats in the forward crew compartment had been proven on many occasions. The Raven seats, however, were a different story. Downward-firing and located just behind the main landing gear, the seats inspired little confidence. No Raven had ever ejected from an RB-47H and lived to tell about it. Rumor had it that the seats were unsafe by design, supposedly because the Ravens were privy to too much sensitive information. The aura of unreliability surrounding the seats caused most Ravens to opt to stay with the aircraft, preferring a belly landing on a foam-covered runway

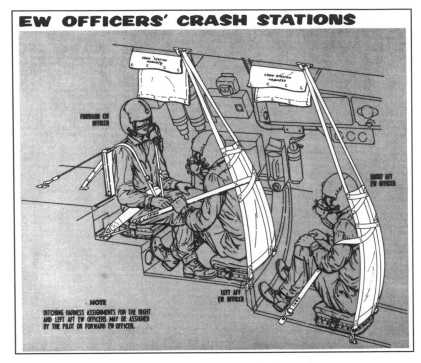

Ravens in their takeoff and landing positions in the forward crew compartment of an RB-47H in the aisle below the two pilots. RB-47H Technical Order, U.S. Air Force.

to an ejection. That choice was exercised by 55th Wing air crews more than once, and in all cases without injury.

The ejection seat was actuated by the Raven raising two leg braces, one at each side of the seat. This action depressurized the aft capsule, locked the shoulder harness, extended two retainers around the Raven's ankles to keep his legs from flying in his face upon ejection, and released a D-ring between his legs. Once the ring was pulled, the seat first cut through a hatch underneath and then ejected itself and its occupant into the airstream. In actuality, the time lapse between the two events was of such brief duration that to the seat occupant it appeared as one.

Crew E96 flew tail number 3-4305 via Alaska to Yokota. On the flight over and on a subsequent test flight over the Sea of Japan, the aircraft could not hold a heading when on autopilot. It was not smart to take such an airplane near Soviet airspace. In case of a navigation error, the Russians would shoot first and ask questions later. The 55th Detachment commander at Yokota, Lieutenant Colonel Gunn, asked for an aircraft replacement. The replacement, tail number 3-4290, was quickly flown from Forbes via Eielson in Alaska down the Aleutian chain to Yokota. Lieutenant Colonel Howard "Rusty" Rust delivered the new aircraft, accompanied by the 55th Wing commander, Colonel Marion C. Mixson, the same man who in March 1952 commanded the RB-45C detachment at RAF Sculthorpe that lent its aircraft to British air crews to fly them over the Soviet Union on daring night reconnaissance missions.

It was 0700 on April 28, 1965, when Colonel Mattison released the brakes and the sleek six-jet aircraft hurtled down the ten thousand–foot Yokota runway. The RB-47H blanketed the air base with thundering noise. The aircraft slowly vanished into the morning mist, leaving behind a trail of black smoke from the water-alcohol mixture injected into its six engines during takeoff to boost power. The takeoff went unnoticed by most, except for the ever-present Japanese photographers at the base perimeter, who took pictures of every arriving and departing aircraft. Mattison flew past snow-covered Mount Fuji and turned north for the Sea of Japan. The mission was scheduled to be a short seven and a half hours, with no need for aerial refueling. The plane was flying one of the canned routes over the Sea of Japan that would take them close to the southern tip of Sakhalin Island; then along the coast of the Soviet mainland past Vladivostok, the major Soviet naval base in the region; and along the east coast of North Korea.

Once the Ravens transferred to their aft compartment, they pressurized and turned on their equipment. By the time the aircraft reached its assigned altitude, the equipment had warmed up and stabilized, the USQ-18 clock was set to Greenwich mean time and was putting its tick marks on every audio and video recording. The Ravens settled back, looking at their world of green scopes and red lights, ready to go on watch once the navigator announced over the intercom that the on-watch point had been reached. The Ravens scanned their assigned frequencies with their APR-17 receivers. The automatic ALD-4 external reconnaissance pod and other automatic systems were turned on at the on-watch point, recording the pulse-recurring frequency, pulse width, radio frequency, emitter location, and other pertinent parameters of every intercepted radar emission. Judging from the activity as they progressed through their mission, it was, according to Raven George Back, "one of those ho-hum missions."

Back recalled, "Nothing exciting came up, other than the usual Soviet early warning radars. Occasionally a height finder gave us four or five scans to confirm our altitude. The Soviets knew what we were doing. They knew the canned route we were flying as well as we did. They knew we were no threat to them as long as we didn't deviate from our route. Consequently, they didn't turn on any of their threat radars or use any unusual techniques. But the Soviet operators monitoring the American spy plane probably passed our track via landline to their North Korean comrades."

"As we passed near Vladivostok," Joel Lutkenhouse remembered, "I picked up Soviet shipborne gun and missile radars. Our pilots looked for them but couldn't see the ships because of a low cloud layer. Bob, our navigator, saw the ships on his radar. They were tracking us with their antiaircraft and SAM radars, but the ships were in international waters and no obvious threat to us."

"We were six hours into our mission," Bob Rogers recalled. "Only another ninety minutes and we would be back at Yokota enjoying a hot shower and a good meal. We turned to a south-southeasterly heading abeam of Wonsan Harbor on the east coast of North Korea. Then we tracked down the Korean peninsula and initiated a 180-degree turn at 37 degrees north latitude, heading north-northwest back toward Wonsan, back the way we had come." At that time, copilot Hank Dubuy recalled, "we were routinely monitoring our instruments. Everything looked normal. The autopilot was tracking, temperatures, fuel flow, everything was within tolerance. Matt and I scanned the horizon out of habit. Nothing but clouds above and below us. We had an unobstructed view from wingtip to wingtip but not to the low rear quadrant, which was obstructed by the aircraft fuselage and wings. There was a layer of stratocumulus clouds below us, preventing us from seeing the water below or the coastline of North Korea. Another layer of gray stratus clouds was above our cruising altitude of thirty-six thousand feet."

"We rolled out of our turn and headed north again," Bob remembered, "and stabilized the aircraft on its new heading, when suddenly a loud single-sideband warning came blasting into our headsets over HF radio. It was a message broadcast in the blind from a secret American monitoring station somewhere in South Korea or Japan, warning aircraft of bogeys in the area around Wonsan. It was a strange warning to a reconnaissance aircraft in international waters off the coast of one of the more hard-line and belligerent communist countries. I had never received such a warning on any other mission. Briefly, I wondered if the monitoring station had heard a radio call of intent to shoot us down. But I was busy navigating my aircraft, and as quickly as the cautionary thought entered my mind, I pushed it aside." Raven George Back put it this way: "No matter how much preparation I had, how much intelligence on the bad guys I knew, I never thought that some North Korean would try to kill me on my first operational TDY. But the North Koreans were deemed unpredictable and their actions frequently irrational. After that mission, I knew this for a fact."

The two pilots continued to scan the horizon, seeing nothing but empty sky. Copilot Hank Dubuy swiveled his seat around. "I raised my camera and took a couple shots off the wings. I had switched the A-5 fire control system to warm up soon after our departure from Yokota. In the off and warm-up positions, the guns remained stowed, pointing upward. Over open water I had switched the system to standby, the two guns pointed straight back. Then I switched to operation, firing a couple of short bursts to ensure the guns were working properly. Everything looked good to me, and I put the system back into standby." The ammunition load for each 20mm gun was 350 rounds. Normally, in an aircraft's standard combat load, every fifth round was a tracer, to give the gunner a visual indication of where he was firing. But Hank didn't carry tracers in his ammunition load.

The gun radar system was designed to automatically track rear hemisphere attackers approaching within forty-five degrees of azimuth to either side of the aircraft and thirty-seven degrees of elevation up or down. Targets outside this automatic tracking window had to be fired on by going to emergency manual operation, using the antenna control handle, manually positioning the antenna on the target azimuth and then spotlighting the target in elevation. The antenna control handle was spring-loaded to position the guns at zero elevation and azimuth, which gave the gunner the ability to quickly baseline his guns and know where they were pointing at that time. As the warning message still echoed in the crew members' ears, Raven 1 Red Winters picked up the distinctive scan of an airborne intercept radar on his APR-17 receiver. The signal was weak and faded quickly, but Red had heard it and seen it long enough on his receiver trace to identify it as an airborne threat signal emanating from their rear hemisphere. It sounded to Red like the scan of a MiG-17 radar in the search mode.

Red notified the crew and simultaneously started his recorder in case the signal reappeared, but it did not. George Back, the Raven 2, was working a Korean GCI radar. "I was unaware of what was happening. I had turned my intercom switch to the 'private' position to eliminate crew communications and was in the process of annotating the signal I was recording to aid in subsequent analysis and evaluation." Raven 3 Joel Lutkenhouse was similarly engaged, "although I was aware that there were probably MiGs prowling in our piece of sky. I did check that I was properly strapped into my seat. The first I knew we were under attack was when I felt the aircraft shudder." Joel felt the impact of 23mm cannon shells exploding into the aft main fuel tank, into the chaff chutes, and probably into the gun compartment.

George related, "I felt the aircraft shudder, pitch nose down, and begin losing altitude. My first thought was that the autopilot or trim had failed, but a split second later, as I went back to the normal interphone position, I found out that a couple of MiG-17s were serious about shooting us down. I noted that the altimeter, which was reading about twenty-seven thousand feet when I glanced at it, was rapidly unwinding. In an instant, my mind seemed to go in a thousand different directions at a thousand different speeds. It was the first time in my life I thought I was really going to die. The irony of it was that I had no control over what was happening. Panic and fear paralyzed my thought processes, and I think I sat dumbfounded for what seemed an eternity, trying to figure out what the hell was going on and what to do. When Matt remarked that we were hit and going down, I thought it was the end. I started the ejection sequence. My mind was still racing and everything I had ever done or witnessed seemed to go whirling by in a kaleidoscope of my life. At the same time, a different part of my brain seemed to be saying, 'Don't panic. You have been trained for situations like this. Do your job and follow the checklist.' I deliberately collected my thoughts and realized that the aircraft was still well above fourteen thousand feet and that my likely time of survival in the fifty-degree water was less than thirty minutes. I didn't pull the D-ring between my legs. As fast as the panic came, it went, and I felt an uneasy calm. I was still scared but starting to think rationally. 'Get your oxygen mask on. Check the flow. Tighten your parachute harness. Remember, you're sitting on an armed seat. Watch out for the D-ring.' During the subsequent MiG firing passes, I could feel the cannon fire impacting the aircraft. I remember thinking that at any time there would be a tremendous explosion, a rush of cold air, and that would be the last I would remember."

Pilot Mattison exclaimed, "They are shooting at us. We are hit. I'm going down!" Raven George Back, who had just come back on intercom, overheard part of the conversation between the two pilots, "We are hit . . . going down," Back heard Mattison say. "I thought the pilot meant we were really going down." Instead, Mattison was telling his copilot that he was going down to a lower altitude and taking evasive action. George Back misunderstood and automatically depressurized the Raven compartment when he raised his leg braces, dropping the back-end crew rapidly from fourteen thousand–feet pressure altitude to the actual altitude in the mid–twenty thousands. Joel saw George pull up the leg braces on his ejection seat, felt the rapid decompression, and immediately pulled down the visor of his helmet in preparation for ejection. He assumed the practiced ejection position—back straight up against the seat, head against the back headrest, feet in the seat stirrups—but he didn't do anything further. He waited for instructions from the pilot.

George and Joel sat side by side in their ejection seats facing aft, their inner turmoil not apparent to each other. Joel listened on the intercom to the front-end crew's conversation as they tried to cope with the situation. He glanced over at George, sitting there ready to eject, looking calm. "Thoughts raced through my mind. How could this be happening to me? My heart was pounding in my mouth. I thought I could feel my blood coursing through my body, my nerves tingling. Suddenly, I was intensely afraid of losing my life. I could feel tears running down my cheeks. I decided to say a prayer, the Act of Contrition. As suddenly as the fear surged through my body, just as suddenly it subsided. I felt calmer and listened to the ongoing battle over the intercom, feeling shells from the attacking MiGs slamming into our aircraft."

The two North Korean MiG-17s, approaching through multiple cloud layers and probably guided by the GCI radar George Back was recording and analyzing, had reached the RB-47H unseen from behind and below, the plane's blind spot. The MiGs kept their radars off, or they would have been detected by the B-47's APS-54 airborne warning receiver and by the Raven 1. When the MiGs commenced their attack, they were still low, directly behind the B-47, firing upward, trying to stay out of the cone of fire of the B-47's 20mm guns. Copilot Hank Dubuy watched the MiGs as they positioned themselves behind his aircraft and took a couple of pictures. The lead MiG suddenly initiated the attack by firing its cannons. It was war. Hank dropped his camera. As the shells slammed into the aircraft, he requested permission from his pilot to fire. "Shoot the bastard down," exclaimed Mattison while calling 'Mayday,' the internationally recognized call for a ship or aircraft in distress, on his single-sideband radio. As he proceeded to drop the aircraft toward the lower cloud layer, Mattison called for the navigator to give him a heading, "to get the hell out of here." The aircraft was plummeting downward to escape the MiGs, seeking shelter in the lower layer of cloud and turning toward open water.

Captain Bob Rogers, the navigator, hunched over his radarscope in the nose of the aircraft, was busy ensuring that the plane remained on its planned track when the attack occurred. "At first I thought Mattison was joking when he said we were under attack. I thought he was joking until I heard and felt the hits." Bob's calm response to Mattison's request for a heading was, "Take a ninety-degree turn to the right, and I'll refine it in a second." Then Bob put his radar crosshairs on the coast of Japan and asked Matt for second station. In second station, the pilot puts the aircraft on autopilot, and the navigator manually controls the aircraft in azimuth. It was a system designed to provide the best possible bombing results for B-47 bombers. Mattison couldn't surrender control of the stricken aircraft to his navigator at such a time, but Bob's request demonstrated the crew's mettle and professional competence. Matt had no idea which systems were still operational. He needed to hand fly, he knew that. "After Matt called out 'Mayday,' everyone in the air was told to clear our frequency, because everyone in the air, including some KC-135 tankers, was offering help," added Bob Rogers.

Unknown to the aircraft's crew, a captain on an airborne Looking Glass C-135 SAC command-post aircraft circling near SAC headquarters at Omaha, Nebraska, picked up their HF radio transmissions of distress. The captain immediately notified the brigadier general onboard his aircraft, which was designed to exercise control over nuclear forces should SAC headquarters be destroyed by a surprise attack. While the general and his staff listened to one of their aircraft under North Korean fighter attack thousands of miles away, they downlinked the radio intercept to the SAC command post at Offutt. The Looking Glass aircraft crew and the command-post staff listened to the unfolding drama over the Sea of Japan but could do nothing to help.

In the meantime, Hank Dubuy was trying to defend the damaged plane against two persistent MiGs. "When I tried to return fire, I couldn't get the attackers on my radar. They were too close and outside the elevation and azimuth limits for the guns to lock on in automatic mode. I immediately went to manual mode and began to engage the MiGs. I had no tracer ammunition, and to increase my probability of hitting the MiGs, I continually reset the guns to zero azimuth, zero elevation—I knew then where the guns were pointing—and I was able to aim the guns at an attacking MiG. I punched the firing button and repeated the process of aligning the guns and firing. The first MiG approached from behind and below, assumed a nose-up position, and fired. Then the MiG fell off on one wing and dove to regain airspeed and altitude for a second pass. While the first MiG recovered, the second tried to down us using the same awkward tactic. The Raven 1 released a steady stream of chaff packages [aluminum strips designed to break lock of enemy fighter radars] into the face of the enemy aircraft, which was trying to get into firing position behind and below us. At one time, the second attacker was totally obscured in a cloud of chaff and broke off his attack."

The two MiGs made three passes each. Although their flying was clumsy and their gunnery abysmal, their shells brought the B-47 close to disaster. In George Back's words, "the hydraulic system failed, boost-pump lights illuminated, and the aft main fuel tank was hit and burning. During subsequent attacks, the number three engine was hit. Shrapnel from broken turbine blades in number three damaged the number two engine. Both engines continued to operate at reduced power; number three engine vibrated like an old car with no universal joints. Engines number four and five continued to run, although number five threw a number of turbine blades into the body of the aircraft. Out of six engines, only the two outboard engines remained undamaged—numbers one and six—continuing to perform at full power. The remaining four engines provided varying amounts of thrust."

"Both hydraulic systems were damaged," copilot Hank Dubuy remembered. "The pumps operated, but there was no fluid. The aircraft was sluggish in its response when I pulled on the yoke, rather like a truck that lost its power steering. In addition, we had to deal with an ever-deteriorating center of gravity. As the main rear fuel tank continued to lose fuel, which was on fire as the fuel spray exited the aircraft through the shell holes, the diminished weight in the rear of the aircraft due to the loss of fuel slowly shifted the aircraft's CG forward. The nose came down. It wasn't that much of a problem flying at 425 knots, but we were concerned that on landing the forward shift in the center of gravity would lead to a severe nose-down attitude, which we couldn't overcome with trim and flap adjustments. The forward shift in the aircraft's CG also precluded us from using full landing flaps because their use would force the nose of the aircraft down even more as our airspeed diminished. Matt knew the landing would be difficult, if we made it that far. I continued to engage the MiGs while Matt did evasive maneuvers and assessed the damage we sustained. Throughout the engagement, Bob, our navigator, continued to provide headings to lead Matt out of the area to Yokota.

"On their third and final firing pass, I thought I scored a hit on the lead MiG. It nosed up abruptly, then pitched over and descended straight down in what appeared to be an unrecoverable position. Matt observed the MiG disappearing through a cloud deck at twelve thousand feet, heading for the water. Then my guns ceased firing—jammed or damaged, I didn't know. I picked up my camera and took a couple of quick shots before the remaining MiG broke off the attack and turned back toward Wonsan. After the last MiG departed, Matt yelled over the intercom, 'Hank, get the Dash-1 out and go to the red-bordered pages, emergency procedures.'

" 'Which page?' I asked. 'Any page will do,' was Matt's laconic answer."

The RB-47 had taken a lot of punishment. The aircraft was vibrating badly, but Matt felt it was responding to his control. He could fly it. Hank could see that the aft main fuel tank was still emitting smoke, but the fire seemed to have diminished in intensity, and the color of the smoke had changed from black to white. A lack of fuel and wind blast had probably put out the fire. But the CG problem was irrevocably with them and would have to be dealt with once they got ready to land. The pilots had no idea if their tires were shot up, if the approach and landing chutes were in shreds, or if there was other damage that might doom their landing attempt. But the aircraft was flying, and they had ample fuel to get back to the base.

Hobart Mattison was an experienced World War II Eighth Air Force combat veteran who in 1944 had bailed out of a stricken B-17 bomber over Hungary, made his way across southern Germany to France, and then escaped to England with the help of the French underground. For him, abandoning a still-flying aircraft, no matter how badly damaged, was not an alternative. After leveling off at ten thousand feet and bringing the three Ravens forward, Matt asked his crew what they thought about punching out over Tokyo Bay or over the runway at Yokota. According to George Back, "When Matt inquired if anyone wanted to bail out, there was a unanimous 'No, Sir.' All fear had left me, and I had the utmost confidence in Matt and somehow knew that God didn't get us that far just so we would end up splattered all over the runway."

In similar situations, such nose-down landings by B-47 bombers most often resulted in funeral pyres. A shredded brake chute or a flat tire could easily spell disaster on landing. As a result of Mattison's Mayday calls, there was no lack of radio assistance, but no American fighters had appeared. Interceptors launched from Yokota were much too far away to provide assistance in a timely manner, and once they arrived on the scene, they could only visually confirm the external damage 3-4290 sustained. Matt turned down a suggestion from the SAC command post at Yokota to recover at a base in South Korea. Instead, he began his en route descent to Yokota. Colonel Mattison was the aircraft commander and, as such, had the ultimate decision-making authority when it came to the safety of his crew. As they approached Yokota, Colonel Gunn, the 55th Detachment commander, came up in a T-39 Sabreliner and looked them over. He couldn't add any new information that would help Matt in the tricky landing ahead.

"Rusty" Rust, the pilot who had delivered 3-4290 only a couple of days earlier, was up in the Yokota control tower making his expertise available in case Matt needed advice. Rusty had been stationed at Yokota for four years earlier in his career, and he knew the area's peculiarities well: "Matt was coming in from the south, heading north to make his first landing attempt. From that direction visibility was half a mile in haze. I wanted to tell him to come in from the north, heading south. Visibility in that direction was three miles. Although I could see him coming in, I had no way of reaching Matt. He was talking on the radio, first to the SAC command post and then to GCA radar. All I could do was watch. The B-47 was built like an automobile, with one UHF radio. There were no backups."

On approach to Yokota, Raven Red Winters manually lowered the landing gear. "One gear stuck and didn't want to lock up positively," Hank recalled. "Red Winters was afraid he was going to break off the handle. 'Do it, Red,' I told him. We had no other choice. Finally, the recalcitrant gear gave, and we got a positive lock indication." The Ravens in their web slings in the aisle below the pilots simply waited. Red, positioned in the aisle, could observe Matt and watched anxiously as the pilot wrestled with the unwieldy aircraft. Matt and Hank determined that they could use one-third flaps for the landing without getting the aircraft in an unrecoverable nose-down position. Matt said a final few words before he initiated his landing attempt. He knew the aircraft was going to porpoise, bouncing back into the air after a hard landing on the forward gear, a situation that frequently led to loss of directional control. "The landing will be rough. We will come down hard on the forward main gear due to our nose-down attitude. Henry, you deploy the [brake] chute and stand on the brakes after the second bounce. I will keep the wings level and maintain directional control." Colonel Gunn cleared the runway for them. Everything was as ready down below as it could be—fire trucks, fire-fighting helicopters, medical teams. The crew did its prelanding checklist.

"Crew discipline and training were important in how we handled the situation," Hank observed. "Crews have scenarios come up in a flying career, and by good fortune the majority make it through. In some cases, they don't. Maybe more discipline and training would have made a difference in those other cases. It probably did for us. On our first landing attempt, we tried to follow standard procedures of descending four thousand feet per minute and keeping the airspeed below 290 knots. As we slowed, the nose of the aircraft began to dip because of our forward center of gravity. We reduced our rate of descent as we approached the runway and continued to experiment with the airspeed and the flaps. We didn't want the nose to drop on us, because we had no idea if we could get it back up. As we continued to bleed off airspeed, approaching the runway, the aircraft's nose continued to drop. We couldn't get low enough in time and had to opt for a go-around. Matt put the power to the engines as we crossed the runway threshold, and slowly the nose began to rise again."

Rusty Rust watched through high-powered binoculars from his perch in the Yokota control tower. "On his first attempt, I saw his nose begin to drop on his landing approach. He was still too high, and then he applied power and initiated a go-around. I hoped he would do a 180 and make his second attempt from the north to give himself the benefit of better visibility, but he opted to go around."

"On our second attempt we got her down to five hundred feet," Hank Dubuy reflected pensively, "then three hundred, then two hundred, and as soon as Matt pulled the power off, the aircraft nose came down and the forward gear slammed into the runway." Said Rust, "When I saw him next he had a good landing attitude. Then suddenly, the nose of the aircraft dropped down and went straight into the ground. He took a tremendous first bounce, nearly up to the level of the rescue chopper, and then he hippity-hopped down the runway until he came to a stop. Recovery from this unusual attitude took great skill and coordination by Matt and Hank."

George Back sat helplessly in his sling in the aisle below the pilots. "The landing was as rough as Matt said it would be. We porpoised about eighty feet into the air, where we nearly hit the fire-suppression helicopter hovering above us. I thought the fuselage was going to break right behind the copilot, but it held together. Matt brought the aircraft

Two pictures of 3-4290 after landing at Yokota Air Base, 1965. MiG-17 cannon-shell hole is clearly visible in the American star. M. Mixson.

to a stop, and we exited, heading for the edge of the runway. I squatted down next to Red Winters, watching the pandemonium around the damaged, smoking craft. Red turned to me and said, 'You know, George, we are now living on borrowed time.' I wondered what Red meant by that. Then I saw Red, our ever-conscientious back-end crew leader, disregard the potential threat of fire, sprint back to the aircraft, climb up the aluminum ladder into the forward crew compartment, and scuttle as fast as he could through the access tunnel into the Raven compartment to retrieve the classified mission logs and other classified materials we had left behind."

Copilot Hank Dubuy remarked, "During the final landing attempt, I watched the airspeed throughout our descent. We were below 160 knots when we touched down. I pulled the brake chute at the top of the bounce. The chute wasn't damaged, thank God. It blossomed and slammed us to the ground and kept us there. I stood on the brakes as Matt had ordered me to do. If the chute had failed? I don't even want to think about that."

Navigator Bob Rogers recalled, "After the brake chute deployed, we hit like a ton of bricks. Everything loose came flying forward, toward my position in the nose of the aircraft. Once the aircraft came to a stop, something else was uppermost in my mind. Get out, of course, but not before I secured the O-15 radar camera film. I held onto it for dear life because I knew there would be a lot of questions regarding our position."

When the aircraft was inspected, it was found that a cannon shell had knocked one of the 20mm tail guns off its mount. Still, Hank Dubuy had fired more than three hundred rounds, nearly half the ammunition the plane carried, and his skillful handling of the guns probably ruined the day for one MiG-17 pilot. Shortly after the crew evacuated the wrecked aircraft, they were summoned to Colonel Gunn's office and debriefed. Were they on course? Yes, the 0-15 camera film confirmed that. Who shot first? The MiGs did. The usual questions were thrown at the flyers. Then they were off to the flight surgeon. He wanted to see all of them and to examine their fitness to fly. All were fine, were served the customary glass of Old Methuselah combat-ration whiskey, and released. That evening, after long, hot showers, the crew met in the bar at the Yokota Officers' Club. They decided that the North Koreans must have sent up their two worst pilots that day. None of the flyers could understand why the MiG pilots failed to shoot 3-4290 down. It was a sitting duck.

It did not make economic sense to repair RB-47H 3-4290. "I remember counting the holes in the airplane. I forget the exact number, but it was in the hundreds," Colonel Rust recalled. The aircraft was used for parts and then cut up. Its loss was not significant, since the advent of a new airborne reconnaissance system was only two years in the future. The new RC-135 aircraft, which would relieve the combat-tested RB-47Hs, did not carry guns. In spite of Vietnam, the Cold War was getting a little less frigid between the two nuclear superpowers. Two days after the North Korean attack on 3-4290, crew E-96 flew again, this time in aircraft 3-4305, taking radarscope photography in the Gulf of Tonkin from the Chinese–North Vietnamese border to the demilitarized zone. The two fighters with them belonged to the U.S. Navy.

Crew E-96 returned to the United States on May 17, 1965. The following month they reported to SAC headquarters at Offutt Air Force Base in Omaha, Nebraska. It was standard procedure for crews to receive a debriefing from the Intelligence people on the quality of their take during their TDY. General Richard O. Hunziker met with crew E-96. Lieutenant Dubuy recalled that during the meeting, the general looked at several pictures Dubuy had taken of the attacking MiGs after the guns quit firing. "How did you have time to take these pictures, Lieutenant?" the general inquired. Hank responded, "I had to shoot at them with something, General, and the camera was all I had left." Crew E-96 was awarded the Distinguished Flying Cross for extraordinary achievement during aerial flight.

Matt Mattison, the competent and courageous pilot with nerves to match his flying skills, died in the early 1990s. George Back was right when he said, "I had the utmost confidence in Matt and somehow knew that God didn't get us that far just so we would end up splattered all over the runway." Military flyers may see the hand of God more often than other mortals, but without the consummate flying skills and self-discipline of a Colonel Mattison, the flight would have ended in tragedy. In a twenty-six-year career, Matt served in World War II with the Eighth Air Force; flew C-54 transports in the Berlin Airlift; tested RB-45C reconnaissance aircraft at Eglin AFB, Florida; and then survived a midair collision at Eglin while testing an F-86D fighter. After his retirement, Matt settled in Florida and worked for another twenty years for the Federal Aviation Administration. Copilot Hank Dubuy left the air force in 1969 to fly for Continental Airlines. He settled in the greater Los Angeles area. Bob Rogers, the navigator, continued to

Flight and maintenance crews posing in front of the last two operational RB-47H aircraft at Yokota Air Base, Japan, March 1967, two years after the North Korean attack on an RB-47H over the Sea of Japan. Captain Lutkenhouse is right front; Captain Samuel (author) is second from right front. W. Samuel.

fly for years with the 55th Wing and after his retirement settled in the greater Boston area. In 1967 Joel Lutkenhouse and this author flew together on another RB-47H crew out of Yokota Air Base, at times retracing the fateful route Joel had flown earlier in 1965. Joel lives in the Washington, D.C., suburbs and is pursuing a successful career as a realtor. Red Winters died young. George Back settled in the greater Cleveland, Ohio, area after retiring from the air force.

In contrast to the descriptive citations issued to World War II heroes, the citations accompanying Crew E-96's award of the Distinguished Flying Cross contain not a word about their unit or what happened. Such factually sparse citations were the norm for awards presented to SAC flyers involved in secretive reconnaissance missions after the Korean War.

Part 4

Vietnam, 1965

In reforming the Pentagon, [Robert McNamara's] talents had served him well, but in the prosecution of the war, they had sometimes failed him. Vietnam was not a management problem, it was a war, and war is about life and death, filled with intangibles that defy analysis. He had never been in a war, and perhaps he did not fully appreciate at first its stupid waste and its irrational emotions, and the elusiveness of facts and truth when men are dying.

Clark Clifford

SAC and TAC pilots, I believe, thought about death in combat. When I went to Southeast Asia, I said to myself, "I am going to assume that I am dead. I am not going to get out of here alive. And I am not going to worry about it one more time." When I came out of it alive, and I arrived back in the United States, I couldn't believe I was alive. I was standing on a street corner saying, "Holy smokes! Yesterday there was flak all over the place, and today I am standing here on the street corner watching the traffic go by, and nobody even realizes there is a war on." I couldn't believe I was still alive, because I really believed I was dead. I didn't think there was any way to get out of that, although I tried hard.

Ralph Kuster, F-105 pilot

˙ In contrast to the Soviet-initiated Berlin blockade of 1948 and the North Korean attack on South Korea in 1950, North Vietnam did not present an immediate military threat to U.S. interests, thereby forcing prompt military action. It is beyond the scope of this brief introduction to deal with the political complexities that led to a national crisis over Vietnam and a political and military quagmire. However, it should be understood that the politicians and military leaders of the time made decisions based on their own backgrounds and experiences—to these decision makers the terms *Munich* and *appeasement* were still meaningful. The chosen strategy of containment of communist expansionism clearly reflected an attempt to avoid repeating the history of the 1930s, when a lack of Western cohesion, resolve, and strategy allowed Hitler to rise to eminence in Germany and threaten the world order. Therefore, containment dictated the nature of the American response once communist expansion was deemed to have occurred. Leaders believed that there was little the economically and militarily powerful United States could not tackle successfully if it set its mind to it. Furthermore, the domino theory of national collapse held that should one small nation be allowed to fall to communist intrigue or aggression, many others would follow. But this theory, although widely touted by politicians, oversimplified the complex process of national orientation and interaction. Finally, personalities, chance, and even outright deceit became factors on the road to Vietnam. William Manchester said in *The Glory and the Dream*, "Soldiers and statesmen misjudged the character of the war and its probable course" (1123).

Vietnam emerged as two political entities, north and south, after the 1950s breakup of the French colonial empire in Indochina. Vietnam, seven thousand miles due west of California, was an uninviting place, a hot and humid land of jungles, mountains, and river deltas. The country possessed neither a critical geographic position nor natural resources the West desired, making American involvement even less understandable. A brief chronology of the Vietnam experience will provide a framework for the stories that follow.

In **1956** the United States established a MAAG in Saigon, supporting

Ngo Dinh Diem's regime, and the first uniformed Americans entered South Vietnam. On **July 10, 1959,** Vietnamese terrorists killed two American military advisers at Bien Hoa Air Base, the first casualties of the war. And in **December 1960,** with the active support of the Hanoi government, the National Liberation Front (NLF) was officially formed in opposition to President Diem's regime in the South. Diem's people labeled the NLF "Viet Cong" or Vietnamese communists (VC). In 1962 President John F. Kennedy approved the expansion of the two thousand–man MAAG contingent to sixteen thousand men and upgraded the MAAG to a military assistance command (MACV), headed by a two-star U.S. Army general.

In **October 1962** the Kennedy administration faced down a Soviet attempt to introduce offensive missiles in Cuba. The nuclear confrontation between the United States and the Soviet Union led to the withdrawal of Russian missiles from the island and was considered a major U.S. military and political victory. This heady victory reinforced some senior politicians' and military officers' belief in U.S. military superiority and in the validity of the concept of gradual escalation of military force to achieve results. In the same month, the United States activated the 2nd Air Division in Saigon to control in-country air support to the South Vietnamese army, which was beginning to be pressed hard by the Viet Cong. (As the American airpower buildup increased, the 2nd Air Division was replaced by the 7th Air Force in April 1966.)

During the first week of **August 1964,** the U.S. Navy, in coordination with South Vietnamese naval vessels, conducted operations off the coast of North Vietnam in the Gulf of Tonkin. The destroyers *Maddox* and *C. Turner Joy* were involved in two controversial naval engagements with North Vietnamese naval vessels. In retaliation, President Lyndon Baines Johnson ordered U.S. carrier-based aircraft to attack North Vietnamese torpedo boat bases and a fuel depot. The president asked Congress for a resolution in support of his actions, which was passed by both the House and the Senate. The United States was at war. American helicopters, first introduced in 1962, were augmented by rotational squadrons of B-57 bombers, and in **November 1964** Viet

Cong guerrillas again attacked Bien Hoa Air Base near Saigon, destroying five B-57s, damaging many more, and killing five American military advisers. The American buildup continued unabated, and more than twenty-three thousand Americans, mostly from the army and air force, were deployed in various capacities in Vietnam by the end of 1964.

On **February 7, 1965**, the Viet Cong attacked a U.S. base near Pleiku in the central highlands, destroying or damaging sixteen army helicopters and killing eight American soldiers. Attacks against American military personnel increased. President Johnson authorized Operation Rolling Thunder against North Vietnam, "a continuing, systematic air campaign," as General William Momyer described it in *Air Power in Three Wars* (18). And on **March 8, 1965,** the 9th Marine Expeditionary Force landed on the beaches near Da Nang to protect Da Nang air base. By **October 1965** the 1st Cavalry Division (Airmobile) engaged North Vietnamese regulars in the Ia Drang Valley in the central highlands. The battle set the political parameters within which America's soldiers and airmen subsequently had to operate, allowing sanctuaries for the enemy. In the case of the Ia Drang Valley battle, Cambodia was the sanctuary for the North Vietnamese survivors of the 33rd, 66th, and 320th People's Army Regiments.

For the air force and the navy, which implemented the Rolling Thunder bombing campaign against North Vietnam, the problem was not only how to persuade a country with few strategic targets to desist from its goal of unification but also how to succeed under severe restrictions. President Johnson and Secretary of Defense Robert S. McNamara insisted on personally directing the campaign from the Pentagon, selecting targets that they thought suited their strategy of gradual and controlled escalation. According to General Momyer, the air campaign's objectives in North Vietnam were defined as:

(1) to reduce the flow and/or increase the cost of infiltration of men and supplies from North Vietnam to South Vietnam;

(2) to make it clear to the North Vietnamese leadership that as long as they continued their aggression against the South, they would have to pay a price in the North;

(3) to raise the morale of the South Vietnamese people. (173)

Only the first of the three objectives was military. The objectives were to be achieved by gradually increasing pressure against small targets moving south through mountain and jungle terrain. The first air attacks under Rolling Thunder launched on **March 2, 1965,** against targets in Route Packs 1 and 2 and were halted between May 12 and May 17, 1965. The North Vietnamese showed no interest in coming to the negotiating table. The flow of weapons from China and Russia increased, offsetting losses. When the air campaign resumed on May 18, targets north of twenty degrees latitude were included. Targets were released incrementally in line with the concept of gradual escalation. American planes could not enter a thirty-mile buffer zone along the Chinese border and around Hanoi, as well as a ten-mile buffer around Haiphong, the principal port.

North Vietnamese air defenses improved. By **July 1965** SA-2 SAMs made their first appearance, and U.S. aircraft losses mounted. After the Christmas truce from December 25, 1965, to January 30, 1966, Rolling Thunder III covered the period January 31, 1966 to March 31, 1966. The F-105 Thunderchief, an aircraft designed to carry tactical nuclear weapons against the Soviet Union, was the chosen bomb carrier. An increasingly sophisticated North Vietnamese air-defense network forced the employment of F-4 fighters as MiG caps to protect vulnerable F-105 bombers, EB-66 electronic-countermeasure aircraft to jam North Vietnamese radars, and modified two-seat F-105F Wild Weasel aircraft to counter SAM sites. The cost to put a bomb on a target escalated both in terms of money and lives lost. Rolling Thunder III was restricted to targets in the lower route packs. Furthermore, air force and navy aircraft were restricted to three hundred sorties per day.

On **April 1, 1966**, restrictions were lifted, and all of North Vietnam was released as a target area, except for the buffer zones and other target restrictions. Among the other target restrictions were airfields from which the MiG-17, MiG-19, and MiG-21 interceptors operated against U.S. Air Force and Navy aircraft. Operations continued with the usual restrictions implemented over Christmas, New Year's, and Tet. Finally, Hanoi's industrial base was released as a target. Production

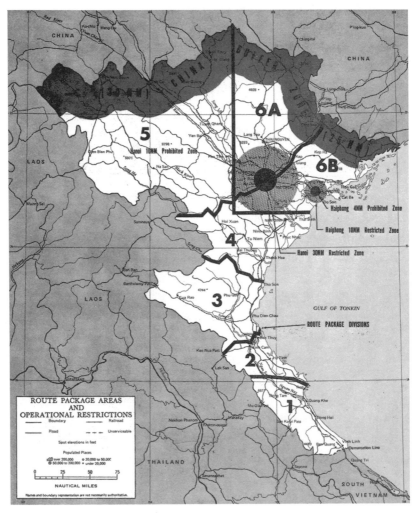

North Vietnam was divided into route packages for targeting purposes. *Aces and Aerial Victories* 9.

losses, however, were quickly made up by communist China and the Soviet Union. On **March 31, 1968**, President Johnson, in a nationwide broadcast, announced the termination of all attacks north of the nineteenth parallel. That meant that only the lower two route packs could be targeted, and they had few targets worth the risk of American lives. On **November 1, 1968**, President Johnson halted all air attacks against North Vietnam. When Richard M. Nixon assumed the U.S. presidency in January 1969, peace talks were in progress in Paris. The talks dragged on, seemingly without end. In 1972, Nixon, under ever-increasing internal political pressure to disengage from Vietnam, decided to act decisively. In an air campaign known as Linebacker I and II, tactical aircraft and B-52 bombers launched massive air strikes against the Hanoi/Haiphong area, and Haiphong Harbor was mined. The North Vietnamese resumed negotiations, signing an agreement on **January 27, 1973**. The Paris Protocol called for a supervised cease-fire, the return of American prisoners of war, and the withdrawal of U.S. troops. In **March 1973** the last U.S. combat forces left Vietnam. On **April 30, 1975**, South Vietnam fell to northern invaders. The war was over.

America's airmen in Vietnam, both in the south and over the north, fought with valor and courage in spite of a lack of relevant training and of flying aircraft built to accomplish other tasks. Steve Ritchie, the only air force Vietnam ace, was quoted in a 1999 *Wall Street Journal* editorial as saying, "The first time I ever saw an unlike airplane was a MiG-21 near Hanoi. In those days, we weren't allowed to train against dissimilar aircraft. They wouldn't let us train the way we were going to fight. Sometimes, I wasn't even allowed to fire back if fired upon" ("Review and Outlook" W11). In addition, airmen had to cope with failing air-to-air missiles and a lack of guns in their newest fighter, the F-4 Phantom—which wasn't a phantom at all, with its black smoke–emitting General Electric engines. (Gun pods eventually were added to the F-4.) America's airmen learned quickly from their early mistakes, as they had in wars past. By the time the air war ended for them in 1973, they had regained their flying skills and technological edge.

By mid-1960 the World War II generation of citizen airmen, many

263

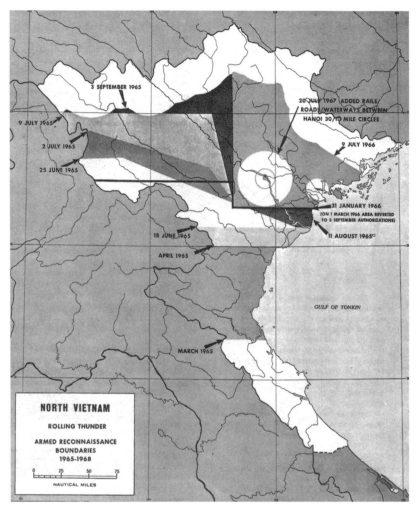

Rolling Thunder bombing boundaries. *Aces and Aerial Victories* 6.

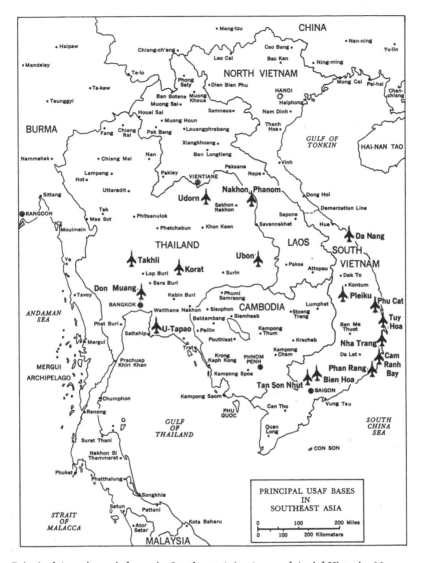

Principal American air bases in Southeast Asia. *Aces and Aerial Victories* 23.

of whom were enlisted men and who flew aircraft powered by recipro-
cating engines, had passed the torch to a new generation consisting
mostly of college-educated officers flying jet aircraft. World War II, the
Berlin Airlift, and Korea were history to the new generation of flyers
fighting the air war over Vietnam. The three accounts that follow tell
the story of how the new generation of airmen took the fight to the
enemy over Laos and North and South Vietnam.

Chapter 14

Hambone 02

By direction of the President, the Purple Heart is awarded to Major Ralph L. Kuster Jr. for wounds received in action against a hostile force on 30 June 1967.

The Distinguished Flying Cross and the 1st, 2nd, 3rd, and 4th oak leaf clusters thereto are awarded Major Ralph L. Kuster Jr. for extraordinary achievement in aerial combat on 14 March, 8 May, 25 April, 30 June, and 7 July 1967. On the latter date Major Kuster was directed to strike at numerous flak sites surrounding Kep airfield. Undaunted when surrounded by exceptionally heavy ground fire, Major Kuster in a voluntary act of bravery, relentlessly pressed the attack and silenced the hostile guns. On the 30th of June Major Kuster, the element leader in a flight of F-105 aircraft, was directed to strike an intensely defended strategic rail yard. Despite his aircraft having received two direct hits during the attack, he pressed on with selfless disregard of his personal safety and delivered his ordnance on target, even though immediately thereafter he was forced to eject from his crippled aircraft over unfriendly territory. The professional competence, outstanding heroism and selfless devotion to duty displayed repeatedly by Major Kuster reflect great credit upon himself and the United States Air Force.

Major Ralph L. Kuster Jr. distinguished himself by gallantry in military operations against an opposing armed force over North Vietnam on 3 June 1967. On that date Major Kuster was a member of a flight of F-105 Thunderchiefs on a strike against a vital highway bridge near Hanoi. After penetrating the intense flak and delivering his own bombs on the target, Major Kuster again jeopardized his life by voluntarily attacking and destroying a MiG that was threatening the remainder of the strike force. For Major Kuster's gallantry and devotion to duty the President of the United States has awarded him the Silver Star for his conspicuous gallantry in action. This award signed:

General William W. Momyer
Commander, 7th Air Force

Harold Brown
Secretary of the Air Force

Colonel Ralph L. Kuster Jr.

Silver Star, Distinguished Flying Cross (5), Air Medal (9), Purple Heart

In 1931 the Kuster family was struggling like many others, watching its pennies. It was not the best of years for the United States or for much of the rest of the world. Ralph was born on August 19 of that year. Fortunately, his father had a steady job as a draftsman at the McDonnell plant in St. Louis, Missouri. When Ralph was old enough to read, his interest was captured by a comic-strip character, Smiling Jack, a daring pilot and a U.S. marshal. Jack flew mostly in the West and landed his biplane in canyons and on top of mountain ridges to get his man. "I always enjoyed Smiling Jack," Ralph said, sitting at his dining room table in Stillwater, Oklahoma, "I especially was fascinated by the way its creator depicted the airplanes Jack flew, and the way Jack skillfully avoided a rock on landing. After the war began in 1941, they put model airplanes into cereal boxes, and my brothers and I collected a whole series of Army Air Corps and navy airplanes. I couldn't get airplanes out of my head."

"When I was fifteen, a friend and I got on our bicycles and cycled ten miles to Wise Airfield, outside of St. Louis. We had eight dollars between us. We asked one pilot after another if he would give us a ride in his airplane. We finally got one pilot to take our money, and he flew us around the airfield for twenty minutes. I enjoyed the ride immensely. From then on, I wanted to be an aeronautical engineer. I wanted to understand what made those machines stay up. Aeronautical engineering was not a real option at the time, since there weren't too many aeronautical engineering programs in the country. I eventually went to the Missouri School of Mines in mechanical engineering, but I took all the aero options they offered. In December 1952, when I was about to graduate, I walked past the library. A big sign out front proclaimed 'Be tested to become an air force officer and a pilot.' My friend and I happened to have a free hour or two, and I said to him, 'It's not going to cost anything to take the test.' So we both took the test and passed.

"When I graduated in January 1953, the air force gave me a ticket to Chanute AFB in Illinois for three more days of testing. The night before I left, we had a big celebration. Then I rode the bus for about a day and a half to get there. At Chanute I was put up in a barracks where the steam pipes were cracking all night long—*ka-pow, ka-pow, ka-pow.* Nobody got any sleep. The next day, everyone's blood pressure was sky high. The flight surgeon couldn't understand it. He had us lay down on the floor. Then he asked us, 'What is making your blood pressure so high? Is it the nurses walking through here?'

"I said, 'It probably is because we didn't get any sleep last night.'

"He said, 'OK. Rest.' We got everyone calmed down, and we passed. At the end of all the tests, they assembled us in a room, and an air force captain came in and read off everybody's name but mine. 'You can be a pilot,' he said after calling someone's name. 'You can be a navigator. You qualify for officer.' And so on. At the end I raised my hand and asked, 'What about me?'

" 'What's your name?' he said, looking at me quizzically.

" 'Kuster,' I said. 'With a *K*.'

" 'Well,' he replied, 'you can be anything you want.' I didn't know if I passed or failed. I took it as a good sign, and before I left Chanute I was given a pilot-training class and a starting date in June 1953. I also received a copy of a form letter signed by the secretary of the air force addressed to my local draft board requesting that they give me a deferment until I reported for duty in June. When I got home, I queried the draft board on my deferment for pilot training. I knew they wanted to draft me. Every time I called, they kept telling me that they would take care of me. 'We'll take care of you'—those were their exact words, not to worry about anything. They said that so many times, I began to worry. I was working at McDonnell engineering, sitting at my desk, and I thought, 'What are they trying to tell me?' I spoke to my boss about the situation, and he suggested I go visit the draft board in person to talk to them. I took along the letter signed by the secretary of the air force.

"I walked into the draft board office on Friday morning. One of the girls working there escorted me to a sweet-looking little old lady. She had white hair and looked like she belonged on a jar of Smucker's marmalade. She had the sweetest smile. She assured me immediately that everything was being taken care of and that they had the letter from the secretary of the air force, and she was going to bring my case before the board the following Wednesday. She said, 'I will make sure that they will react honorably toward your request for deferment.' She finished by saying, 'You don't have a thing to worry about.' Then she flashed her beatific smile at me, concluding our conversation. I was about to say goodbye when the phone rang. She picked up the telephone and after listening for about five seconds she yelled into the phone, 'I don't give a damn if you are going to be a doctor in two weeks. If you don't get down to the train station as directed, I'll have the military police haul you out in a jeep with your hands in cuffs.' By then she was screaming at the top of her voice. I had heard people screaming before—that's not what shocked me. What she said to that person was what shocked me—a doctor nonetheless. I walked out of the place dazed.

"Across the hall from the draft board was a National Guard office, and I spoke to the recruiting officer. I asked him if they were still giving commissions to engineers with experience. I had quite a bit of experience working at McDonnell. He said, 'I have enough engineers.' Then I asked him, 'How far would you trust the draft board to do the right thing by me?'

"He kind of smiled and said, 'Well, about as far as I can throw this building.'

"So I asked him what he thought I should do.

"He said, 'I think you should go and talk to the air force recruiters. Their offices are only three blocks from here.' The air force major at the recruiting office listened to my story sympathetically and suggested that I take the air force enlistment test right away. He would then hold my papers and defer my departure from St. Louis until June, when I was to report for pilot training. In the meantime I should go back to work at McDonnell. If the draft-board letter arrived at home—and he told me exactly what it looked like so my mother would recognize it—she would then call me at work, and instead of going home, I would go to Union Station and take a train to San Antonio, Texas. Without me getting a draft notice, it was legal for me to do that. I thought this was the best of all worlds. When I was through with the air force paperwork, they told me to clear the police and the draft board. It was late in the day when I walked back into the draft board office. The young lady who had greeted me in the morning jumped up and said, 'You're back. What's happened?'

" 'Well,' I said, 'I enlisted in the air force.' She got a grave look on her face and ushered me over to the sweet little old lady, who was sitting behind her desk piled high with papers. She had three stacks of paper in front of her, varying in height from a couple of inches to eight inches. She looked at me and said, 'You're back again. What can we do for you now?' I said to her, 'I enlisted in the air force.' She screamed at me, 'You what?' Then she brought her left hand down and whipped the three stacks of paper off her desk. Paper was flying everywhere. The girls sitting at the sides of the office rushed over, trying to catch the papers. Two tried to sit the sweet little old lady down in her chair. Two others grabbed my elbows, and one was yelling in my ear—she had to yell with all that was going on—'What did you do to her?'

"I backed away and said, 'I didn't do anything. I only told her I enlisted in the air force.' The girl let go of me and walked around the little old lady's desk, and I saw her bend over. I pulled the one girl still holding onto my other elbow over in that direction so I could see what was going on. On the floor was a canvas U.S. mail pouch, and she was riffling through it. She pulled an envelope out of the pouch and put it in front of the sweet little old lady, who took the envelope, tore it open, and waved a letter in my face. She screamed, 'This is your draft notice. If you're not in the air force on February 27, we are going to come out with the military police on the 28th and pick you up and take you away in handcuffs.'

"She did sign my release, and I was in the air force on February 27, 1953. I missed three and a half months of good salary at McDonnell. I had planned on buying a used car with that money. At Lackland I went through two months of basic training before entering the aviation cadet program. I graduated from aviation cadets in Bainbridge, Georgia, on August 17, 1954. I was at the top of my class, and with that distinction, I got my choice of assignment. The Korean War was over, so they weren't sending any more pilots there. Most of our assignments were to SAC or to T-29s at Harlingen AFB, Texas, a navigator training base. At that time, the air force started an experiment. They thought that guys who had just completed pilot training would make good instructors. I volunteered and got one of those slots. After a short tour of instructor training at Craig AFB in Alabama, I was assigned to Laredo AFB, Texas, a small town smack up against the Rio Grande. The four of us picked by the air force to be first assignment instructor pilots (FAIPs) turned out to be good instructors. From then on the air force took the top graduates of each pilot graduating class and made them instructor pilots, until eventually most of our instructors were inexperienced pilots.

"At that time, we were losing three pilots every two months, on average, at Laredo to aircraft accidental deaths. A lot of that wasn't the pilot's fault, but rather the blame should go to the airplane. The air force changed engine controls on the T-33 trainer. If you came back on the throttle too fast, you'd blow the fire out the end of the tailpipe (a compressor stall), and if you were close to the ground, it was too bad. The other thing the air force changed was the airspeed indicator, going from miles per hour to knots. Our airplanes at Laredo converted to the new speed dials, but frequently planes from other bases would be shipped to us to replace our aircraft losses, still with the old instrumentation. A guy would be on final approach and think he was flying knots when he was actually on miles per hour and be three to four miles below the stall speed of the airplane. As he approached the ground and tried to round out, the airplane of course wouldn't round out, and he plowed into the ground instead. So we killed a lot of guys.

"At Laredo we flew off a six thousand–foot runway. Another runway was five thousand feet long. When the six thousand–foot runway was closed with a flat tire, which was frequently, we had to land on the five thousand–foot runway. I remember landing one time on the five thousand–foot runway, and there were three airplanes off the end—one off the end and one on each side of the end. You had to put that bird down within fifteen feet of the end of the runway, and then it took pretty much forty-five hundred feet to stop. You had hot brakes when you got there. And if you stepped on the brakes too heavily, it blew the tires. The air force finally extended one runway to ten thousand feet and built another twelve thousand–foot runway, but we still had that five thousand–foot runway, which we used whenever the other two were closed.

"I graduated twenty-nine pilots. I never had any of my pilots flunk out. Then they made me an elimination test pilot. The wing policy was that if the elimination test pilot passed a candidate, he would have to pick him up as a student. I picked up about half a dozen guys and got them back into the program. I always hated to wash a guy out because I knew it affected his life. But at the same time, I thought it would be worse if he got killed or got a lot of other people killed. To wash someone out of pilot training was never an easy decision.

"In 1962, around the time of the Cuban Missile Crisis, the air force leadership decided they better get some more fighter pilots, and I was assigned to Nellis AFB in Nevada to check out in the F-100 Super Sabre. The Fighter Weapons School at Nellis, its pilots were our instructors, because most of the other instructor pilots were down in southern

Florida because of the Cuban thing. The Fighter Weapons School pilots were absolutely top-notch instructors. We got to fire the cannons and drop real bombs on the range. When we graduated, we were rated as weapons officers. Then I went up to McConnell AFB in Wichita, Kansas, and we opened up the first TAC fighter outfit there—F-100Cs. Our job was to train and become proficient in the use of nonnuclear weapons. Then the F-105 came along. The F-105 was a tremendous airplane. It was like a Cadillac compared to the F-100. We all enjoyed the F-105, but we didn't understand the airplane well. I became a weapons officer in the F-105. My job was to teach the guys to fly the airplane to survive in combat, to shoot the gun, and to drop bombs. As we pilots got more skilled in flying the F-105, we discovered that when we rolled the airplane over and pulled it around at altitude, high drag would slow it down, and then it would almost fall out of the sky. It wouldn't turn at all at the speeds its builder, Republic Aviation, told us to fly the airplane. Generally, when you are in a dogfight, it is to your advantage to be in an arc, because it makes it more difficult for a pursuer to get a lead on you and hit you. The F-105 wouldn't let us do that, at least not the way we were flying it.

"About that time, the air force needed pilots in Germany, and I volunteered to go. A bunch of us went over to Bitburg and Spangdahlem. The two bases are close together. I became the weapons officer in the 7th Fighter Squadron at Spangdahlem, and once again I was keeping all the scores of all the gunnery and running a bombing school at the same time. But I was still interested in why the F-105 wouldn't perform like a fighter when it had enough power to be one of the best. One time the Republic Aviation guys came out and briefed us. I will always remember what one engineer said to me: 'The airplane will pull 8.33 Gs. Aerodynamically, you can't get more Gs than that out of it. But the wings are stressed for 12 Gs. So there is no possible way you can pull a wing off an F-105.'

"While I was still at McConnell AFB, I also tried to get information from Republic on the aerodynamics of the airplane and its lift and drag curves. The data finally caught up with me at Spangdahlem. I found that the airplane had to do 285 knots to pull two Gs. Two Gs, in practical terms, is a sixty-degree bank at a steady rate and steady airspeed. But the F-105 in a sixty-degree bank turn would get such an angle of attack that it would slow down and fall out of the sky. I started experimenting with the airplane, and I discovered that I had to have it well over 300 knots. Then I could pull up to five Gs. But below 285 knots indicated airspeed, the airspeed would bleed off rapidly, and I would fall out of the sky. There was a guy named John Boyd, an air force colonel, a fabulous fighter pilot. He wrote a book called *No Guts, No Glory*. He collaborated in his theoretical work with a fellow named Davis. Davis and Boyd wrote a book together—this is before computers, mind you—called *Through Gs Maneuverability*. They developed a whole series of energy maneuverability curves. I wrote a letter to John Boyd and asked him if he could do the curves for the F-105. Boyd and Davis did the curves. From those curves I learned a lot about the aerodynamics and capabilities of the airplane. At 350 knots it had enough power to sustain the momentum to swing into a five-G turn, and it would maintain its airspeed. The energy curves let me extend what the 105 could do, and I started teaching it in the F-105 combat weapons course. All pilots had to attend the course every six months. It finally dawned on us that the 105 could be used in an air-to-air engagement if you kept your airspeed up and stayed down low. Then the 105 was a going machine. I think the training we gave the pilots at Spangdahlem and at Bitburg really turned it around for the F-105.

"John Boyd's contribution was really significant to the development of F-105 tactics. I would give Boyd and Davis credit for making an airplane out of the F-105. Before their work, the airplane was a straight and narrow thing to be afraid of. The curves they developed for us gave us an understanding of why you came into the pattern at 300 knots instead of 220: it was because the silly thing would fall out of the sky if you pulled it sideways at 220 knots. Also we learned to understand why the F-model, a longer two-seater version of the D, would go straight for two seconds longer than the D. Because of the extreme slope of the wing and the engine inlets, there was a two-second lag in the buildup of lift on the wing on the longer F model. A lot of engineering was done in those days on the new airplanes. We didn't understand the swept-back wing that well, with its extreme forty-five-degree angle and high wing loading. It was the last fighter to be built that way.

"By early 1966 we knew that everybody was going to go to Southeast Asia. We scrapped competition between squadrons because it was teaching the pilots to get in too close to the target, and they would get killed if they did that in Vietnam. We started teaching more realistic weapon-release methods on the range at Wheelus in Libya. I also taught the guys how to avoid getting shot down. I recommended to them that if you didn't have to fly below 4,500 feet, don't. And don't ever fly straight and level. Always have a wing down at least fifteen degrees right or left, and don't be mechanical about it. Never fly a straight line, and never slow down below 350 knots. The antiaircraft and SAM radars at that time calculated a linear projection for an aircraft's track, whether you were flying a curve or not. That meant if you were in a curve with the wings down at least fifteen degrees, by the time a projectile got up there, you were out of range. If you flew these tactics, you would be about one hundred feet off a straight-line projection away from where the shells were exploding. Overall, I think the Spangdahlem and Bitburg pilots were pretty well trained when they arrived in Southeast Asia.

"In October '66 my transfer to Southeast Asia came through. En route I dropped the family off, bought a house, and spent three weeks in the Philippines in the jungle, camping out and learning how to survive. Then I went over to Thailand. I arrived in Bangkok on Christmas Day. On the 26th I caught a C-130 shuttle out of Bangkok for Korat Royal Thai Air Force Base. I flew my first mission the next day, December 27, 1966, over Route Pack 1 and bombed Ron Ferry. That was considered the low-risk training ground. We got shot at, so we knew what flak looked like. On the 28th I flew my second mission. I went up to Route Pack 6, flying wing on a Wild Weasel lead (the two-seat F model configured to kill SAM sites). We were circling at about six thousand feet, looking for SAMs to come up. I was on the high side of lead, looking down at the ground, and I saw all these blinking lights below me and wondered what the hell was going on down there. Somebody dropping CBUs? That can't be. We don't have that many CBUs. Then I looked up, and there was flak all over the sky.

"Lead was zigging and zagging all around, and I was following and didn't know what was going on, while the North Vietnamese gunners were laying 57mm and 85mm barrages on us—big, rectangular barrages. It really amazed me how they could do that. I counted eight explosions across and six down. There were nearly fifty guns firing together and moving this rectangle of AAA fire as we were flying along. I don't know how they kept all those guns coordinated. The barrages followed us wherever we flew. We finally got out of there. That was my introduction to Route Pack 6, my second flight. From then on, I just got to go bombing and have a good time." There was no humor in Ralph's voice as he made this comment. His eyes had narrowed and assumed that distant, trancelike look of a combat veteran.

"I was assigned as weapons officer in the 469th Tactical Fighter Squadron of the 388th Tactical Fighter Wing. There were two other squadrons in the wing, with eighteen aircraft assigned to each squadron. All of us flew every day for three weeks straight. We regularly flew twenty ships in the morning and twenty in the afternoon. Then we had various four-ship flights go out over Route Packs 1 and 2 and into Laos. We flew about ninety-six missions a day total from Korat. Korat's sister wing, the 355th at Takhli, also had three squadrons of F-105s plus two squadrons of EB-66 electronic-countermeasure aircraft. Ubon and Udorn had F-4s. Every morning and every afternoon, over two hundred strike and support aircraft launched against the North. Air refueling was the critical node, and all scheduling revolved around the availability of SAC tankers. There were never enough of them. As a result, air operations against the North became predictable and routinized, a deadly way for the offense to conduct an air war.

"On March 14 I led a flight of four aircraft into northern Laos, near Dien Bien Phu. There was a key highway snaking down a narrow valley. The highway made a loop around a mountain, a prominent ridge with

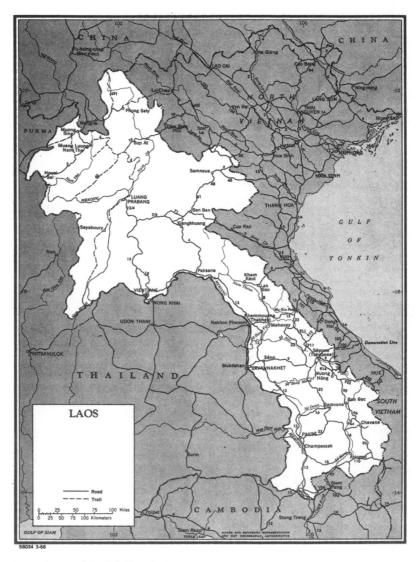

Laos. *Aces and Aerial Victories* 86.

a level outcropping at the top, straight down on all three sides. The outcropping was probably one hundred feet across, but it jutted out for perhaps four hundred yards. The communists had made a fortress out of the rock and hollowed it out. On top they had mortar emplacements, machine guns, and gun pits. From that rock they could command ten miles of road. Number four aborted as we approached the area. I sent number three back with him. A flight of F-4s was being controlled by a FAC in an OV-10 when we arrived in the area. The FAC asked us to hold. The F-4s were attacking with rockets. There was a cloud ceiling at eleven thousand feet, and the elevation of the rock was four thousand feet, leaving us little altitude to work in.

"We were circling around watching the F-4s. The FAC fired a smoke rocket designating the target, and the F-4s fired their unguided rockets at the side of the cliff, doing no damage. We had six 750-pound bombs each. With time to play around, I calculated a thirty-degree dive angle (we generally used forty-five degrees) at 350 knots. Using those parameters, I thought, we might be able to stay underneath the cloud layer and still have enough altitude at pullout to clear the exploding bombs. When the F-4s went home, they hadn't done any visible damage to the mountain. The FAC indicated that the Laotian Royal Army was just to the north of the outcropping, waiting to attack the rock. I had to drop the bombs from north to south so as not to hit the Laotians. I called the readings out to my wingman—'Thirty-degree dive, 350 knots, kind of slow. Try to follow me.' I lined up and came rolling down. I pickled five of my six bombs. The sixth would have gone down into the valley. I set my bombs for individual release so I could spread the 750s out and not have them all fall in the same hole. As I pulled off, I looked at what I had done. My first bomb hit a hundred yards from the lip of the cliff, and the others walked along right up to the opposite edge. Number two rippled his off, and his first bomb hit right at the edge and walked up to my third bomb. The FAC nearly jumped out of his airplane, he was yelling so loud, 'They are running out at the base of the cliff!' I couldn't see them, but we went in strafing the sides anyway.

'I have a bomb left,' I told the FAC. 'How about me putting it in the side?' 'Go ahead, if you can do it.'

"The FAC got out of the way, and I made a flat fifteen-degree dive and pulled up real sharp. I hit the side of the cliff about two-thirds up. The FAC was ecstatic. We strafed some more at the people we couldn't see, and he kept yelling 'They are all coming out.' So we strafed some more. On the way back, I still had some 20mm left. I wanted to get a counter for the mission, and you had to fly into North Vietnam to get a counter, so I went to a truck park in Route Pack 5. With the radar, I was able to pick up the highway through the clouds. We came in underneath the clouds, and there was this truck park ahead of us, and I swear there was a yellow road grader parked under the trees. We went in and strafed the hell out of everything. By the time we got back to base, the FAC had sent a message to Korat saying that the Laotian army walked in and took over the mountain fortress. They found nobody left alive. He put us in for a Distinguished Flying Cross.

"We kept a separate tally of Route Pack 6 missions north of the Red River. We called that 'Indian country.' Most of the pilots leaving then with one hundred missions had fifteen to twenty missions in Route Pack 6; all the rest they flew in the lower packs. When I got my one hundred, I had twenty-nine missions in Route Pack 6.

"On June 3, 1967, my call sign was Hambone 02. I was number two in a flight of four. We were going to bomb a highway bridge ten miles northeast of Hanoi. Zigzagging at fifteen degrees, wings down, we flew in from the water. We were going in north of the flak, and then we were going to fly southwest into the target, hit the target, and come out to the northeast. They were shooting 85s at us. I was watching the 85s and their movement. They were radar controlled but weren't accurate that day. I wasn't too worried about them. I was flying with my left hand. For some reason I was relaxed. The arming switch for the bombs was over on the right side panel. I had the bombs all set up. I reached over with my right hand and flicked on the arming switch, and I felt a *thunk*. The three thousand–pound bomb on my right wing dropped. Why that happened, I don't know. I had one bomb left, on my left

280

wing. We rolled in on the target to the right. When we rolled in on a target, we ended up upside down and then released the bombs. As we were going down on the target, I wondered how the lone bomb on my left wing was going to affect my roll. I was doing about 550 knots. I tried, but the aircraft wouldn't roll over the top. I finally cut the bomb loose. It missed by a mile.

"With all that maneuvering, I got separated a bit from lead. I was supposed to be on his wing. He was about a thousand feet in front of me and snaking out across the ground. I saw three MiG-17s crossing a little bit under his nose from left to right at about thirty degrees. I thought they were going to jump our 105s as they came off the target. John Flynn, my lead, decided to attack. He put his airplane into a ninety-degree hard right turn. I followed. I figured if he put his airplane in a hard turn, I would do the same, but I wouldn't be able to see where he was, so I continued into a 180. We were at five to six thousand feet, still at 500 knots indicated airspeed. I pulled around as tight as I could. When I came out, I was kind of abreast of him, and all I had to do was slide over into position. We were going faster than the MiGs, and he was closing on them. Then the MiGs went into a left 360—a pretty tight turn. John rolled into a 360 with them. We chased them around one half of a turn. We were carrying full belly tanks—850-gallon tanks, I think they were. John pulled probably between two and three Gs. I sat right below him. He said, 'Releasing belly tank.'

"John pulled the release, and I watched his belly tank come off his airplane. The tank turned sideways and barely cleared the tail section of his airplane. It narrowly cleared my right wing. I thought to myself, 'I'll hold my tank a little bit.' We went around and made almost another 180. Larry Wiggins was number three. I forget who was number four. As we were coming off the target, all strung out, number four looked back. When he looked forward again, the three of us were gone. We had made that 180. All of a sudden, number four had lost the flight. Larry Wiggins thought the other plane was still on his wing, though, and that he was covered. You can't look back in a sixty-degree cone behind an F-105 and see anybody. The MiGs were in a fifteen-degree bank. Larry Wiggins, the number three, hosed off a Sidewinder. The MiGs were in an arrow formation, one on each side of their lead. The one to the left was about 1,500 feet trailing, the right one was about 1,000 feet to the right in trail. Larry went after the one on the left. At the time of his shot, the MiG was at my nine o'clock position, and I was really worried about him. All he had to do was straighten his wings and slide across my rear, and he had me cold.

"I watched the Sidewinder snake up behind that MiG and go off right under the horizontal stabilizer. The MiG started streaming fuel, went from a fifteen-degree turn into a ninety-degree turn, and pulled out slightly. About that time, Larry came in and hosed him down with the 20mm gun. The MiG blew up like in the old World War II movies of the Japanese zeros. I said, 'That was a good shot, Larry. You got him.' I was glad to see him get that one. I called John Flynn, my lead, and said, 'We got one at ten o'clock going to two o'clock. We ought to do something about him. He's starting to get behind us.'

"John said, 'If you can get one, go get him.' John thought he was talking to number three, Larry Wiggins. He didn't realize that I was still with him.

"I said, 'OK. I'll pass on your right.' I figured he would pull in on my tail. I thought his guns or his gun sight were jammed, that's why he didn't go after the MiG. I went ahead and pushed the afterburner up and passed him on the right. I went after the MiG at our eleven o'clock position. He went into a ninety-degree bank right turn. I was basically coming ninety degrees into him. I started shooting when I thought I was within range. I had to have a forty-five-degree lead on him. I didn't. I quickly realized I had no chance of hitting him. He went on past, and I went into a climb and slowed her down and rolled in and dropped behind him. As I came down on him, for some dumb reason he almost leveled out, which allowed me to slide in behind him. I figured I was at 1,500 feet. I fired a whole bunch of rounds and didn't hit him. I raised, lowered, went around him a couple of times, and never did hit him. I thought, 'Where are those bullets going?' About that time I saw his right aileron go down, his left aileron go up. 'You dumb ass,' I thought, 'I got you now.' I knew the MiG couldn't get through the stream of bullets if I set it up like a saber in front of him. I threw all I had into a hard turn, all the rudder and all my aileron, and I was able to roll a lot faster than he was. I pulled the nose of the airplane in front of him and was closing. I moved the stick back as far as it would come, snapped the nose of the airplane up, and let it slide through him as I fired the cannon.

"We were pulling 8 1/2 Gs. He was flying at 580 knots, and I was flying at 680 or 690. I fired three hundred rounds in that burst. One round caught the top of the left wing and may have punched out the fuel line and gone through the wing and possibly penetrated the tank that was underneath the wing and set it on fire. That fire acted as an anchor on his left wing, and he immediately slid into flat spin. It was like someone grabbed hold of his left wing. He was on his third spin when he hit the ground. I don't think he had a chance to get out. I went through the fire from his airplane. My windshield and left intake were covered with melted aluminum. My engine started coughing and sputtering. I came back to idle to let the engine clear out. I turned for the water. Somebody else had seen the MiG explode and called me and said, 'Good shot.' As I turned for the water, I thought I wasn't going to keep the engine running. I probably got aluminum on the rotor blades. Then an F-105 pulled up on my right wing. I thought it was John Flynn, my lead. We were talking but not making any sense.

"What happened when I went after the second MiG was the lead MiG ran across John's nose and came after me and started shooting at me. I wasn't worried about it because we were going faster than they were, and I didn't think he'd get a lead on me. But John pulled in behind him. John didn't have a gun sight, as I had suspected, and he was trying to shoot him down without a sight. He didn't. I was sinking lower and lower, to about one thousand feet above the ground. I was thinking I might have to eject. I took the gun-camera film out and put it in my flak vest. Then I reestablished communication with the guy flying to my right, and it turned out it wasn't John Flynn but Larry

Gun-camera film of Ralph Kuster's MiG-17 kill, June 3, 1967. R. Kuster.

Wiggins, our number three. Larry thought I was his number four. There is a lot of confusion in combat.

"About the time I was ready to eject, the engine started working again, and I was able to hold the airspeed and altitude. But I knew at a thousand feet I was flak bait. When I got to 315 knots I started climbing. When we went over the harbor at Haiphong, where I knew they had a lot of 85mm guns, I figured we'd get shot down for sure. But I guess they thought the raid was over and had left their guns for tea. I flew over the water, pretty low on fuel. My engine was humming along real good. We climbed up to twelve thousand feet. I called on guard channel and said, 'I am about out of fuel, and I am going to punch out near one of the navy ships.' Some KC-135 tanker driver heard me and said, 'Hang on, I may have some fuel for you.'

"I said, 'Don't waste your time. I won't have time to wait for you to get here.' I pointed the airplane south and turned on my air to air radar and swung it back and forth. I picked up a target. It was the tanker, way up north in the Gulf of Tonkin. When he was about ten miles out, I swung into a hard turn, right behind him, and right on the boom. He started pumping gas immediately. After two thousand pounds, I slid off to let Larry have some fuel. I looked down and realized we were right back over Haiphong Harbor. We were still over water but within easy 85mm range. Larry was on the tanker taking on fuel. I called the tanker pilot. 'Hey, turn this thing to the right, or we'll be in China soon.' He said, 'I can't turn while we are refueling except in an emergency.' "I called him back and said, 'Bend it around to the right. He can stay on.' He rolled it into the standard KC-135 30-degree bank. It took forever to make a 180. I said, 'That won't do. Bend it around. Put it into a 45-degree emergency turn.' He bent it around. Larry sat right on his tail and took on four thousand pounds. Then I rolled in and took on a couple more thousand pounds, and we wrote that tanker crew up for saving two F-105s. We would have lost those airplanes if the tanker had sat around in the orbit where it was supposed to have been.

"In the meantime, John, my lead, also came out in the gulf, low on fuel because we were using afterburner a lot. Somewhere, he found a tanker and the three of us managed to join up. We were way behind the rest of the formation because they hit the target and headed for home fast. They were about two hundred to three hundred miles ahead of us. We were flying along, feeling good. When we were abreast of Route Pack 2, I called the ground radar and informed him that we would turn across Route Pack 2 into Laos. 'No, you can't do that,' he responded. 'They have SA-2s in there and 85mm.' 'Well,' I said, 'we'll spread out and turn our music boxes (ECM pods) on.' The radar guy said, 'They have guns in there. They'll shoot at you.' So what's new? We flew across Route Pack 2 without incident. John was feeling kind of bad because the MiG had gotten away from him. Larry went over the field and made a victory roll. I followed and made two rolls to let them know we got two MiGs.

"I had my film in my flak vest. Larry left his in the airplane. The film guy came out to meet us, and I took him by his shirt collar and said, 'There is a MiG kill on this film, and if you lose this film, I'll come to kill you.' They took care of my film. They lost Larry's gun-camera film, and Larry was the one who blew his MiG up. Maintenance inspected the engine on my aircraft and cleaned the melted aluminum from the MiG off the windshield and the engine air intakes, and it was ready to go again. Two days later the airplane was shot down. That MiG kill cost me eight hundred dollars. I bought drinks in the Officers' Club. That didn't cost much, maybe fifty dollars. I bought a round of drinks at the NCO Club, and that cost me about two hundred fifty dollars. And I bought a round of drinks at the Enlisted Club, and we drank until about three o'clock in the morning. That cost me over five hundred dollars. I wasn't fit to fly the next day.

"The day I was shot down, June 30, 1967, I was number fifteen out of a flight of sixteen aircraft. I was getting close to going home. Our ingoing altitude was 18,000 feet. Above 8,000 feet, the flak was pretty low. SA-2s started coming up at us, but they went all over the sky. We were using ECM pods and a staggered pod formation, staggered horizontally and vertically by 500 feet between airplanes. I flew at 18,000, my wingman would fly at 17,500 feet, and so on. With a sixteen-ship formation, we were spread across the sky for about two miles horizontally and 2,000 feet vertically. It was a nice, steady bomb run at 16,000 to 18,000 feet. Of course, on clear days the 85s could fire visually. The SA-2 Guideline missile doesn't guide for six seconds or so—until then, it accelerates. When the rocket booster drops off, the guidance fins deploy, and that's when the missile starts to follow operator commands. The SAM radar operator has an eight-by-eight-degree window on his screen, so a sixteen-ship formation with ECM pods denies him the target information he needs to guide the missile. Our loss rate to SAMs really dropped when we went to ECM pods, but it took discipline to fly such a formation.

"As long as you could see the telephone pole (SA-2 missile), you had nothing to worry about. With the spread in our formation, the missiles flew through and by us and exploded harmlessly. If the SAM was a threat, the missile would turn to a pinpoint in your field of vision. You knew it was heading for you. To evade the missile, you turned into it, down and up, forcing the missile into a turn it couldn't follow. The missile would lose energy, become unguided, and explode harmlessly. Takhli, our sister wing, insisted on staying with the twenty-second pop-up maneuver for bomb delivery instead of using ECM pods and the pod formation. The North Vietnamese started picking off their number fifteen and sixteen aircraft two or three times in a row. Then PACAF (Headquarters Pacific Air Forces, Hickam AFB, Hawaii) finally ordered Takhli to use the pod formation. ECM pods were scarce at the time. We heard some F-4 wing didn't believe ECM pods were useful and weren't using theirs, so I grabbed a C-130 one day, went there, and brought all their pods to Korat. Every one of our aircraft then carried an ECM pod.

"Our target was the Thai Nguyen rail yard. This was the one day I had brought along my camera because I thought it would be a no-sweat mission. Before, I always felt I would be too busy flying to stay alive to take along a camera. I took pictures of KC-135 tankers, of SAM launches, of two MiG-15s who flew underneath us, and of the 85mm batteries cooking off below. As I came in over the target, I felt a thump.

I looked left and right, but I couldn't see anything out of the ordinary. I continued my bomb run. Then something hit underneath, jolting the aircraft, and I knew I was hit. I quickly lost my electrical system and radio. I suspected I had a fuselage fire. I had never known an F-105 to blow up, so I didn't worry about that, and I figured I had time to get out of the area.

"I broke away from the formation and ran along the east side of Thud Ridge. Then I discovered I couldn't come out of afterburner. I thought, 'Hell, this airplane is going to run out of gas.' Smoke was coming into the cockpit. I shut off the air-conditioning, and I opened the auxiliary air vent. Then I started losing my hydraulic system. The F-105 had three systems. Two are redundant, and I knew the second one would carry me for a while. Instead of following the route out across Thud Ridge and over Yen Bai, I cut straight across the valley, and I stayed low and swung up when I got to the mountains. My wingman was still with me, both of us going supersonic in afterburner. I knew the way the airplane would go down with a fuselage fire. The fire burns through the hydraulic lines, and when the hydraulic lines give out the horizontal stabilizer tilts up. The stabilizer was aerodynamically loaded, so that when the hydraulics failed, air resistance would cause it to go up and throw the nose of the airplane down. When the nose dropped, you were going to get thrown against the top of the canopy—a real neck stretcher. And you couldn't bail out, because when you activated the ejection seat, the canopy was going to pick up forward velocity and hit you in the butt and crack every vertebra in your body.

"I was going supersonic and I thought, 'Boy, if the horizontal stabilizers go straight up at this speed, I'm really going to get a neck stretching.' What to do? I couldn't shut the engine down because I would crash. I rode it out. I thought, 'If I take her up high into thin air, then the aerodynamic forces on the wing would be less, and I wouldn't get such a neck bend, and I might be able to eject.' I pointed the nose up, and she went up to forty-four thousand feet like a skyrocket. I was cruising supersonic at forty-four thousand feet. I tried to get the attention of my wingman. I waved at him to get him to join up on me. He was an ADC pilot and didn't understand my hand signals. Finally, he pulled alongside of me, trying to figure out what was going on. I tried giving him SAC signals with my hands, telling him what was going on. He wasn't reading any of them, either. The airplane flew for ten minutes. Then I ran out of gas. My wingman still had 650 gallons of fuel in his bomb bay tank, as did I, but I couldn't get to mine without an electrical pump. When my number two hydraulic system gave out, I kicked out the ram air turbine, which activated the third hydraulic system. It didn't have as much hydraulic fluid as the other two, but it would run for a while. Then the engine came back to idle, or it flamed out and it was windmilling, I don't know which. I started losing altitude, but as near as I could tell the engine was still turning at 30 percent.

"I tried slowing her down as I lost altitude, trying to get to ejection speed, to around 200 knots. I had it down to about 220. I came through twenty thousand feet, and there was a big thunderstorm right in front of me, too wide to get around. I thought about circling down to a lower altitude, but when I looked down, I realized no matter what I did, I would come down in the mountains. I had come one hundred miles in ten minutes. I couldn't see any roads or villages. There was a river down there, and the big thunderstorm was on the other side of the mountain range. I didn't want to bail out in that thunderstorm. I had my camera with me. The whole time I was trying to figure out how I could bail out with the camera. I couldn't come up with a way. As soon as I got back to Korat, some guy said to me, 'Why didn't you take the film out?' I didn't think of it at the time. She was at 220 knots, nose heavy. I couldn't trim her up because I had no trim, no electricity. I tried to figure out how to eject. Obviously, I had to hold the stick back as I got out, or I would come off the seat as she tried to go down pulling negative Gs. How was I going to do that? I knew my right hand was more coordinated than my left. I would hold the stick with my right hand and squeeze the trigger with my left, and I would pop my right hand back into the seat and get out that way. I thought that was the best way. I ejected. I remember seeing the canopy floating by, the fire in the bottom of the cockpit from the charge that blew my seat out, and the nose of the airplane as it went down and away from me. All that seemed to happen very slowly.

"I sat up there, looking at the world, thinking, 'Well, it's not so bad.' By the time I settled in on this nice ride, the butt-snapper went *pow*, and I flew out into space. About that time, I felt my right arm just about being torn off at the shoulder. 'Hell, what is that?' I thought. I looked over at my right arm, and I was still holding onto the seat handle. I shoved the seat away from me and started tumbling end over end. I had ejected at twenty-two thousand feet, so I got into a skydiving pose. Unfortunately, I ended up looking at the sky instead of the ground. What to do? I pulled in an arm and a leg, and I flipped over. I brought them back out straight, and I was again looking at the sky. I thought, 'The next time, I'll kick them out sooner.' It worked. I was stretched out, looking at the ground, trying to figure out where to land. The automatic timer opened the parachute. The opening shock was in my groin. It really hurt. I looked down at my legs. I had a bottle of water in a lower pocket of my flight suit. The zipper was open. I remember seeing that bottle floating out of my pocket. I tried to grab it, but it floated away.

"The next thing I was supposed to do was deploy the survival kit and the life raft. I pulled the lanyard, and the pack didn't open, but the life raft decided to open up. I heard a *poof*, and the orange life raft started forcing its way out of a tiny opening in the survival pack. I finally got the life raft out, and it floated up into the parachute. I was carrying a long bolo knife, which I had one of the natives make me at the jungle survival school at Clark out of an automobile spring. He had beaten the knife out over a charcoal fire. The reason I liked it was because I could go through a two-inch piece of bamboo with one chop. The blade was heavy at the end and light toward the back. I pulled the knife out of its scabbard and stabbed the life raft a couple of times and then cut it off. *Poof.* Off it went into space.

"I looked around and saw I was going to miss the ridge. I was two miles or so into Laos, a small piece of Laos that cut into North Vietnam. I could see a big tree, and I determined I was going to come down right in the middle of the tree. I blew up my Mae West life preserver and put my arms across my chest. I saw the tree rise up on my right. Somehow, the wind blew me over, and I came down beside the tree. The slope of the mountain was a steep forty-five degrees, but it felt much steeper than that. I tried to figure out how to land on the side of a mountain. They didn't teach that in survival school. I decided to hit the mountain sideways, extending my right leg, keeping my left leg up, and throwing myself into the mountain. It worked perfectly, except that I bounced off the mountain into space. I tumbled down the mountain and stopped with a jerk. The parachute had caught the tree and jerked me off the mountainside, anchoring me to the tree. The tree saved my life. I tested all my fingers and toes. I did a push-up off the mountain. To my right and left I saw pine trees. The elephant grass was three to four feet high. I unhooked the chute and sat down. I got out one of my radios (I had three with me and six batteries) and tried calling my wingman. I never reached him, and he finally flew away.

"I looked at my watch. I had been ten minutes in the air before I bailed out. I was in the parachute for fifteen minutes before I hit the ground. On the ground I would be seventeen minutes, as it turned out. When my wingman left, I thought I saw a clearing on top of the ridge. If I got to that clearing, it would make it easier for a helicopter to get in and pick me up. I figured I'd climb up there and wait. I started up the side of the mountain. I stayed in the path I had made when I tumbled down. The elephant grass was as thick as my thumb and got hooked on my boots every step I took. I chopped at it with my bolo knife to free myself. I finally got myself up to the tree in which my chute got tangled. I looked to the right, and there was no opening, only more trees. But there was an opening to my left. So I made my way past the tree. Suddenly, I noticed I was walking but not getting anywhere. I seemed to be going deeper into the grass instead of making forward progress. I laid down my radio and helmet and bent over to look into the thick grass. I saw the tops of two black boots sticking out of the grass. I thought, 'What the hell is going on?' I wiggled my feet. The boots were on my feet. I refocused my eyes downward and found I was about 250 feet up in the air on a thick layer of grass matting. I had walked off the cliff onto a carpet of dried grass. I knew I couldn't use my feet. I thought, If I was in quicksand, I would swim out on my back.' I got on my back and kind of swam off the grass until I was sure I was on solid ground again.

"It was a hell of a place for a chopper to put down his jungle penetrator, so I decided to go back to my initial landing place. I started down the hill. Every time I took a step, I slid a couple of inches and got locked up in that elephant grass. I rolled down sideways. Eventually, I ended up at the exact place where I started. About the time I got there, I heard an A-1 Sandy (a heavily armed, single-engine, rescue-support aircraft) coming into the area. I got one of my radios out and called him on guard channel. He said, 'We have a chopper coming in. He should be here in a few minutes. Meanwhile, let's see if I can spot where you are.' He flew around, trying to spot me. I said, 'I am trained as an FAC. Why don't you let me direct you?'

" 'OK,' he said. While he was circling, I told him 'You are now at my nine o'clock position, eight o'clock position, and so on.' 'OK,' he finally replied, 'I think I know where you are.' About that time, I heard the *whomp, whomp, whomp* of an incoming helicopter. I called him and told him, 'You are about a ridge over from me.' He came right overhead, but he couldn't see me. I told him, 'I am right below you.' I popped a flare, and he spotted me. He moved the helicopter slightly forward, then the penetrator came down until it was level with me. As it swung toward me, I thought it was going to hit me. I put up my arms to ward it off. Instead, it dropped right between my legs—really close. I grabbed the top of the penetrator, released the pedals, stepped onto them, and hooked myself in. The chopper then backed off the mountainside, and I swung out over the valley, hundreds of feet up in the air. I started to get dizzy, so I kept my eyes focused on the ground. They pulled me up and in and gave me a shot of Old Methuselah. I had a second shot, maybe more.

"The rescue chopper took me to a helicopter base, and I transferred to another chopper, which then ferried me to Udorn, where the flight surgeon checked me over. I drank about half a bottle of Old Methuselah while the flight surgeon poked at me. He asked me, 'How do you feel, Ralph?' I said, 'I feel OK—now.' He said, 'Do you hurt anywhere?' 'I hurt all over,' I told him, 'but nowhere in particular.' I got back to Korat on a C-47 transport at two o'clock that morning. That day, we lost two F-105s and two were damaged. The other pilot also got picked up, and the two damaged aircraft recovered at Korat.

"I guess the worst mission I flew would be July 7, 1967, against Kep Airfield, only a week after my shootdown. Usually out of twenty airplanes we put into Route Pack 6, two would be Weasels and two would be flak suppression. We flew the flak suppressors in a flight of two, and each airplane pretty much operated independently. We were armed with four CBUs that we could drop individually or in twos. The idea was that when you saw some batteries firing, you dropped the CBUs over the batteries and had the gunners dive into their little foxholes, and the CBUs went off as they came back out. We had a formula for the attacking formation. The goal was to get all sixteen airplanes on and off the target in twenty seconds. The goal of twenty seconds was established as the time it took a gunner to pick out an airplane; track the airplane through the dive, bomb release, and pullout; and then crank the gun back up to vertical and try to select another target. We wanted him not to have a target when he got the gun back to vertical.

"Kep Airfield was on the northeast highway from Hanoi to China. Mine was one of the flak-suppression airplanes. We split up and took on the flak on the field. There were two batteries firing: one 85mm, which consisted of six guns, and one 57mm battery. I dropped two CBUs on the 57mm battery and two CBUs on the 85mm battery. Apparently, they got ticked off at me and decided I was going to be their target for the day. I went checking out to the south, jinking right and left, and they did their damndest to shoot me down. I flew along and thought, 'I go to the right. No, I go to the left.' Actually, I had to go left to get out of the area and into the protection of the mountains. I turned back to the left, they'll think I'd turn right, so I turned a little more left. I tried to outguess those batteries, and they were trying to outguess me. And they were winning. Boy, they were really getting close with their big rectangular barrages. Those 85s must have been firing one barrage every two seconds. The barrages would overlap, and before one rectangle ran out, they would have another rectangle up there. And they were tracking me with those barrages, back and forth across the sky, until I didn't know which way to turn. You can jink up and fly over a barrage, but you can't fly through the rectangle, because of the fragments in there. They'll tear your airplane apart. You have to kind of dive and roll, the thing I used to do with clouds.

"I finally pulled to the left—all the time in afterburner, the 85s still tracking me—and I headed for the other side of Thud Ridge. Then I jinked from one side of the ridge over to the other, back and forth, not to give any gunners a chance to line up on me. When I finally leveled out at altitude, getting ready to join my tanker, I was drenched in sweat. I happened to look at my right hand. There is an area where the glove ends and the sleeve of my flight suit had pulled up. The hairs on my arm were standing straight up. I brushed them down like you brush down the hairs on a dog to get them to lie down. I touched the back of my neck, just below the helmet, and my hairs were standing straight up. That was my worst mission.

"The allowable loss rate over North Vietnam was 6 percent. I think we were losing 18 percent over Route Pack 6—on average, two airplanes a mission. And sometimes we lost up to four from one squadron. With the other squadrons together, we sometimes lost eight to ten airplanes a day. At least we would have some of them severely damaged—they wouldn't all crash. The way the air force controlled the 6 percent was by fragging targets in the lower route packs, where we seldom lost an aircraft. So the overall loss rate was only 6 percent. But a 6 percent loss rate on a one hundred–mission basis gave you a little less than a 50 percent chance of getting shot down. Of the pilots shot down, almost one-third were picked up by helicopters, one-third became POWs, and one-third got killed. That's an Air Force statistic, not my statistic. One-sixth of the F-105 pilots got killed, and one-sixth became POWs. And I was fortunate enough to be in the sixth that got rescued. Let me tell you a little story. When I was having lunch with my family over at Spangdahlem one summer day, out of the blue my son, Ralph, who was about five at that time, said, 'Daddy, don't go to Vietnam.' "I was shocked, because I was going to Vietnam. I said, 'Ralph, why would you say that?' And he said, 'Daddy, you'll get killed.'" Ralph Senior's voice trembled as he told this story. "That comment haunted me and stayed with me throughout my tour in Vietnam. And when those guys were shooting the hell out of me, I'd hear his little voice. That did more than anything else to keep me alert, to keep me working, to keep me trying to second-guess those North Vietnamese gunners. When my airplane was on fire, I recall saying to the Lord, 'I know I'll get killed when you are ready, but I'd appreciate it if you didn't take me now. I have a little boy, and he needs a father, and I'd like to be around when he grows up.' And he granted my wish. Any fighter pilot who doesn't believe in God—I don't know.

"The spread ECM pod formation we developed worked well for us. The North Vietnamese tried to run MiG-21s up on us, and initially, they were getting our altitude. So we'd see the MiG-21s taking a look at us, and we'd change altitude, maybe 1,500 to a couple thousand feet. And we think that helped to throw the gunners off a little bit. But then the MiG-21s got a little more assertive and started making a 180 and coming in behind us. The first time they did this—I wasn't on the flight—half of the guys dropped their bombs to flee from the two MiGs. When they asked me what to do about it, we three squadron weapons officers got together and discussed the MiG tactic. We decided if we had to drop our bombs, we'd have only one flight do it to chase the MiGs. We designated a MiG flight.

"We got to the point where we could predict on which side the MiGs would show up. We designated the flight that was on the opposite side from the MiGs to be the MiG flight. If the formation was flying toward the west, and if the MiGs were flying south of us, then the flight on the north side was the MiG flight. This went on for a few days, and the MiG flight would pickle its bombs and start turning toward the MiGs, and then the MiGs would turn away. All the MiGs were trying to do was to get us to get rid of our bombs. We decided to roll the airplane up sideways and not pickle our bombs. If they turned away, we would roll back into formation and continue on. That worked, because as soon as the MiGs saw the planform and knew the airplanes were sideways, they turned away from us. Once they'd turn away, they could never complete the turn and catch up with us again. That worked and got to the point where we didn't lose a bomb except over the target.

"Turnover of experienced pilots because of the one hundred– mission tour was a constant problem. Replacements took six to eight missions, sometimes more, to get a feel for things. After that, they seemed to be OK. I had a horrible time because it got to a point where I could talk to a new guy at the Officers' Club and in my mind I would say, 'This guy's going to be shot down.' There wasn't anything I could do. It was the way the guy thought, the way he moved, the way he picked up his drink, the way he handled his cigarette. I don't know what it was. But I got to where I could predict the guy was going to be shot down. And I hated doing that. And I thought, 'What should I do?' Should I say to him, 'Pack your bag and get the hell out of here. Go AWOL(absent without leave, a courts-martial offense)? Get arrested. Go to jail. Do anything rather than get killed.' I didn't know what to say to those guys. I was so damned accurate on that, I felt horrible about it.

"After I came back to the States, I was at the Weapon Systems Evaluation Group in Washington. We were doing the Red Baron air-to-air-combat study. Later, we did an air-to-ground-combat study. I brought this up. There is something about pilots, and I don't know what it is, something about their backgrounds which makes some of them good combat pilots and others not. I don't know what that is. I can't identify it. When, in our analysis, we stacked the capabilities of pilots in combat in fighters, TAC fighter pilots generally were the best. On a scale from one to ten, TAC fighter pilots at that time were about an eight. Then I would put SAC pilots on the scale and put them at about a seven. They generally were pretty decent. Some of them were easily as good as TAC pilots, better than a lot of TAC pilots, especially the older ones. But when I got off of TAC and SAC, the two combat commands, and went to the Air Defense Command, they were down to about a four. And Air Training Command pilots would be about a three, and other pilots would be down in the grass, like one and a half. Those were the pilots we were losing.

"There is something in their backgrounds that makes them what they are in combat. SAC and TAC pilots, I believe, thought about death in combat. When I went to Southeast Asia, I said to myself, 'I am going to assume that I am dead. I am not going to get out of here alive. And I am not going to worry about it one more time.' When I came out of it alive, and I arrived back in the United States, I couldn't believe I was alive. I was standing on a street corner saying, 'Holy smokes! Yesterday there was flak all over the place, and today I am standing here on the street corner watching the traffic go by, and nobody even realizes there is a war on.' I couldn't believe I was still alive, because I really believed I was dead. I didn't think there was any way to get out of that, although I tried hard. We made a film at Korat called *There Is a Way*. The idea was that you could survive a hundred missions.

"Was a hundred missions too many? I don't know. I had been at Korat six months and was getting ready to go home. Three guys I knew from Spangdahlem arrived. We all ate in the Officers' Club at the squadron table. I sat right across from them, watching them eat. I thought there was something strange about the way they ate. What was it that seemed so strange? I couldn't figure it out. I leaned back in my chair, put my fork down, and tried to figure out what it was that was so strange about the way those three were eating. I was bringing my glass of ice tea to my lips, and the ice was jingling in my glass. Then I looked at my hand: it was shaking. I put the glass down. They picked their glasses up smoothly, brought them to their lips, and brought them down again, not shaking. I thought, 'Oh my God, I'm in bad shape.' I looked to my right and to my left at the other pilots. All the old pilots were picking up their glasses, and their hands were shaking. They were bringing their forks up and trying to find their mouths. They reminded

Ralph Kuster at his home in Stillwater, Oklahoma, demonstrating coming off a bomb run, March 1999. W. Samuel.

me of drunks who had to look at their ties to get their drinks to their mouths.

"After I got home, I woke up nearly every night soaking wet, seeing the flak going off in the bedroom. I found myself in the living room staring out the window trying to get things to calm down. One night, I remember looking at the houses across the road. There were some tall silver maple trees, beautiful trees. A thunderstorm came up, and these trees were rocking back and forth, and I was looking out the window. I didn't know how I got into the living room. I told myself, 'You are in Vienna, Virginia, and those are trees waving out there in the storm. They are not flak.' But I was still seeing all those 85s and SAMs going off, and I was hearing those voices in my ears screaming, trying to get a message through, because everyone was always talking on the radios at the same time. I told myself, 'You are not there. This is all in your head. Those are trees over there.' Finally, I started getting through to myself, and the flak melted away, and I saw the trees waving, and then the flak came back. That went on for ten years.

"On some days we'd lose no airplanes over Route Pack 6. On others we'd lose two, three, or even four. Not all of those aircraft crashed. Nevertheless, they were heavily damaged and out of commission for days or weeks until they were again flyable. I think we had pretty smart pilots over there at the time, guys I flew with and trained at Bitburg and Spangdahlem. As weapons officer, it was my job to figure out why we lost so many airplanes one day and none the next. I finally thought I figured it out. I was shot down on June 30. Two vertebrae in my back and two in my neck were off-center. They were going to send me to Clark until I got better. I said, 'No. I have eleven more missions up north. I think I'll go fly them.' So I was back in the cockpit in five days. For some time I had kept arguing that their gunners were tracking our IFF and TACAN. Intelligence kept saying the North Vietnamese didn't have the capability to track either the IFF or the TACAN. I didn't believe it. The guys who told me they were going to leave the IFF/TACAN on kept getting shot down.

"On my first flight back into Route Pack 6 after I was shot down, we were about ten miles in when an 85mm battery decided I was the one to shoot down. 85s went off in my 12:30 position. I could almost reach out and touch them. I didn't get hit, but I heard the *crack* and *smash*. When the second barrage went off closer than the first, I thought, 'All right, Kuster, what the hell is going on?' I looked down and saw the TACAN was on. I turned the TACAN off. That was the end of it. I was positive then they were tracking the TACANs and possibly the IFF."

Ralph Kuster survived one hundred missions over North Vietnam. He retired as a colonel after serving thirty years in the U.S. Air Force. Ralph settled in Stillwater, Oklahoma, where he had attended Oklahoma State University and obtained a master's degree in aeronautical engineering. This was also the place where he met his wife, a peaceful place filled with lots of good memories. But there are summer nights when storm clouds come racing across the Oklahoma Hill country, and Ralph Kuster in his sleep fights SAMs and MiGs, trying desperately to stay alive.

Chapter 15

Lincoln Flight

Citation to Accompany the Award of the Air Force Cross
Captain Kevin A. Gilroy distinguished himself by extraordinary heroism as Electronics Warfare Officer of an F-105 aircraft engaged in a pre-strike, missile suppression mission in North Vietnam on 10 March 1967. On that date, Captain Gilroy guided his pilot in attacking and destroying a surface-to-air missile installation protecting one of the most important industrial complexes in North Vietnam. He accomplished this feat even after formidable hostile defenses had destroyed the lead aircraft and had crippled a second. Though his own aircraft suffered extensive battle damage and was under constant attack by MiG interceptors, anti-aircraft artillery, automatic weapons, and small arms fire, Captain Gilroy aligned several ingenious close range attacks on the hostile defenses at great risk to his own life. Due to his technical skill, the attacks were successful and the strike force was able to bomb the target without loss. Through his extraordinary heroism, superb airmanship and aggressiveness, Captain Gilroy has reflected the highest credit upon himself and the United States Air Force.

Colonel Kevin A. "Mike" Gilroy
Air Force Cross, Silver Star, Distinguished Flying Cross (3), Air Medal (11),
Purple Heart

"I was born on June 4, 1936, in Menlo Park, California, about fifty miles north of the small town of Gilroy. Gilroy is named after my great-

great-grandfather. He was a Scottish sailor on a Hudson Bay Company ship, the *Isaac Todd*. He came from Liverpool and landed here in 1814. He was the first non-Spanish settler in California. He was put off in Monterey with scurvy, which was a fairly common disease among sailors at that time. The ship went on up north to trade with the Russians for furs and was supposed to come back and pick him up. He stayed in Monterey for about six months, waiting for his ship to return. But for whatever reason, the tides or the prevailing winds, the ship never came back. He took a liking to California and decided to make his life here. He changed his name from John Cameron to Gilroy, which was his mother's maiden name. This was just after the war of 1812, when it was still a common British practice to impress seamen. They'd go in the riverfront bars, hit some likely prospect over the head, and take him out to the ship. The next thing he knew, he was on the high seas. If they came looking for John Cameron, there wouldn't be anyone living there by that name.

"John married Maria Clara Ortega, the daughter of the Spanish don who had the local land grant. At that time, under Spanish custom, the land always went to the husband, so he inherited eleven leagues square. That is a lot of land. When John died, I believe it was 1869, he didn't have much land left. In his lifetime, control of the area had gone from Spain to Mexico to the United States. And during each change, some land was taken away. A year after he died, the town of Gilroy was incorporated, and they named it after him."

Today, Mike Gilroy, the great-great-grandson of John Gilroy, is the mayor of Gilroy, California, a small town on the highway between San Jose and Monterey. "After finishing high school, I went to one of the local junior colleges for a while. One day in early November 1953, a couple of my buddies and I decided to go in the military. One went in the navy, the other in the army. I looked at the marines. But the Marine Corps recruiter was at lunch, and the air force office was open. I went through jet-engine-mechanic school at Chanute AFB in Illinois and then was assigned to the 11th Bomb Wing at Carswell AFB near Fort Worth, Texas. I was a mechanic on giant B-36 bombers with six conventional engines and four jet engines. I got there in '54, about the time Jimmy Stewart was shooting the movie *Strategic Air Command*. Around Thanksgiving 1957 my enlistment was up, and I briefly got out of the air force before again reenlisting. That time I was stationed at March AFB, in Riverside, California.

"At March I was assigned to the 320th Bomb Wing, which flew the new, all-jet B-47. It was interesting work. I carpooled to Riverside Community College with Bob, a friend of mine. Bob was a pretty ambitious type. One night he said to me, 'Mike, I took the OCS test.' I said, 'Good for you.' A month later, Bob said, 'I passed the test.' Bob would get Cs when I would get As in classes we took together. I thought, 'If Bob can take that OCS test and pass it, I surely can.' I had no burning ambition to be an officer. I thought I might stay in the air force and retire as a warrant officer or a master sergeant. But Bob's casual comments sort of became a challenge for me. I took the OCS test and actually got a class starting date ahead of Bob. I entered OCS in March 1960 and was commissioned a second lieutenant that September. I wanted to be a pilot. I remembered when I left March, one of the maintenance officers had taken me aside and said, 'You need to be a pilot. Pilot is the only decent job in the air force. That's what you need to ask for. Above all, don't be a navigator.' When it came time for assignments, I put down pilot training. We took our physicals, and a lot of us wound up in navigator school, some for eyesight, some for different reasons. My sitting height was too great. There were a couple of us in that fix. The medics said, 'Come back tomorrow. We'll measure you again.'

" 'What am I going to do by tomorrow?' I thought. 'Cut a vertebra out of my back?' Actually, the word was passed from class to class how to get by these things. The way to pass in my situation was to get up early and walk around, because when you first get up your back is stretched out and you are taller. Then, just before going down to the flight surgeon's office, have two guys sit on your shoulders to compress your spine. I sat in a chair that morning, upright. One guy sat on my left shoulder, the other on my right. When I was measured again, I was still an inch too tall. The medics suggested I go to navigator training. I thought that's what that captain told me not to do. But we had other guys in my OCS class who had flown as enlisted men. One had been a loadmaster on a C-124 transport. He said, 'No, no. Navigator is a good job.' In fact, that's what he put in for. He didn't want to be a pilot. I went to navigator training at Harlingen AFB in Texas. I graduated in August 1961 and requested electronic-warfare training. A friend told me that EWOs did neat things. Even in peacetime, they were doing dangerous things such as flying reconnaissance missions around the Soviet Union. That sounded exciting to me, and that's what I put in for. Instead, I ended up with an assignment back to Carswell in B-52s. I was assigned to the 7th Bomb Wing, 9th Bomb Squadron. They didn't have a flying slot available when I arrived, and while I was waiting, I met a pilot who said to me, 'I know you.' 'I used to be here in the 26th Bomb Squadron as an enlisted man,' I said. He replied, 'I was in the 26th too. I'll need an EWO in a few months. I want you on my crew.' 'Why do you want me on your crew?' I asked. 'You don't know any-thing about me.' 'Anybody who went from enlisted man to become an officer and worked that hard should do well on my crew.' Several weeks later, I got on his crew when the slot opened up. It was a select crew. I got a spot promotion to captain a short while later. I thought I had arrived in hog heaven. I worked hard and tried to do everything really well, not to let my crew down.

"Because we were a select and STANDBOARD crew, we were picked to participate in varied things. In 1964, for instance, we went to Eglin AFB in Florida to do the first tests dropping iron bombs from the B-52. We spent a couple months down there, flying on the range, with F-104s and F-100s flying camera chase while we dropped 750-pound bombs. We flew the B-52D model, which eventually became the Vietnam-era workhorse.

"In January 1965 we were sent to Andersen AFB on Guam. The Vietnam War had begun. We sat on alert with our B-52s loaded with 105 750-pound bombs, I believe. The bombs were carried in the bomb bay and on underwing racks. We flew only training missions on this

Crew S-11, B-52D, 7th Bomb Wing, Carswell AFB, Texas, 1965. Captain Mike Gilroy is third from right. K. Gilroy.

deployment. Then in June '65 we were at Andersen again with a wing from Mather, near Sacramento. We had targets assigned in both South and North Vietnam. Some of our targets in North Vietnam were airfields, but luckily we never went. It would have been a disaster, if you can imagine twenty-seven airplanes, flying in trail formation, with one-minute separation between airplanes, going in at about twenty thousand feet. I was on the first B-52 mission to bomb in South Vietnam. My airplane was in the second of two waves. By the luck of the draw, the wing from Mather led the first wave. I believe there were nine aircraft in that wave in three cells of three. There was five-minute separation between the first and second waves. We took off from Guam after dark. We were going to refuel over the Philippines. The lead airplane in the first wave was five minutes early to the refueling point.

"What do you do in SAC when you are five minutes early? You do a 360-degree turn, and they did. The turning B-52 lit right into one of the B-52s behind it. There were two airplanes down, and we were not even halfway to the target yet. Beepers were going off everywhere. I think we lost five people from those two crews. Of course, we were all pretty well hyped-up for the mission. Our target was in the Iron Triangle, near Saigon. Intelligence had given us a threat briefing and put these big combat radii of the MiGs on their briefing charts. The MiG circles were well down where we were. We knew we were going to get bounced by MiGs. Over the target, it was all uneventful. We dropped our bombs and began the long flight home. When we got back to Andersen, there was a congratulatory telegram from the army commander in the Iron Triangle area saying what a wonderful job we had done, that we saved their bacon and killed all these people. Then the SAC inspector general came to investigate the accident and asked our wing commander, 'Did you tell the air crews not to make 360-degree turns?' The wing commander, a colonel, replied, 'No.' And then he was gone. From that time on, the new wing commander—it was the most stupid thing you ever saw in your life—at the end of every mission briefing got up and said, 'Don't make 360-degree turns to kill time.' That was the fix. One of the interesting differences between SAC and TAC was that SAC probably never made the same mistake twice. Once you made a mistake, there was a procedure put in place to keep that from happening again. In TAC you were supposed to be a free thinker. 'We are not going to give you any unnecessary restrictions' was the message. 'Go do it.'

"We flew nineteen missions into South Vietnam and then came back to the States, back to pulling nuclear alert—seven days straight on alert, in on Thursday morning, off the following Thursday morning. A little boring, yes, but it had its compensations. We went in there Thursday morning and took a series of tests. We took an emergency-procedures test, of course. Then the EWOs had to take a radar-signal-recognition test. We listened to radar-signal tapes. The Intelligence people would play a Fansong SAM missile radar tape, and if you identified it correctly, you had to mark down on your sheet 'Fansong.' If you missed, you listened again until you got it right. They played Whiffs and Fire-cans and Firewheels—all the AAA radars: the YoYo, a missile-defense radar deployed around Moscow; Scan Fixes, Scan Threes, and Spin Scans, fighter intercept radars. That was tremendous training for the Weasel program later on, because the Weasel program didn't do any of that. SAC EWOs moved into the Weasel program effortlessly. The ones that came from ADC or ATC had problems.

"Of course, we flew airborne alert too—'Chrome Dome,' as it was called. Our missions from Carswell were over the Mediterranean. We flew through the Strait of Gibraltar on to the eastern end of the Mediterranean Sea, back and forth. Chrome Dome duty lasted only about three months, after which you wouldn't get it again for about a year. Those were long missions, twenty-seven hours or so. There wasn't much for the EWO to do, most of the time, so I used to sit in the pilot's seat and fly the airplane manually.

"I was on the golf course one day at Carswell, playing with this pilot who had just transferred in from Barksdale AFB in Louisiana. He said, 'I got an EWO friend who just went to an F-100 assignment.' I said, 'Oh? What's that?' 'It's something about killing SAM sites,' he said— some real secret stuff. I thought, 'That sure sounds interesting.' I sort of had itchy feet. There was a war going on, and I thought it would be fun to do some of that. I went down to Personnel and said, 'I heard about this program where EWOs can get into fighter aircraft and do this SAM site stuff.' Of course, they didn't know anything. They got out the books that had all the courses listed. 'There is no course like it,' they insisted after reviewing the course listings. I talked to some of the guys in the squadron, but none of them had heard anything either. Then there was a guy who ran our electronic warfare simulator. He had an assignment to the Weasel program. He was going through a divorce and was fighting for custody of his daughter. He called me and said, 'Mike, I heard that you are looking for this kind of an assignment. I got it. Would you want to take it?' I said, 'You bet.' He and I went down to the personnel section to swap assignments. This time they said, 'You can't do that.' 'There has to be a way,' I insisted. They shook their heads. We made an appointment with the wing deputy for operations, a colonel. He called the chief of personnel at SAC Headquarters and made it happen.

"Three weeks later, I left. My orders were cryptic: 'Report to the American Motel, Sepulveda Boulevard, Long Beach, California, for three weeks of training at the North American facility at Long Beach Airport.' It was January 1966 when I drove into the parking lot of the American Motel. As I checked in, I asked the clerk if she knew anything about a school. 'I have orders to report there.' She replied, 'I don't know anything about that, but there is a hospitality room back there,' and she pointed down a hallway, 'and some guys asking questions like you are down there. They may be able to help you.' There I learned from other guys who drifted in that come Monday morning, someone would pick us up and take us out to Long Beach Airport.

"Come Monday morning, there were eight of us. Way in the back of the airport, there was a fenced-in area with concertina wire on top of the fence. We went into this hangar, and in the hangar was an F-100, a couple of classrooms, and a cockpit simulator. There were some North American Aviation (builders of the F-100) guys there and some Applied Technology guys. They gave us the academic portion of the Weasel school. We students were four pilots and four EWOs. An instructor from North American told us to pair up, one pilot and one EWO. 'You'll be a crew,' he said. 'That's how you'll fly your combat tour. However you guys want to do this. It's up to you.' The flamboyant pilots immediately paired with the flamboyant EWOs. It got all the way to the end, and I hadn't picked anyone. Ed Larson and I remained. Ed Larson was an OCS guy like me, a little older than most, a little junior in rank than most. We paired up—a wonderful choice for me. Ed was a superb individual. That night, most of us went out to dinner. We had a drink beforehand and shot the breeze. I looked at my pilot, and he was asleep with his face about a quarter of an inch from his soup bowl. I thought, 'What the hell have I got myself into, here?' Later I learned that Ed would fall asleep almost anywhere at the drop of a hat.

"The simulator training was fun—pretty basic. They had an operable stick and a vector scope. All you did was fly and put the SAM signal at the twelve o'clock position, until you had station passage. The classroom instruction was terrible. An engineer from Applied Technology gave us four hours on how the SAM system worked, how the associated Fansong radar worked, and how the guidance signal worked, and how the triplets moved. 'Why do we need to know that stuff?' I thought. I wished he would get on with it. We were falling asleep and dozing. I remember three months later, thinking, 'What the hell was that guy saying?' How the triplets moved was really important then, but it didn't seem important at the time. We were supposed to go from there to Nellis to get training in our airplanes, but the airplanes weren't ready. They were still being modified. 'Come on back to Nellis with me,' Ed said. 'I'm an instructor pilot there in the F-105. When I instruct, I get an F model, a two-seater, and you can fly with me.'

"For six weeks I flew every working day. I flew three times a day, if I could, with Ed Larson. It was a lot of fun. On one of the first missions we flew down the Grand Canyon. That was exciting, after having flown B-52s for years. We went down to Death Valley and flew below sea level. I had my own stick and throttle in the back seat, and Ed encouraged me to fly. I was really impressed with Ed Larson as a pilot, and my earlier misgivings vanished. Our airplanes finally arrived, and we transferred to the Weasel squadron. My Weasel class had eight pilot-EWO crews. By then I felt I was born to be in that airplane. The instructors were the guys who had originally gone over to Vietnam and checked out in the F-100F two-seater. Some of them had killed SAM sites; most of them hadn't. They had maybe twenty missions each.

"The instruction was general. We had two SAC RBS sites that we flew against—one at Walker Lake, Nevada, and one at Saint George in Utah. We would make passes on the RBS sites from different directions to get used to the equipment. I had a panoramic scope in the back and a vector scope. The receiver had a variety of functions. One was a direction-finding capability. When you tuned to a specific signal, two tuning bars appeared on the scope, and it would either tell you the signal was in front of or behind you. As you flew by the SAM site, station passage, you only got a brief indication that you were abeam or over the site. If you missed the instant of station passage, the tuning bars looked the same if you were approaching or leaving the site. I would soon learn that in the heat of combat, detecting station passage was difficult but critical to the success of our mission. You could also gate the Fansong signal, and the receiver would display the scan and the fly-back time. You could actually tell where you were in the scan of the enemy radar. And if he launched a missile, you could tell if he was launching at you or at someone at the left or right of you—if you had the presence of mind to do that when you were being launched at. I didn't have the presence of mind to do that. I just assumed they were launching at us.

"The first six seconds the missile was unguided. Then, after the booster rocket fell off, the guide vanes in back of the sustainer rocket deployed. Above a thousand feet, the missile became a real threat—not below, although Intelligence was liable to exaggerate and say it could operate down to five hundred feet. I learned that between the SA-2 SAMs and the MiGs they could force us down where they had their real capability, their antiaircraft guns. The flak was capable because there was so damn much of it. We had six training missions at Nellis. Our primary weapon was the Shrike, the AGM-45 antiradiation missile. We never fired one at Nellis. We carried them on the airplane but never fired one. And we carried CBUs, and we never dropped any of those either. But all the pilots were experienced and had lots of time in the airplane. They all came from Bitburg or Spangdahlem in Germany.

"We had six aircraft to ferry to Thailand. Two crews went over by Military Airlift Command aircraft. Those of us lucky enough to fly our own aircraft across the Pacific went to McClellan, from where, on June 29, we took off for Hickam AFB in Hawaii. It was great. I flew manually most of the way. I did everything but the takeoff and the landing, including joining up with the tanker. We got to Takhli on July 4, 1966. We were there with six airplanes and eight crews. Forty-five days later, we had no airplanes. We had four people killed, three wounded. Two were wounded so badly, they had to fly them back to the States. Two more were POWs. One guy quit. Not a great start.

"After we arrived at Takhli, we started off with a typical week of briefings of what we couldn't do—targets we couldn't hit, places we couldn't fly over. The rules of engagement. The 105 wing from Korat went in a certain time every day, and the 105 Wing from Takhli went in a certain time of day. The biggest driver was the tanker schedule, controlled by SAC. What a way to fight a war. The targeting was a disgrace, we all knew that. A lot of times we would go after suspected truck parks, river crossings—worthless things. Then we were sent to someplace like the thermal power plant, or the Thai Nguyen steel mill, or some other heavily defended target. We'd hit it the first day and get the crap shot out of us, lose several airplanes. Go back the next day, and the next day, and we'd lose about half as many airplanes because of the damage we'd done before and the defenses being out of shells and missiles. Then, invariably, there would be a bombing halt—it was either Christmas, or Easter, or Tet, and we stopped bombing. They resupplied. Then we'd go back to the thermal power plant or the steel mill and we'd lose several airplanes again.

"At Takhli we really had no checkout at all. We didn't know how to do anything against SAM sites. No Weasel crew we talked to had any experience in a real tough area such as Route Pack 6. It was still an evolving program. Our first five missions we flew into Route Pack 1. One SAM site at Vinh would come on the air occasionally. He was a crafty guy. I don't think anybody ever took him out. Then, on August 7, 1966, we got a mission up to the northeast railroad in Route Pack 6. You talk about a transition: from doing nothing to going up to the northeast railroad, probably the most heavily defended piece of real estate in North Vietnam. We were lead of a flight of two. Pete Pitmann was on our wing with a D-model. One Weasel and one D to take out the SAMs. We refueled over the water. The weather was crappy. Clouds covered half to three-fourths of the area, and then there was a haze layer below us. We were about ten minutes ahead of the strike force.

"I picked up a SAM signal as soon as we entered the Cam Pha area on the coast northeast of Haiphong. I lined up on the SAM site, and Ed fired a Shrike—the first Shrike either one of us had fired. The radar went off the air at the appropriate time, so we figured we hit it. Another SAM site at our two o'clock position lit us up and immediately launched at us. I called the launch to Ed. He lit the burners, got some airspeed, and pulled up. We dodged the first missile, leveled out, and dodged the second missile. Then we were right next to this huge towering cumulus cloud, and the third missile came out of the cloud and blew up directly in front of us. When it exploded, it knocked the aircraft five to seven feet straight up in the air. The cockpit immediately filled with black smoke. As it turned out, we had taken a hit in the front end of the aircraft, where the 20mm cannon is. The cannon had a big can full of ammunition behind it. The missile exploded some of the ammunition, blowing our nose section right off the aircraft.

"With all the black smoke in the cockpit, it was hard for me to breathe. My mask was leaking, and I was choking. The only thing I could see through the smoke was the master caution light and the red fire warning light. The intercom was useless. I thought, 'What now?' as I was choking and fighting to breathe. 'I better get rid of that canopy.' On the left-hand panel was an auxiliary canopy jettison handle. If I pushed on one end of it, it rotated up, and I could pull the handle and blow the canopy. I couldn't find it. I just couldn't find that handle. I was running out of air. I was nearly asphyxiated. I thought, 'To hell with it. I'm getting out of the airplane.' And with that I rotated the ejection handles. It was a two-action ejection—you rotated the handles and the canopy went, then this trigger pops down, and you have to open your hands and squeeze the trigger to actually eject from the aircraft. I rotated the handles up, intending to get out of the aircraft. As I opened my hands to grab those triggers, I decided, 'Maybe I should stay.' When the canopy blew, it cleared the smoke from the cockpit, and I could breathe again. I could look outside, and I noticed it was a pretty day. I went to call position on the intercom, 'Ed, are you still there?' He replied, 'Yeah. Are you still there? Are you hurt?' 'No, I'm not hit at all.' 'Well, we're going to fly out of here.' 'Good. I couldn't find my auxiliary canopy ejection handle,' I said. 'I had to fire my seat.' 'Me too, Mike.'

"We headed east toward the water, the closest way out of there. We were north of Haiphong. We had lost sight of our wingman as we were dodging the missiles, so we were by ourselves. In our open-cockpit airplane and without a nose section, we were going only about three hundred knots—much too slow to survive the flak. I could look back on the leading edge of our intake and saw a big hole. In spite of all the damage, we were still flying. It was a great airplane. It had a dry wing, unlike the F-4, which had a tendency to flame when hit in the wing. Sometimes we carried a 650-gallon centerline tank. That would absorb a lot of flak. The rest of the fuel was on top of the fuselage and in the former bomb bay.

"We were getting close to the coast. I looked back, and about 1,500 yards behind us, there was a burst of 85mm. I said, 'Ed, they are shooting at our eight o'clock.' 'I see it,' Ed answered. The next burst of 85mm was about 500 feet behind us. The rounds would go off in sequence—*pow, pow, pow, pow, pow,* in a circular burst. Then the third burst hit us underneath and threw the aircraft up in the air. At that time, our wingman rejoined us. Pete must have had at least a hundred knots overtake speed on us. He flew directly beneath us and overshot by about 200 yards. Then the next burst of flak hit him. I don't know whether he pulled the AAA radar's range gate off us, or they thought they had us and wanted to get another kill. Pete's maneuver saved us and gave us enough time to get over the coast. Once over the water, Ed said, 'Mike, the controls are gone. We have to eject.' The flak had taken out our hydraulics. The plane went into a slow left bank, heading toward China. I said, 'OK, Ed. See you in the water.' We were both pretty calm about it. Ed said, 'OK, Mike. Good luck.' I sat up straight in the seat and ejected. Ed ejected right after me. Then I wondered, 'Is the chute going to open?' Next thing, I am under that beautiful canopy and everything is so calm and quiet. All the radio noise is gone. All the SAM and AAA radar signals, which only seconds earlier were blasting in my ears, were off the air. I sort of had the feeling that everything was OK. I observed our plane going down. It exploded about 1,000 feet above the water. It was good we got out when we did. I really wasn't scared at that time. In fact, I released my survival kit and held onto the kit handle. I thought it would make a good souvenir. I unzipped my G suit pocket and put the handle in there and zipped it back up. I still have the thing on the wall at home mounted on a plaque: It says 'Aircraft 358, 7th August 1966, Gulf of Tonkin.'

"I pulled out my survival radio and listened to the rescue effort on the way down. I tried to talk, but I was really garbled, and no one could understand what I said. Ed and I were coming down outside Haiphong Harbor, amongst those big karst islands. I was sure there was a pretty good chance we would be picked up. As I drifted downward, I was going over all the things I learned in survival school about water landings. The raft hits the water, pull on your risers and face into the wind, release the clips when the feet hit the water, release the canopy so it blows away from you. I thought I was Joe Cool, remembering all that stuff. All that repetition in survival training was invaluable. You'd think under stress you'd tend to forget those things, but most of it came back. The raft hit the water. My feet hit the water, and I released the canopy. The next thing I knew, I was under water and sinking fast. I forgot to inflate my Mae West. I couldn't find the little tabs that hang out beneath your armpits. I couldn't find them, and I was still going down. I thought I was about to run out of air. I couldn't find the tabs no matter how hard I tried. 'They are right under my arms,' I thought in rising desperation, but I couldn't find them. And just then, the white nylon cord that attaches to the life raft above me floated in front of me. I grabbed it and pulled myself up to the raft and hopped in. 'How stupid can you get,' I thought. But I still didn't inflate my Mae West. Once securely in the raft, I retrieved my survival kit and opened it up. The only thing in the kit was two pairs of black wool socks. The Thais on the base had gone through the survival kit and taken everything out they knew what to do with. They probably did not know what to do with the wool socks. I pitched them over the side. We carried sea dye marker in our survival vest, pen gun flares, smoke flares, two or three radios, and baby water bottles. I had a drink of water then listened for

313

the rescue on a survival radio. Our wingman was flying cover for us. He said, 'There are boats in the water. I see one.'

"Ed had let out a sea dye marker so they could see him. I was closer to the islands than he, and I wasn't going to let anybody know where I was until I was sure we were going to be rescued. At that time, there were seven aircraft flying cover for us. A ship was coming out of the harbor toward us. One of the F-105s went after him and dropped his bomb load near the ship. The ship turned around and went back. We were in the water for about an hour and a half before we were rescued. I could hear Crown Alpha on guard channel saying, 'Where are they? I see them, I see them.'

"Ed let go with an orange smoke flare. Crown Alpha came in and landed and picked up Ed, and then I heard him say, 'I don't see the other one.' Then I let my flare go. Crown Alpha was an amphibious SA-16 Albatross out of Da Nang with no markings. I listened to all the conversation on the radio, and I knew they were there to pick us up. As the aircraft taxied over toward me, I saw an Oriental face in a wet suit standing in the door. I was confounded. A trick by the North Vietnamese? I reached down and pulled my thirty-eight and pointed it at the rescue man standing in the aircraft door. He waved at me and shouted, 'Don't shoot, I'm Hawaiian.' Then he jumped in the water and swam over to me, grabbed my raft with one hand, and pulled me over to the airplane.

"Once in the aircraft, I saw Ed, all bundled up in blankets. He hurt his back. The seat gave him a massive compression fracture, and he never flew jets after that. As soon as I got in the airplane, the SA-16 rescue men looked at me and smiled. One said, 'You forgot to inflate your Mae West, didn't you?' I looked down, and sure enough, there were the inflation tabs where they were supposed to be. 'Yeah,' I said sheepishly, 'I forgot.' Then they handed me a cup of coffee. The SA-16 had one bad engine, and the breeze was off the shore, so our takeoff was toward shore. They taxied out a ways and then pushed the good engine up to full power. Then they tried to push the bad engine up. We aborted two takeoff attempts. At the end of every takeoff, we received mortar fire from the nearby islands. The guys had the side door open and were shooting their M-16 rifles at the shoreline. The bullets probably got about halfway there.

"The most frightening part of that entire experience was the takeoff. The SA-16 started bouncing on its belly as it gathered speed. It would go a few feet in the air and crash down again. It seemed like every rivet in the airplane popped. The plane groaned and creaked. I envisioned a wing falling off or the floor caving in. On our third and final try, they bounced their way five feet into the air, and the next thing I knew we were airborne. They flew us to Da Nang. There Ed and I were met by the base flight surgeon. After he examined us, he told Ed he was not going back to Takhli but would be hospitalized at Clark in the Philippines. My back was hurting, too; in fact, I had a compression fracture, but it didn't bother me much at the time. It wasn't until years later when I had a CAT scan that I learned I had two crushed disks in my back.

"The next day, my wing, the 355th Tactical Fighter Wing, sent a C-47 to pick me up and take me back to Takhli. There I learned that we didn't have any Weasel airplanes left. We had lost seven aircraft that day—the highest toll for a single day. 'What do you want to do?' I was asked. I said, 'How about thirty days leave?' I hopped on a KC-135 tanker and went to Okinawa, then to Fort Worth. I got back a month later. How did I feel about coming back? At that time, the chances for anyone to complete a tour were poor. When I first arrived at Takhli, we were told that as Weasels we could count on getting shot down 1.6 times. 'One out of the way,' I thought. I believe everybody was pretty fatalistic but not overly concerned. Most thought that they themselves wouldn't get shot down. The guy next to you may get shot down because he doesn't have your abilities, but not you. Getting shot down, being taken prisoner, or getting killed was not something you sat around and talked about.

"That doesn't mean the next time I went up to the northeast railway, about three months later, I didn't have some second thoughts. And the guys in the squadron were giving me a bunch of good-natured crap, too. 'Eh, Gilroy,' I heard someone say in the briefing room, 'you are going back to the northeast railway today. Didn't do so well the last time you were there, did you?'

"We learned. A couple months after I was shot down, we wouldn't have gone in that day under those weather conditions. You have to give yourself a fighting chance. At a minimum, you have to be able to see the missiles coming. The conditions we flew under that time, two months later I would have positioned us further away and probably been content to stand off and throw the Shrikes in there. You learn every time, and it makes you a little more capable.

"Of course, everyone had to deal with the stress of the mission and with fear. How did we do it? There was a lot of letting off steam during our off-duty hours. When I first got to Takhli, we'd go to the stag bar at ten o'clock in the morning. A lot of people would be there, and they drank all day, until evening. Then they got four or five hours sleep and flew the next day. We had five squadron commanders while I was there. Four were shot down. The last one, Phil Gast (he retired as a lieutenant general), came in as a brand-new lieutenant colonel. He said, 'No more of that.' I really admired Phil for doing that. He wasn't popular when he did it, but the squadron went from one with the highest loss rate to an average loss rate.

"Our tour was one year or one hundred missions, whichever came first. You could take a month off your tour for every ten counters you flew against the North—eleven months at ten missions, ten months at twenty missions. Only one Weasel crew member I knew ever took advantage of that. Everybody thought you were a coward if you did that.

"The thing that really kept us going was the peer pressure from the people we flew with. When we went to the bar at night to have a drink, we wanted to have been as brave as they were that day or braver. We didn't want to go in there having put our tail between our legs and done something embarrassing. Again, it is something like the Weasel crew feeding off each other to become something greater than what they were individually capable of. The whole squadron was like that. It wasn't spoken peer pressure, although if someone did something stupid, we'd give him a hard time. Everyone wanted to be able to stand up as tall as everyone else and be able to look them in the eye.

"When I got back to Takhli from thirty days leave, the Weasel crews had gone over to Korat because Korat still had airplanes. We got our new planes a couple weeks later, in early September. My new pilot was Glen Davis, whose EWO had quit. Glen was one of the original Weasel pilots, and he was good. We had quite a bit of operational flexibility as Weasels, and as a result, we did a lot of low-level work when we were by ourselves. We'd be on the deck at one hundred feet. That's a good altitude for a Weasel. Our weapon of choice was the 20mm Gatling gun. A lot of times we'd attack a site, end up dodging missiles, and need a gun because we were eyeball to eyeball with the SAM site. There was no time to climb back up to do a dive-bomb maneuver. The gun killed as many SAM sites as any other weapon we had available to us.

"When our primary target was weathered in, and we were sent to Route Pack 5 near Dien Bien Phu for road recce, we would go and make one pass in the area to see if there were any radar signals up. There rarely ever were. Then we drove over into Route Pack 6 and went SAM hunting. That was the most fun of all. We could really control the situation when we didn't have a strike force to protect. We could pick our approach. If it looked bad, we'd call it off. If it looked good, we'd go in and kill them. We probably killed more SAM sites when we were by ourselves than when we were protecting a strike force. Some of our wingmen (Iron Hand bomb–carrying F-105Ds) didn't like it at all when we headed back into Pack 6 to hunt for SAMs. Nobody was ever hit by a SAM when flying with me. Nobody. That, I think, was a measure of success.

"We carried two Shrikes on the outboard stations and two containers of CBUs on the inboard stations. The CBUs were good for killing SAM sites. After we dropped the CBUs, they opened up, and numerous small bomblets were released in a shotgunlike pattern. Those small bombs exploded into a multitude of fragments. One is enough to take out a radar. The Shrike had a small warhead with a proximity fuse, and the missile homed in on the radar antenna. It usually didn't kill any people. It took the radar off the air, with no great damage to the site. We didn't call that a kill if all we did was take the radar off the air. Unless we could follow up with CBUs, 20mm cannon fire, or an accompanying strike aircraft with bombs, we didn't consider it a kill. Most of the time, when we were protecting a strike force, we trolled for SAMs at 8,000 feet above ground level. We wanted to be above the 4,500-foot level, where we picked up the 37mm and 57mm stuff. At 8,000 to 9,000 feet, it left us enough room to go into a good dive, track the target to see which way the wind was blowing, make our adjustments, drop CBUs, and still be able to get out without going below 4,500 feet. That time all the Weasel airplanes were shot down, Glen Davis flew single-seat missions. He led a lot of them because of his Weasel experience. When he finished his one hundred missions, I had sixty-five. At his hundred-mission party, Glen said, 'Mike, if you want me to stay and finish your hundred missions with you, I will. But I hope you don't ask me to do that.' I didn't.

"Then I flew with Merlyn Hans Dethlefsen. Merl came as a replacement pilot for Buddy Rheinhold, one of the original guys who got shot up. Merl was a strange guy, I thought. He went through a class at Nellis that had one more pilot than EWO. All the pilots and EWOs paired up. Merl was the one who didn't select anybody. He was a loner, a quiet guy. I soon regretted pairing up with him. We didn't get along at all. He was the only nondrinking fighter pilot I've ever met—a Pepsi drinker and a born-again Christian. I was a hell-raiser, as many of us were. I figured I wasn't going to live long. Merl and I were different. Merl never came to the bar at night as we all did to bullshit about what went on that day. We got along OK the first couple of missions, and then we didn't. It got so bad, he wouldn't speak to me except in the line of duty.

"The day Merl got his Medal of Honor, March 10, 1967, we didn't get along well at all. We were flying the number three position of a flight of four SAM-suppression aircraft. Our call sign was Lincoln: we were Lincoln 03. We headed up to the northeast railway. The strike target was the Thai Nguyen steel mill. We went in on the overland route, rather than coming in from the Gulf of Tonkin side, at 8,000 or 9,000 feet. As we approached the target area, we started descending. I said to Merl, 'We are really getting awfully low.' He said, 'Yeah.' We were down to about 4,500 feet and still descending. At 4,000 feet I said, 'Merl, something is wrong. We are going to get our asses shot off down here.' Then we heard beepers. Lead had been shot down by AAA. Both guys bailed out and were captured. Number two was shot up so badly that he, too, had to leave the area. We pulled up. Merl and I were lead now. Major Kenneth Bell, who later made general, was on our wing.

"There was a SAM site slightly to the south of the target, which dominated the approach. We went for it. The flak was terrible—absolutely awful. At the apex of our turn, when we were the most vulnerable, a pair of MiG-21s made a pass at us, and one fired a heat-seeking missile. We went down into the flak, and the MiGs pulled off. We fired a Shrike at the SAM radar. It didn't do any good. The second Shrike didn't do any good either. Both missed. We had CBUs and the gun, and I tried to direct Merl to the site. He said, 'I can't see it, I can't see it.'

"I told Merl when we passed over the site where it was. He said, 'Where is it? Where is it?' He still couldn't see it. Merl did a tight turn about a quarter of a mile from where the site was. I said, 'Merl, it's down there. If you want me to show you, give me a run-in from about five or six miles out, and I'll take you right over it.' My equipment was good, but it had its limitations. One of the difficulties of localizing a SAM site was that I had to reduce my bandwidth to only this one signal. It blocked everything else out, so I didn't know what else was going on. To get an accurate alignment on the site, I had to get far enough away to be sure we were heading toward the site. Then I had to watch carefully because the indicators on my scope moved quickly once we passed the site.

"The site was obscured by smoke and dust caused by the flak and the bombs from the strike force. Out we went. We were getting the crap shot out of us the whole time. It was the only mission I was ever

Lieutenant Colonel Phil Gast, squadron commander, and Colonel Bob Scott, wing commander, congratulate Mike Gilroy after he returns from his one hundredth mission over North Vietnam, 1967. Captain Merl Dethlefsen, Mike's pilot and a Medal of Honor winner, is standing at the front of the aircraft. K. Gilroy.

apprehensive on. I was scared shitless. I didn't have the feeling that Merl could handle the situation. We got out about seven miles and headed back in. Another MiG-21 made a pass at us. Again the flak took him off our back. Our wingman got hit—one of his flaps came down due to flak damage. He could only make right turns. We continued to take lots of hits. They counted 137 holes in the airplane when we got back to Takhli. We got station passage. I called it out to Merl, and he rolled over to look down and again couldn't see the site.

"I said, 'OK, let's try it again.' So we went out six or seven miles and tried it a second time. The whole time the flak was all over the place. It's the worst I had ever seen. It was bursting all around us. On my scope I saw what looked like a whole lot of apostrophes. I thought, 'What the heck is that?' They appeared in clusters, disappearing and reappearing. When I looked out, I realized it was the proximity fusing of the flak. We came back in the second time. I called station passage to Merl. He flipped up the wing and said, 'I got it,' nosed over, and dropped the CBUs on the site. The site went off the air. Merl made a tight turn and returned and strafed the site with the 20mm cannon.

Mike Gilroy kneeling by a carpet showing the names of everyone in the 354th Fighter Squadron who completed one hundred missions over North Vietnam, 1967. K. Gilroy.

"We headed for home. We didn't have enough fuel to get to Takhli, so we got an emergency tanker way up north in Laos and then landed at Udorn. We got more gas and continued on to Takhli. I got out of the airplane at Udorn, walked up to Merl, and shook his hand. 'You did really good,' I said to him. He really did. He deserved the Medal of Honor for that mission. He displayed the kind of courage and professionalism all Weasels liked to think they had. When we got back to Takhli, our squadron commander wanted to know what happened. We chatted with him for about half an hour. Then he called in Ken Bell, our wing man, and the number-two guy who had to leave the area because of flak damage, and asked them what happened. Then he got the guys who flew that day and talked to all of them. He then wrote us up for two Air Force Crosses. I finished up the first part of April, and at my hundred-mission party at the Officers' Club, our squadron commander came in and said, 'I want to propose a toast. Mike has been put in for the Medal of Honor.' Merl's and my award recommendation for the Air Force Cross had gotten to 7th Air

Force in Saigon, and they had changed it to Medal of Honor recommendations. Mine eventually became an Air Force Cross. I am very proud to have it. Merl and I worked well together from then on. April 13, 1967, was my last mission, my one hundredth mission over North Vietnam. I never thought I'd make it out alive."

When interviewed after the March 10, 1967, mission, Merlyn H. Dethlefsen humbly replied, "All I did was the job I was sent to do." Merl and Mike, a team after all, did a lot more than just their job. Merl Dethlefsen is deceased.

Chapter 16

Yellowbird

The Air Force's most effective truck killers were the AC-119 and AC-130 gunships, the B-57, a few C-123s equipped with special detection devices, and the A-26.

Carl Berger, ed., *The United States Air Force in Southeast Asia*

I had many harrowing experiences in my three years there, but I kept extending. I liked the flying. When I left, I had more combat time in the B-57 than anybody else, 450 missions or something like that, many of them night interdiction in Route Packs 1 and 2 and in Laos. On my party suit I had a patch that read "Laotian Highway Patrol."

Ed Rider, B-57 pilot

Major Fred E. "Ed" Rider
Distinguished Flying Cross (3), Air Medal (23)

Ed was born in 1937 in a farmhouse somewhere in the rural Alabama countryside. There were mules and cotton and not much else for him to remember, except for the airplanes he occasionally saw flying overhead. "I was fascinated every time one came over my house," Ed said,

323

his eyes shining brightly. "I used to draw airplanes when I was a kid. I thought at times, 'Maybe someday I can fly an airplane.' But then I had no idea how I would learn to fly. I remember reading stories about zeppelins dropping bombs on England in World War I. I dreamed about them at night. In 1953 I read about dogfights between F-86 Sabre Jets and Chinese MiGs in Korea. I was having trouble staying in college because I didn't have any money, so I joined the air force. It took six years before I made it to pilot training. I worked on B-57 bombers as an electronics technician. A captain who took a liking to me occasionally took me along on a test hop and let me take the controls if it was a dual-control model. It was fun to fly the plane. I was good at it. He encouraged me to go to OCS and then to pilot training. I followed his advice. I was high enough in my class to get any fighter I wanted, but I found out they didn't get much flying time, so I stayed in ATC. I wanted to fly. In five years in ATC I racked up 3,300 flying hours in T-33, T-37, and T-38 jet trainers. I loved every minute of it.

"By 1965 I was tired of the place and volunteered for Vietnam duty. An ATC general came to speak to us on personnel policies. During the question-and-answer period, I put up my hand. When I was recognized, I said to him, 'Every month, I fill out a form volunteering for Vietnam. Every month my commander throws it in the wastepaper basket. Why is that?' It got deathly quiet in the room. The general said, 'You and your commander see me afterwards.' We did. I got reassigned, and so did my commander. I went to Kansas to some National Guard base to get a transition check into the B-57, the type of airplane I worked on as an airman. From there I went to Clark Air Base in the Philippines. I was assigned to the 8th Tactical Bomb Squadron, the Yellowbirds. Our sister squadron was the 13th, the Redbirds. The 8th and the 13th rotated back and forth to Da Nang. The 8th was at Da Nang when I arrived. I sat around the squadron building for about a week, and no one offered to train me or even took notice of me. One Friday afternoon, somebody came into the ready room looking for someone to fly the courier to Vietnam. I said I'd go. He said, 'Who are you?' 'I just got here, and I am sitting around doing nothing,' I replied, 'so I might as well fly to Vietnam and do something.' He said, 'You can't go. You don't know what's going on yet.' But he couldn't find anybody else. It was Friday afternoon, and everybody was looking forward to the weekend. So he came back and said, 'OK, you're it. Go see the sergeant. He'll cut you some orders. In Saigon go to this hotel on Tudo Street. Our guys have rooms there, and they'll tell you what to do.'

"I jumped on a contract flight out of Clark to Saigon and found the hotel on Tudo Street in Saigon. I said to the Vietnamese desk clerk, 'I'm here with the B-57 guys. I understand you have a room for us.' The Vietnamese laughed and said, 'I don't know anything.' 'Just get me a room,' I said. He laughed again and said, 'There is no room in town.' There was a little bar in back, and it was already curfew, so I sat down next to a guy and ordered a drink. 'This is the most screwed-up war I've been in,' I said to him, 'and it's my first war.' He laughed and said, 'What's the matter?' I told him my story. He gave me a long look and said, 'I'm a B-57 guy. We have a room upstairs. It has eight bunks, and you are welcome to one of them.'

"The next night they gave me a navigator, and a transport picked us up and took us to Intelligence at 7th Air Force Headquarters, where we signed for a bunch of top-secret documents. They told us to put them in the tail section of the aircraft. We went out to Tan Son Nhut Airport and cranked up. It was pouring rain. I couldn't see, and I was on a VFR clearance. I mentioned that to the navigator. He said, 'Yeah, yeah.'

"I called the tower and told the controller that I had never seen this airfield before and didn't know where the runway was. 'I know where you are parked,' the guy in the tower responded. 'Pull out to the taxiway and turn right. Call out the markers as you go down the taxiway.' When the tower determined I was at the end of the runway, he said, 'You're cleared for takeoff.' The rain was pounding down. I couldn't see a thing. I went down the centerline, and when I hit takeoff speed, I pulled back on the yoke. That was my first takeoff in Vietnam. We hit all the fighter bases—Takhli, Udorn, Ubon, Korat. By that time of night there was no GCA, only tower operators. At the first stop I made two approaches without seeing anything. Finally I climbed back up to altitude, got my letdown book out, and studied where the TACAN was, where the runway should be, and what the needle had to look like for me to hit the runway. I really concentrated and let down to about two hundred feet over the TACAN, and sure enough there was the runway. I landed. The runway had a dip in it, and the dip was full of water. I hydroplaned like crazy. My brakes didn't do anything. I went onto the overrun—all mud. I was going down the right edge of the runway to stay out of accumulated water, so when I hit the overrun, I cranked up the right engine, stepped on the left brake, and turned around, blowing mud all over the place. When the Intelligence people showed up, they unlatched the rear compartment and took their sack of documents. They signed a release, even though I had no idea what they had taken out of there. Away I went to the next place—VFR again. I was really good on instruments, otherwise I couldn't have done it at night and in that weather. We finally got back to Saigon at nine in the morning. I did this about eight times.

"Then one morning I got a call from the command post, and they told me to bring all my gear on the next flight because I would be getting off in Da Nang, where my squadron was. In Da Nang I crawled out, another guy crawled in and took the airplane. The next day I was on the schedule to fly a bombing mission into North Vietnam. I told the scheduler, 'Look, I've never been on a bombing range. I don't even know how to work all the switches.' He handed me a -34 and said, 'I guess you have to study tonight. Learn where all the switches are.' He was serious. I talked to some of the guys and asked, 'How do you do this?' 'Well,' one of them said, 'you get up close to the target, roll upside down, throw the nose down onto the target, roll right side up in about a forty-five-degree dive, and when it looks about right, you pickle.' That was my instruction in bombing technique. The next day, I dropped my first bomb over North Vietnam. Fortunately, it was daytime.

"My lead—we always flew two ships during the day—was experienced. All the people in the squadron were experienced. They'd been

with the airplane since it came from the factory. They'd all been together in the 3rd Bomb Wing up in Japan, and all they ever did was
practice dive bombing and strafing. They were good at it. The B-57
was a fantastic airplane, a stable platform with lots of fuel and lots of
armament. We could take off with ten thousand pounds of ordnance,
climb to thirty-five thousand feet, go out to a target five hundred miles
away, let down and do an hour of road recce, make twenty-five hot
passes, climb back up to fifty thousand feet, and go home unrefueled.
The B-57 came to Bien Hoa a year before I did, in '64. Those guys did
a terrific job. The Viet Cong put up a reward for anyone who shot
down a B-57 or killed a pilot. At Bien Hoa, to save time, they lined up
the airplanes in a straight line and had the next reload stacked right
behind them. When the Viet Cong attacked the base with 81mm mortars, the whole flight line went up when the mortars hit. Pieces of airplane flew all over the base. A couple of the guys ran out and got some
of the airplanes airborne and saved them. When it was all over, five
B-57s had been destroyed; fifteen more were damaged.

"Those early Bien Hoa guys were iron men. They'd fly out of Bien
Hoa with a full bomb load up to Da Nang, refuel, and then take off
and go way the hell up into northern Laos, around Dien Bien Phu in
Route Pack 5, and then hit bridges and other strategic targets—really
stressful. They did that every day. Finally, the airplanes moved to Da
Nang. We evolved into night flying to go after trucks on the Ho Chi
Minh Trail. We were pretty successful at that.

"We had two models of the B-57. The B model had eight fifty-
calibers, four in each wing. When you fired them all at once, you fired
at a rate of 6,000 rounds a minute. They carried 2,400 rounds. The E
model had four 20mm guns, M-60s, and also fired at a rate of 6,000
rounds per minute. The E carried 1,160 rounds. Normally, if I had a
pinpoint target, I'd fire two-second bursts. I got about six passes out of
the 20 mike-mike (20mm cannon). Seldom did all eight of the fifties
fire at the same time. At times, it took me twelve to fifteen passes to
fire out. We had tracers for the fifty-caliber but not for the 20 mike-
mike. After a fifty-caliber pass, I'd retract all the breaches and reset

B-57 formation near Phan Rang, 1968. F. Rider.

them before rolling in for the next pass. It cooled the barrels; otherwise, they got so hot, rounds would start cooking off. When I first got over there, I was on a target with one of the old heads. I had a hard time keeping up with him. He flew a five-G pattern. I was working myself to death trying to keep myself from getting lapped by him. And I did get lapped a couple of times, that's how tight his turns were. He'd fire two passes to my one. The FAC timed me, and it was eighteen seconds between passes—a real tight pattern. After I came off the target for the last time, I pulled up to join up with him on his right wing. Just then, a few rounds cooked off. The tracers went right in front of his nose. He looked over at me and said, 'Rider, are you pissed at me?'

"I had many harrowing experiences in my three years there, but I kept extending. I liked the flying. When I left, I had more combat time in the B-57 than anybody else, 450 missions or something like that, many of them night interdiction in Route Packs 1 and 2 and in Laos. On my party suit I had a patch that read 'Laotian Highway Patrol.' One time me and my nav were up north looking for trucks. At low altitude you sometimes could see their combat lights. I saw something on the road, and I said to the nav, 'There is a truck.' We went after him. We carried funny bombs (Mark 35 firebombs that split open a few hundred feet above ground, spilling a cascade of bomblets that at night looked like a fiery waterfall). I went after the truck in a shallow high-speed dive. I released. When the bomb fuse went off and it split the canister to release the bomblets, the antiaircraft gunners saw the flash. They knew instantly where I was and where I was heading. Both sides to the left and right of the truck lit up like a Christmas tree. I pulled up thirty degrees, and the rounds went by parallel to me. I quit pulling up until the volley passed me. It wasn't a truck after all. It was a trap. I got up to altitude where the guns couldn't reach, and I sprayed bombs all over the area where the guns were. The nav had hooked a tape recorder to our intercom. After the mission, we listened to the tape. For that bomb run all there was on the tape was one exclamation, J—— C——!' then silence.

"A friend of mine fell for a trap in the daytime. He thought he spotted a truck on the trail. To his wingman, he said, 'I'll get this one. You go ahead and look for more.' You should never do that and send your wingman off. You need someone looking out for you. It wasn't a truck after all but concrete, and the sides of the road had 57mm emplacements. He got hammered good but managed to get out with one engine out and a round below the rear cockpit. It shredded the nav's legs and his right arm. The pilot had a briefcase with a bunch of flight manuals behind his seat. That's what saved him. The briefcase took most of the shrapnel. One of the wings was missing sheet metal bigger than a dining room table. The tail was shot up, and he lost electrical, hydraulics, and oxygen. Without radios and oxygen, he dropped down low and flew along the coast, looking for Da Nang, planning to make a belly landing. He didn't know his gear had come down. He made his first approach to Da Nang and saw no fire trucks and decided to make a low pass. On one engine, that is quite a feat. There was an F-4 in the pattern, and he cut off the F-4. The F-4 pilot screamed over the radio, 'What the hell is that B-57 doing cutting me out of the pattern?' As the F-4 driver looked down, he could see right through the B-57. He then got all the fire trucks out, since the B-57 had no radios.

A 57mm shell did this damage to the wing of a B-57, 1968. F. Rider.

"At night it was too hard to go two-ship. We couldn't keep up with each other. I had my own night tactics. If there was any kind of moon, you could see the road, because the roads were white sand along the coast. We'd turn off all the lights in the cockpit, and with no lights you could really get your night vision. Only the nav kept his altimeter light on low. I couldn't see any instruments. I set the power beforehand to give me the speed I wanted and let down to 200 to 300 feet. That's where I wanted to be. I experimented in the daytime. The guns were harmonized at 3,200 feet. That's where I wanted my target, where the guns intersected. I figured the altitude and airspeed that would give me convergence. Then we flew down those white roads, and when I saw a black dot on the road, that was usually a truck. When he got to the right angle on my windshield, I'd close my eyes, squeeze off two seconds, open my eyes, and make a hard break to the right or left, because the muzzle flashes would tell them where we were. One night we hit a fuel tanker. The world lit up like you wouldn't believe.

"There was a river that ran down from the northwest to the coast. Right at the coast was a ferry crossing, Ron Ferry. From thirty thousand feet I saw lights on the road. My target was actually further north. I said to my nav, 'Bill, I can't believe there are lights on the road down there. It's got to be some kind of a trap. Should we go and take a look?' 'Let's,' Bill curtly replied. As we got closer, I suddenly saw muzzle flashes and two strings of lights. 'They have radar, Bill,' I said. He grunted into the intercom. They were twin 57s, two of them, one in front and one in the rear of the column. I jinked as the red-hot beer cans came streaking up toward us. I said to Bill, 'There must be a bunch of trucks down there lined up at the ferry. We can't just leave them.' 'No, we can't,' Bill responded in his usual curt manner. I looked over the situation, and Bill and I decided to come in from over the water, the Gulf of Tonkin, low level. And we'd toss the bombs in there and see what happens. We carried eight funny bombs, four internal and four external. We got out over the water and entered a steep dive. There was no way to tell altitude because the altimeter was always be-hind where you really were. But I had a string of trucks out there as a point of reference. As they got more and more level on my horizon, I leveled out. When I was about two miles from them, I pulled up in a four-G pull and started pickling off the bombs. Some fell short, some long. As I got about vertical, the red-hot beer cans started coming by. I rolled over to the water and out to sea, then up to twenty-five thou-sand feet. We could see what we'd done. There were trucks burning from one end of that line to the other. I tried to call the C-130 com-mand ship over Laos to get some recce aircraft to take pictures, but there was no reply. We sat up there for nearly thirty minutes, watching them burn. We counted what we thought were twenty-seven individual fires, the most trucks we ever got in one pass. The North Vietnamese thought no one was going to get close to them with their radar con-trolled twin 57s. We fooled 'em.

"Then F-4s arrived in Thailand, and someone decided to let the F-4s kill the trucks at night and use the B-57s for close air support down south in the Delta. They moved us to Phan Rang. When we got there, the only airplanes at Phan Rang were four squadrons of F-100s. They didn't know anything about B-57s and quickly let us know that they

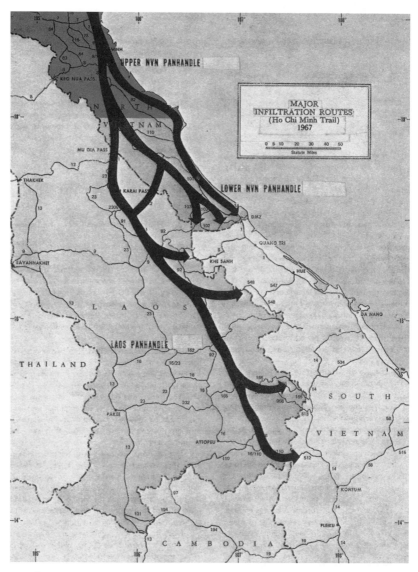

Ho Chi Minh Trail, 1967. Ban Karai and Mu Gia passes were bombed by B-52s and Thailand-based fighters throughout the war. *Aces and Aerial Victories* 2.

didn't care for us. Our new wing commander at Phan Rang didn't know anything about B-57s either. He was a Hun (F-100) driver. But we were in his command. The Hun guys called us multiengine bomber pilots. In the Officers' Club, they had their end of the bar, we had ours. They drew a line across the bar. Nobody met in between. The first mission I flew out of Phan Rang was a four-ship formation. Each of us carried twenty-one 260-pound frags (fragmentation bombs), four cans of napalm, four rocket pods, and the guns. We're in the Delta. When we got to the FAC, I told him to clean up a great big place on his windshield. FACs use a grease pencil to record your ordnance, and they cross it off as you expend it. The FAC said, 'OK, I'm ready.'

" 'We got eighty-four 260-pound frags, sixteen 750-pound napes (napalm canisters), ninety-two 2.75-inch rockets, 2,320 rounds of 20 mike-mike, and 4,800 rounds of fifty-caliber. And I'll give you two hours over the target.' There was silence. I guess he was still scribbling on his canopy. Then he said, awestruck, 'J—— C——, there aren't enough targets in the entire Delta for your ammo load.'

"A couple of days later I was on a two-ship monkey-killer mission near the Cambodian border—monkey killer because we couldn't see what we were bombing in the jungle. On the way back, I still had my guns. I was yelling for a FAC to find me a gun target because I hated to take ammunition home. I finally got a target north of Phan Rang. After I checked in with the FAC, a flight of F-100s also checked in. They had taken off from Phan Rang. I said, 'Do you guys mind if I go in first because I am kind of short on fuel?' One of the Huns said, 'No, go right ahead. We still have our tanks. We couldn't do anything anyhow. We'll hold overhead at about two thousand.' I said, 'You better hold a little higher than that.' 'Why?' 'Because I fly a vertical pattern.' 'Bull-shit,' was the response from the Hun driver.

"I had a new guy on my wing. He was supposed to be pretty good, from what I heard, so I thought I'd give him a test. When the FAC fired a rocket into the target area, I was right on the tail of that rocket. I started firing two seconds after that rocket hit—fired, pulled straight up for a couple of thousand feet, rolled on my back, and held it there and flew back over the target, inverted. When I was at the other side of the target, I pulled it straight down and reattacked from the same direction as before. Normally, everyone would pull off the target to the left. On my second pass I looked for my wingman. I looked to the left—I was expecting him to be there. I didn't see him. I looked right, and I didn't see him. I happened to look in my mirrors, and there he was right behind me, inverted. He was as good as they said. We made eight passes.

"At the bar that night these four Hun drivers came in. One said, 'Guys, you wouldn't believe what I saw those damn bomber pilots doing,' pointing at us. 'Well, what'd they do?' one of the others finally said. 'They were out there strafing and flying a rectangular pattern.' 'They'll get their asses killed flying those rectangular patterns,' another Hun driver volunteered. The first pilot answered, 'No, you don't understand. This is a vertical rectangular pattern.' We had impressed some of the single-engine guys with our acrobatics.

"The wing commander finally flew with me on a ride to get some experience. The target was over on the coast—a Viet Cong regiment. At the briefing he wore his G suit. I said, 'Sir, it won't do you any good. There is no place to plug it in.' He said, 'I know. I don't need a G suit in a B-57.' I thought, 'You'll learn.' Anyhow, we got to the target, and I made several bomb runs and dropped our napalm. I was pulling four to five Gs, but it didn't last long. Then the FAC gave us a strafe target. On the first pass, my wingman discovered his guns wouldn't fire. I said, 'You orbit and watch for ground fire and tell me where it's coming from, and I'll go in and strafe.' I flew a constant five-G strafe pattern. I had trimmed the airplane up for five Gs. When I got my pipper on the target, I pushed forward a bit and fired for two seconds, then I went back to five Gs. When we got into debriefing, we gave Intelligence the BDA the FAC had given us, and how many dive-bomb and strafe passes we made. I said, 'I made six strafing passes.' The wing commander looked over at me and said, 'No, Captain Rider, you only made one pass.' I said, 'No, Sir. I made six. You were asleep after the first one.' He had blacked out after the first firing pass. After a while, they found that the F-4s that were supposed to take our job on the trail couldn't hit the trucks. They sent us back up north. It was much further from Phan Rang than from Da Nang. If we couldn't make it home we landed at Nakhon Phanom in Thailand or Udorn. We were doing good work up there, and the FACs loved us. The ground fire was mostly 37mm and ZSUs (Soviet-made mobile antiaircraft systems). The ZSU looks like a fire hose with green tracers—unbelievable how much stuff they can crank out. Anyway, someone found out that the wing commander didn't believe our reports, and before he submitted them to Saigon, he'd divide our numbers by four. My squadron commander found out about that and went over and raised hell. 'If you don't believe we are doing anything,' he told him, 'why don't you crawl into the backseat and go up there with us one night.' Since he had flown with me before, I ended up with him in the backseat again. Phan Rang had the 101st Airborne on the perimeter to protect the base. They had a whole bunch of artillery and fired all night on suspected VC areas. There were specific egress areas to keep us from flying through their artillery fire. Our departure took us east, then south, then up the coast to Cam Ranh Bay, and then inland. It wasted about three thousand pounds of fuel. I took off toward the east. As soon as I got the gear in the well, I turned off the external lights so the tower couldn't see me and made a steep 270, heading northwest. I flew right across the 101st compound and shook all the grunts out of bed and headed up a valley toward Da Lat. Once out of the valley I turned north.

"The wing commander in back didn't like my maneuver. 'What are you doing?' he said, when I turned off the lights and did the 270. 'Saving three thousand pounds of fuel, Sir.' He didn't say anything else. Over Laos, I checked in with the FAC, and he had a string of trucks on a road he wanted me to take care of. He had a nightscope and could see them. He dropped two log flares on either side of the road. The flares just lie there and burn for a long time. Then he told me how many funny bombs north or south of the flares the trucks were. We used the dispersal pattern of the funny bomb as a measurement. There was a string of 37s about a mile apart on each side of the road. On my first pass they were hammering at me from both sides. They were shooting at sound. I pulled straight up after each pass and hung inverted, zero Gs over the top, until the FAC told me where to put the next one, and I went straight down and lobbed the next one. We finally got rid of all of our funny bombs. The target wasn't good enough to strafe, so I called the FAC and told him I had my boss along and would like the BDA. His reply was, 'I can't give you your BDA right now. I'm busy.' I said, 'I have my boss along, and he wants our BDA.' The FAC got the message from my tone of voice, so he said, 'Take two trucks destroyed and ten secondary explosions.' He had an A-26 coming in which he was working and who was following the trucks down the road. We orbited for a while. The longer we orbited, the more trucks were blowing up because the bomblets from the funny bombs got inside of them, and eventually it got hot enough in there, and the stuff they were carrying cooked off. We had about eight trucks burning and blowing up, and secondaries going off all over the place.

"At home we had our standard intelligence debriefing. When Intelligence asked me about ground fire, I said, 'Light and inaccurate.' 'Light, hell,' was my wing commander's comment. 'That whole damn sky was full of that stuff—57mm, too.' I had to correct him. 'No, Sir, 37mm. They come out in clips of four, so we know it's 37mm.' Next question, BDA. 'Two trucks destroyed, and ten secondaries,' I reported. He said, 'Bullshit.' I said, 'Sir, we must report what the FAC gives us.' He jumped up and down over that. After that mission we were his B-57s.

"I never took any hits, and I killed more trucks than most. I tried to fly smart, not stupid and get killed. My normal tactics at night against a well-defended target were to get directly overhead at about eight thousand feet, roll inverted and pull the nose down to the target, drop my bomb at about five thousand feet, and pull up into a vertical climb. Just before I ran out of airspeed, I would pull the nose down to level and roll upright. This faked out the gunners, because they expected me to be off to the side of the target. I was only vulnerable in the first part of my pull-up.

"We were taking off about midnight to hit a truck park way up in

Ed Rider posing in front of his bomb-laden B-57, 1968. F. Rider.

Laos. I went around the airplane with the armorer and checked the fuses on the bombs for proper settings and the arming wires for proper routing. Then I spread my maps and showed them where we were going and what we were supposed to hit. We were in the northeast monsoon and had forty-knot winds down the runway. I flew my usual unorthodox night departure over the 101st compound up the valley to Da Lat. We stirred up a hornet's nest when we got to our target. The flak was thick, and when it got close you could hear it popping like popcorn. When we left, we still had our 20 mike-mike. I called the airborne command post, a C-130, and he sent us down to Tchepone. A FAC had spotted some trucks at a ferry crossing. We contacted the FAC to coordinate altitudes before we got into his area. We used a secret base altitude which changed every twelve hours so the enemy couldn't listen in and find out our altitudes and set the fuses on his shells. That night the base altitude was eight thousand feet. The FAC said he was at base plus four, meaning he was at twelve thousand feet. I wondered what he was doing up there. I said, 'You must mean minus four.' 'No, plus four,' he repeated. His flares were floating so high that they did not illuminate the ground, and I had to circle until I got their reflection on the river before I could see. I asked, 'Why are you at plus four?' He replied, 'This thing won't climb any higher.'

"Bill, my navigator, suddenly piped up and said, 'Bingo fuel,' the minimum fuel we needed to get home plus a two thousand–pound reserve. I ignored him. A few guns were shooting at our sound but not coming close. I knew there were no radar-controlled guns because otherwise we would have been tracked and fired on accurately while we were circling. I finally got it worked out and caught the ferry in the flare reflection on the river. I rolled in, firing a three-second burst in a thirty-degree dive from 1,500 feet. The muzzle flashes lit us up like a Christmas tree, saying, 'Shoot me.' And they did. I knew why the FAC was flying so high. I pulled five Gs trying to get away from them, going straight up.

"The FAC was encouraging, saying that he had seen lots of hits on the ferry with his nightscope, so I got set up to go again. Bill didn't think it was such a good idea. There were lots of guns protecting the ferry, most of them twin-barrel 37mm. The red-hot beer cans came in strings of eight. On my second pass, I had to use the same heading as on the first in order to see the ferry—not a smart thing to do. When our muzzle flashes lit us up again, I had the feeling that if I pulled up as usual, every gun would be aimed at our recovery path. Instead, I turned ninety degrees and continued at low altitude with a low power setting until I was far enough away from the guns. Then I pulled up. The sky behind us was filled with a spectacular display of fireworks. The FAC was jumping up and down because we had torched off some of the trucks on the ferry and on the south shore of the river, where the ferry was resting. We could approach from any direction and still see the target. My nav was getting insistent about our fuel situation— 'Bingo minus two,' Bill said. Our two thousand–pound reserve was gone.

"After two more passes, we headed for home. Relieved of most of its fuel, the B-57 climbed like a homesick angel. In short order we were passing thirty-five thousand feet and we had to tighten our oxygen masks and start pressure breathing. The B-57 was old and had poor pressurization. As we passed forty-five thousand feet, we had to forcefully breathe out and relax and let the pressure blow up our lungs to breathe in. At fifty-three thousand feet we were above 95 percent of the atmosphere. At that altitude, the engines used little fuel. When we arrived over Pleiku, we were 150 nautical miles from home and had eight hundred pounds of fuel remaining. Normally, when we land with a two thousand–pound fuel reserve, that is considered an emergency. But I had done it many times before and was only concerned about being able to taxi to the ramp. To expedite our descent from fifty-three thousand feet, I shut down the right engine because we would be flying a left-hand traffic pattern. I flew a Mach .84 descent, which meant that it got progressively steeper as I entered hotter, denser air at the lower altitudes. I let down inside the 101st artillery donut at Phan Rang, and once inside the donut I extended the speed brakes. At five hundred knots, it's like running into a brick wall. Our shoulder harnesses locked as we were thrown forward in our seats. I pushed the nose down and crossed the end of the runways at ninety degrees at about eight thousand feet. Then I did a 270-degree split S, leveling at fifteen hundred feet, heading down the runway; got an air start on my dead engine; and landed.

"There were many problems unique to flying in Vietnam. Call signs, security, and the rules of engagement were just three of many. We always used the same call sign. Ours, in the 8th Bomb Squadron, was Yellowbird. Our sister squadron's, the 13th, was Redbird. Anyone listening to us knew immediately who we were and how many bombs we carried. There was a ferry crossing near Tchepone in Laos. Sometimes we'd drop our bombs, and they wouldn't shoot at us until we told the FAC that it was our last bomb. Then the whole world would open up. I knew the North Vietnamese were listening to our radio chatter. One night, I went there alone as usual. When I was in the area I came up on freq and said, 'Yellowbird, flight check.' And I called out two, three, four, and so on to eight, changing my voice every time I called out a number. Then I called the FAC, this is Yellowbird flight with a flight of eight. We are loaded with one thousand–pounders and are after those guns. The FAC told me where to put my bombs, and I hit both sides of the ferry crossing. He asked me about the rest of my flight. I told him they were holding high, waiting for the guns to open up. Then I went in, dropped my remaining bombs, and did some strafing. Never got shot at.

"Security. We listened to Hanoi Hannah. One day, she said, 'It is really too bad, but last night we shot down tail number 1234'— whatever it was, I can't remember. We checked if that aircraft was missing. Maintenance said it was way down at the end of the flight line, behind the hangar, being washed. It wasn't on the ramp any more. Somebody was calling in our tail numbers, and when one was missing, they thought it was lost.

"Many rules of engagement were stupid. We had a rule that we couldn't bomb dikes and dams. Guess where the North Vietnamese put their guns? One day, I was working with a Fast FAC over North Vietnam—a two-seat F-100, their call sign always was Misty. We were after some trucks. He was holding away from the target because a 57mm gun was right on the dike. Every time I rolled in, the stuff popped all around me. Then I rolled in from twelve thousand feet, going nearly straight down. I dropped a one thousand–pounder, and after I pulled out of my dive I called the FAC and told him I had an inadvertent release. The FAC said, 'Oh, well. By coincidence it hit right in the gun pit.' "

After three years of flying the trails of Laos and North Vietnam, Ed Rider went home. In spite of all the Yellowbirds' efforts, the war was no closer to being won. Ed Rider and his B-57s were part of Operation Steel Tiger, an air campaign against the Ho Chi Minh Trail in Laos that complemented Operation Rolling Thunder against North Vietnam. *The United States Air Force in Southeast Asia* states, "the Air Force's most effective truck killers were the AC-119 and AC-130 gunships, the B-57, a few C-123s equipped with special detection devices, and the A-26" (Berger 108).

The Magic of Flying
Concluding Thoughts

Regulations Concerning Operation of Aircraft of the U.S. Air Service (1920)

Don't take the machine into the air unless you are satisfied it will fly.

Never leave the ground with the motor leaking.

Don't turn sharply when taxiing. Have someone lift the tail around.

Never get out with the motor running until the pilot relieving you can reach the engine controls.

Pilots should carry hankies in a handy position to wipe off goggles.

Riding on the steps, wings or tail of a machine is prohibited.

In case the engine fails on takeoff, land straight ahead regardless of obstacles.

No machine must taxi faster than a man can walk.

Do not trust altitude instruments.

If you see another machine near you, get out of its way.

Hedge-hopping will not be tolerated.

Pilots will not wear spurs while flying.

If an emergency occurs, land as soon as you can.

L. R. Carastro, comp. and ed., *Of Those Who Fly*

Many airmen who fought the Cold War succumbed in their youth to the lure of flying, drawn by its promise of freedom and adventure.

They may have been next-door neighbors—average kids—but their imaginations were far from average, captured by passing barnstormers, by five-dollar rides in open-cockpit airplanes, by the sight of Ford tri-motors on the tarmac, by planes passing overhead, or by Lindbergh's epic Atlantic crossing. Some watched in fascination as airliners took off from airports near their homes; others built their dreams into the balsa-wood models they fashioned at the kitchen table. But all spoke of being inspired by the magic of the airplane, the magic of flying. "I always wanted to fly," Ralph Kuster, Sam Myers, Ed Gorski, Joe Laufer, Ed Rider, Moe Hamill, Dave Taylor, Hal Austin, and Hack Mixson told me, "just to fly." I know what they mean. Flying was also my dream as a child living in post–World War II Germany, watching the Americans flying their heavily laden C-54 transports overhead during the Berlin Airlift. Those Cold War airmen did not see themselves as heroes or patriots. During many of my interviews, these flyers tried to convince me that their experiences were not extraordinary and that they merely did what anyone else would have done in similar circumstances. But there is no doubt in my mind that these men were patriots. There is no doubt that they achieved extraordinary things. There is no doubt that they were leaders, each in his own way.

I believe we need to continue to foster the magic of flight that captured the youngsters who became the airmen of the Cold War. We need to foster dreams of new frontiers in the minds of our youth, tomorrow's airmen and airwomen, if we are to sustain our enviable tradition of success, often against great odds. The odds of which I speak surely will be different in the future, not necessarily the odds of greater numbers fielded by an enemy, but rather approaches to warfare ingenious and unconventional, designed to diminish the viability of the United States.

The effectiveness of the air force past, present, and future was and is dependent on a number of things—the enemy, the operational environment, information and how it is put to use, adequacy of numbers of aircraft, supporting and complementary systems, and enough of the right armaments to sustain a prolonged conflict. Maybe even more important to success is a clear understanding of political and military objectives to be attained. The bitterness many Cold War airmen took away from the Vietnam War was precisely over the absence of both. Finally, once objectives have been articulated, they then need to be implemented by a military leadership that understands airpower history and its attendant principles of employment, which were hammered out in the skies over Germany, Korea, and Vietnam.

It is the men and women of our air force who make the ultimate difference, not weapons or rules. More than fifty years ago, young men took obsolescent B-17 bombers in daring daylight raids over Germany and destroyed the Luftwaffe. Flying the leftovers of America's World War II airpower, the same men then destroyed the North Korean People's Army in a "come as you are" war. The following generation of flyers took the Thud, designed for nuclear war, and wrote a proud record in the flak- and missile-tainted skies over North Vietnam. The message is clear: we can prevail with second-rate equipment but never with second-rate people; nor can we prevail without conviction— conviction gained through clarity of vision, which in turn comes from doing the right thing.

I Always Wanted to Fly tells the stories of airmen who took whatever airplanes they were given and then did the best they knew how with them. These men frequently dealt with their fears and mortality as abstractions, deliberately using the rush of adrenaline to sharpen their responses—*it has always been that way.* Berlin, Korea, Vietnam, strategic reconnaissance, and many other armed clashes large and small were Cold War way stations. Some of those Cold War clashes were more difficult than others, some were better led than others—*that too has always been that way.* The courage displayed by airmen in these Cold War encounters was no accident. It was the courage nurtured by every generation of America's military flyers and passed on to the next—*that has always been that way.* The challenges of the future will obviously differ from those of the past, but they will come mostly unannounced, just as in the past. Our airmen and airwomen will have to meet those challenges with whatever they have on hand—*and that has always been that way, too.*

The huge air forces of World War II consisted largely of aviation enthusiasts and of men so aptly described by historian Stephen Ambrose as "citizen soldiers," many of them barely out of high school yet motivated, even inspired, by the magic of flying. Over the years of the Cold War, the flying air force turned into a relatively small, all volunteer, largely college educated professional force of officers, men and women. Air crews shrank in size as vast technological improvements in aircraft made the enlisted air crewman a rarity. Even the loss of life in training military flyers was reduced to the absolute minimum. While losing several pilots each month in training, as described by Ralph Kuster in "Hambone 02," was not newsworthy in the 1960s, such training losses would be unacceptable today.

Not only is today's air force much smaller, highly technology focused, safety oriented, and flown by men and women, but it also has to recruit the next generation of flyers in an environment where the airplane has become a public utility. The sight of aircraft in flight has become a common occurrence and does not necessarily arouse youngsters' interest, let alone inspire them. For many Americans, flying in an airplane as a passenger has become as common as driving a car to the supermarket. As a result of this changed environment as well as an economy vastly different from that of the 1930s, '40s, and '50s, our challenge for the future may no longer be the technology of flight but rather one of inspiring and motivating the hearts and minds of youngsters to want to be America's future military flyers and the explorers of the new frontier—space. That is a different challenge from the past, and *it hasn't always been that way.* I believe flying is still magic. And what better example do we have to inspire the flyers of tomorrow than the men who fought the Cold War?

Glossary

AAA	antiaircraft artillery
ADC	Air Defense Command
AFB	air force base
aileron	moveable control surface at back of wings to bank airplane
ATC	Air Training Command or air traffic control
BDA	bomb damage assessment
bingo fuel	minimum fuel to get home, plus a reserve
CIA	Central Intelligence Agency
CBU	cluster bomb unit
CFC	central fire control position on the B-29
CG	center of gravity
counter	mission over North Vietnam counting toward the one hundred missions that had to be flown before a tour of duty was over
DMZ	demilitarized zone (Korea/Vietnam)
DP	displaced person
EATS	European Air Transport Service
ECM	electronic countermeasures
EGT	exhaust gas temperature
ELINT	electronic intelligence
EOB	electronic order of battle
EWO	electronic warfare officer
FAA	Federal Aviation Administration
FAC	forward air controller

fast FAC	two-seat F-100 fighter employed as a FAC aircraft in Vietnam; call sign Misty
FEAF	Far East Air Forces
flak	antiaircraft gun
flaps	extensions at trailing edge of wing to provide increased lift at reduced airspeed
GCA	ground control approach radar
GCI	ground control intercept radar
G force	force of gravity toward center of earth
G suit	air bladders used to fight gravity
HF	high frequency
IFF	identification friend or foe
IFR	instrument flight rules
indicated	airspeed as shown on an airspeed indicator
IP	initial point
MAAG	Military Assistance Advisory Group
Mach	speed in relation to speed of sound
MiG	Soviet fighter aircraft from the Mikoyan and Gurovich design bureau, such as the MiG-15/17/19/21
Mickey	radar and communications operators or aircraft configured to conduct electronic reconnaissance—WWII term
NCO	noncommissioned officer
OCS	officer candidate school
pickle	release bombs
PSP	perforated steel planking
punch out	eject from a jet aircraft
PX	post exchange
RAF	Royal Air Force
Raven	electronic warfare officer (55th SRW)
RBS	radar bomb scoring site
RIAS	radio in the American sector of Berlin
ROK	Republic of Korea
route pack	one of six areas into which North Vietnam was divided for targeting purposes during the Vietnam War
SAC	Strategic Air Command
SAM	surface-to-air missile
Sidewinder	infrared air-to-air missile
SNAFU	situation normal, all fucked up
SRS	Strategic Reconnaissance Squadron
SRW	Strategic Reconnaissance Wing
stall	the point where the wing no longer produces lift

STANDBOARD	standardization board in SAC; selected air crews who administered flight-standardization checks to other combat-ready air crews
TAC	Tactical Air Command
TACAN	tactical air navigation system using a ground-based UHF transmitter providing bearing and distance information to the ground station from an aircraft
TDY	temporary duty
TRS	Tactical Reconnaissance Squadron
UE	unit equipment (a table of authorization)
UHF	ultrahigh frequency
USAFE	U.S. Air Forces Europe
USSR	Union of Soviet Socialist Republics
Viet Cong	Vietnamese communists (also called VC)
VFR	visual flight rules
Wild Weasel	aircraft modified to locate and destroy SAM sites or any other ground-based gun or missile system using radar for aircraft targeting
ZSU	zenitnaya samokhodnaya ustanovka (antiaircraft self-propelled gun); the Shilka ZSU-23-4 consisted of four liquid-cooled 23mm cannons guided by gun-dish radar

Bibliography

"Aborted Rescue Haunts Santa Fe Pilot." *Santa Fe New Mexican,* December 29, 1997: A1, A4.

Aces and Aerial Victories: The U.S. Air Force in Southeast Asia, 1965–1973. Washington, D.C.: U.S. Air Force, 1976.

Acheson, Dean. *The Korean War.* New York: Norton, 1971.

————. *Present at the Creation.* New York: Norton, 1969.

Austin, Harold R. "A Cold War Overflight of the USSR." *Daedalus Flyer* 35 (spring 1995): 15–18.

Bailey, Bruce M., comp. *"We See All": A History of the 55th Strategic Reconnaissance Wing, 1947–1967.* N.p.: 55th ELINT Association Historian, 1982.

Berger, Carl, ed. *The United States Air Force in Southeast Asia, 1961–1973.* Washington D.C.: Office of Air Force History, U.S. Air Force, 1977.

Berlin Airlift: A USAFE Summary. N.p.: Headquarters, USAFE, 1949.

Blum, Allen H. "War Diary of Lieutenant Colonel Allen H. Blum, 1943–1944." Unpublished manuscript in possession of author.

Burns, Robert. "Forty-four Years Later, Families Finally Get Answers." *Norfolk Virginian Pilot and Ledger Star,* December 4, 1994: A6.

Carastro, L. R., comp. and ed. *Of Those Who Fly.* [Maxwell Air Force Base, AL]: Air Force ROTC, Air Training Command, 1972.

Clifford, Clark. *Counsel to the President.* New York: Random House, 1991.

Collier, Richard. *Bridge across the Sky: The Berlin Blockade and Airlift, 1948–1949.* New York: McGraw-Hill, 1978.

Dupuy, R. E., and T. N. Dupuy. *The Encyclopedia of Military History.* New York: Harper and Row, 1970.

Early Cold War Overflights Symposium, Bolling AFB, Washington, D.C. February 22–23, 2001.

Bibliography

Frederiksen, Oliver Jul. *The American Military Occupation of Germany, 1945–1953.* N.P.: Historical Division, Headquarters, U.S. Army Europe, 1953.

Freeman, Roger A. *Mighty Eighth War Diary.* London: Jane's, 1981.

Hall, R. Cargill. "Strategic Reconnaissance in the Cold War." *MHQ: The Quarterly Journal of Military History* 9 (summer 1996): 107–25.

———. "The Truth about Overflights." *MHQ: The Quarterly Journal of Military History* 9 (spring 1997): 24–39.

Hopkins, J. C. *Development of Strategic Air Command, 1946–1976.* [Omaha]: Office of the Historian, Headquarters Strategic Air Command, 1976.

Johnson, Sue. "A Special Holiday for Korean War POW." *Novato (California) Advance,* May 29, 1985: A-20.

Kennan, George F. *Memoirs, 1925–1950,* Boston: Little, Brown, 1967.

Lashmar, Paul. "Shootdowns." *Aeroplane Monthly,* August 1994: 6–11.

———. *Spy Flights of the Cold War.* Annapolis: Naval Institute Press, 1996.

LeMay, Curtis E. *Mission with LeMay.* New York: Doubleday, 1965.

Lyon, Peter. *Eisenhower: Portrait of the Hero.* Boston: Little, Brown, 1974.

Manchester, William. *The Glory and the Dream: A Narrative History of America, 1932–1972.* Boston: Little, Brown, 1973.

McCullough, David. *Truman.* New York: Simon and Schuster, 1992.

Miller, Roger G. *To Save a City, the Berlin Airlift 1948–1949,* College Station: Texas A&M University Press, 2000.

Momyer, William W. *Air Power in Three Wars (WWII, Korea, Vietnam).* Washington: Department of Defense, Department of the Air Force, 1978.

Moore, Harold G. *We Were Soldiers Once . . . And Young.* New York: Random House, 1992.

Myers, Howard S., Jr. *Sky Spy,* Air Classics, March 1998.

Palmer, Bruce, Jr. *The Twenty-five-Year War: America's Military Role in Vietnam.* Lexington: University Press of Kentucky, 1984.

Peebles, Curtis. *Shadow Flights,* Presidio Press, Novato, 2000.

"Review and Outlook: The Last Ace." *Wall Street Journal,* January 29, 1999: W11.

Rich, Ben R. *Skunk Works.* New York: Little, Brown, 1994.

Ridgway, Matthew B. *Soldier: The Memoirs of Matthew B. Ridgway.* Westport, CT: Greenwood Press, 1956.

Schneider, Donald K. *Air Force Heroes in Vietnam.* Maxwell Air Force Base, AL: Airpower Research Institute, 1979.

"Secrets of the Cold War." *U.S. News and World Report,* March 15, 1993: 30–36.

Smith, Jean Edward. *Lucius D. Clay: An American Life.* New York: Henry Holt, 1990.

A Special Study of Operation "Vittles." New York: Conover-Mast, 1949.

Summers, Harry G., Jr. *Korean War Almanac.* New York: Facts on File, 1990.

————. *The Vietnam War Almanac.* Novato, CA: Presidio Press, 1999.

Technical Order 1R-47H-1 Flight Manual Performance Data. N.p.: U.S. Air Force, 1962.

Thompson, Warren E. "The Mustang's Last Hurrah." *Wings* 12 (February 1982): 26–42.

Truman, Harry S. *Memoirs.* 2 vols. Garden City, NY: Doubleday, 1955.

United States Air Force Combat Victory Credits Southeast Asia. Washington D.C.: Office of Air Force History, U.S. Air Force, 1974.

The United States Military Experience in Korea, 1871–1982: In the Vanguard of ROK-US Relations. N.p.: Headquarters U.S. Forces, Korea, 1983.

Yeager, Chuck. *Yeager.* New York: Bantam, 1985.

Bibliography

Interviews, Letters, and Tapes

Provided by:

Martin Allin
Harold R. Austin
George V. Back
Marshall M. Balfe
Byron A. Dobbs
Henry E. Dubuy
Thomas W. Etherson
Kevin A. Gilroy
Edward Gorski
Joseph J. Gyulavics
Robert S. Hamill
Harold Hendler
Ralph L. Kuster
Joseph F. Laufer
A. E. Lidard

Joel J. Lutkenhouse
Francis T. Martin Jr.
Howard S. Myers Jr.
George Nelson
Charles L. Phillips Jr.
Fred E. Rider
Robert J. Rogers
Howard L. Rust
Charles E. Schreffler
Richard G. Schulz
Joseph Studak
Leonard W. Sweet
David M. Taylor
Chester J. Vaughn

Index